PRIVATE INVESTIGATIONS I

AN INTRODUCTION

The Role of a P.I. & Business Development

Criminal Investigation Series

Carol Malia Hawks, BS
Diane Evans, CPI

D1500925

LawTech
Custom Publishing

LawTech Custom Publishing Co., Inc.

(949)498-4815   Fax: (949)498-4858

E-mail: sales@LawTechCustomPublishing.com

www.LawTechCustomPublishing.com

Comments and suggestions are welcome.

v.04.03.07

pp. 282

ISBN: 1-889315-41-9

Carol Malia Hawks

Carol has worked defense investigations involving death penalty cases and violent crimes. She has worked state and federal investigations in the criminal and civil realm. She has a B.S. in Criminal Justice and holds certifications in crime scene investigation and fingerprint classification. Carol is a notary public and private process server. She also has experience as a curriculum developer for homeland security programs.

Diane Evans, CPI

Diane is a California licensed private investigator. She is a member of the California Association of Licensed Investigators, where she qualified and earned their "Certified Private Investigator" designation. In the last 20 years, Diane has taught classes for a well-known detective academy, presented related Community Services workshops in over 30 Community Colleges across the state, and created four class instructional manuals. She operates her own agency in Claremont, California and prepares candidates to pass the state licensing exam through an organization she created for that purpose, ISS Network.

About this Book

Private Investigations Part I provides an introduction to the private investigation profession. Topics include the not only the historical perspective, but an overview of career opportunities, basic investigative methods, investigative resources, interviewing and interrogation, surveillance and the organization of an investigative firm. The material includes special "From the Files" sections where experienced investigators share true stories and experiences. Part I provides students with a strong base of general knowledge, and prepares them for the more in-depth material presented in Part II.

Contents at a Glance

Chapter 1   The History of Private Investigations, 1

Chapter 2   Career Fields For Private Investigators, 29

Chapter 3   Methods of Investigation, 65

Chapter 4   Sources and Resources, 95

Chapter 5   Interview and Interrogation, 139

Chapter 6   Written And Recorded Statements, 175

Chapter 7   Surveillance, 191

Chapter 8   Law and Ethics, 213

Chapter 9   Organization of a Private Investigation Firm, 243

Articles and Figures

Chapter 1

    Article 1.1 Gum Shoes and "Hard Boiled" Private Eyes: The P.I. in Fact and Fiction 24

Chapter 2

    Figure 2.1 Who PI's Work For and What They Do 39

    Table 2.1 Cost of Insurance Fraud 40

    Figure 2.2 Sacramento (CA) County Sample Policy 50

    Figure 2.3 U.S. Diplomatic Security Policy 54

    Figure 2.4 Entry Level Positions 57

    Figure 2.5 Specialized Areas of Investigation 58

Chapter 4

    Figure 4.1 Sample from the Nevada Marriage Index 106

    Figure 4.2 Directory of Resources 123

    Figure 4.3 General Directory of Resources 133

Chapter 5

    Figure 5.1 Arizona Constitution Article II 154

    Article 5.1 Strategies to Avoid Interview Contamination 171

Contents

Chapter 1   The History of Private Investigations, 1
TERMINOLOGY, 2
HISTORY OF PRIVATE INVESTIGATIONS, 3
  Filling the Void, 3
AMERICA'S PRIVATE EYES, 8
  Allan Pinkerton (1819-1884), 8
  Kate Warne: First Female Private Investigator, 11
  William J. Burns (1861-1932), 17
THE WORLD'S FIRST PRIVATE EYE, 20
  The French Detective: Eugene Francois Vidocq (1775-1857), 20
  INFLUENCE OF FICTION ON PRIVATE EYES AND PRIVATE EYES ON FICTION, 22
  From Fact to Fiction to Future, 23

Chapter 2   Career Fields For Private Investigators, 29
PUBLIC/GOVERNMENT INVESTIGATIONS, 32
CHARACTERISTICS OF PRIVATE INVESTIGATIONS WORK, 32
WORKING CONDITIONS, 33
INVESTIGATOR LICENSING, EDUCATION AND TRAINING, 35
  Licensing, 35
  Education and Training, 37
EMPLOYMENT OPPORTUNITIES, 38
  What P.I.'s Do and Who They Do It For: Areas of Specialization, 39
  General Investigations: Calls for Diversity, 55
  Types of Cases, 57
CAREER OUTLOOK, 59
  Financial Prospects, 60
RELATED OCCUPATIONS, 60
  Private Security, 61
  Bail Enforcement Agents, 61

Chapter 3   Methods of Investigation, 65
INTRODUCTION, 66
  Reality Checks, 67
  Wire Tapping, 68
PROFESSIONAL INVESTIGATIONS, 69
  What Investigators Do, 70
PURPOSE OF INVESTIGATIONS, 71
  Insurance Companies, 71
BIG BUSINESS, 75
  Pre-employment, 75
  In the Workplace, 76
  Stopping Losses, 77
  Executive Protection, 78
SMALL & RETAIL BUSINESS, 78
  Shoplift Detail, 79
  Employee Theft, 80
  Shopping Services, 82
  Undercover Operations, 82
  Counterfeit Products, 84
  Legal Investigations, 86
  Hate Crime, 87
  In the Field, 88
INDIVIDUAL CLIENTS, 89

Contents

Chapter 4   Sources and Resources, 95
INTRODUCTION, 96
  Definition of Public Records, 96
  What's Out There?, 96
  State Records, 98
  Businesses, 99
  Public Business Records, 100
  Record Vendors, 101
  Creation of Documents, 102
  Indexing Records: Logic or Illogic, 104
  Companies, 105
  Keep Thinking, 107
  Notes from Index, 107
  Certified Copies, 108
  Perusing Public Records, 108
  On-Site Record Review, 110
  Case Dockets, 110
  Court Record Briefs, 111
  Certified Copies, 111
  Ordering Copies, 112
  Grantor-Grantee Index, 112
DOING BUSINESS AS (DBA), 114
ACCESSING PUBLIC RECORDS, 114
  Local Records, 114
  Record Content, 115
  Obtaining Federal Records, 116
  WWW Sources, 116
  Buyer Beware, 118
  Investigators and Information, 118
  Getting Hooked Up, 119
  Internet Use and Content, 119
  Government Searches, 120
  Website Evaluation, 120
ONLINE RESOURCES, 121
  Invisible Web, 121

Chapter 5   Interview and Interrogation, 139
THE INTERVIEW, 140
  Purpose, 140
  Related Considerations, 141
  The Interpersonal Orientation Personality Types, 144
  The Problem Solving Personality Types, 144
  Interviewing Elderly Persons, 146
PREPARING FOR THE INTERVIEW, 148
  Review Available Information, 148
  Time is of the Essence, 148
  Determine the Location of the Interview, 148
  Ensure Resources are Available, 148
  Interview One at a Time, 149
  Background Check, 150
CONDUCTING THE INTERVIEW, 150
  Establishing a Rapport, 150
  Inquire as to Witness Knowledge of the Incident or Case, 151
  Protected Information, 153
THE INTERROGATION, 155
PURPOSE OF THE INTERROGATION, 157
  Establishing an Initial Belief in Guilt or Innocence, 157
  Establish the Law or Crime that is to be Proved, 157
STAGES OF THE INTERROGATION PROCESS, 158
  Preparation Phase, 158

THE INTERROGATION AND TECHNIQUES, 161
  Detecting Deception, 161
TECHNIQUES, 164
  Making Accusations and Handling Denials, 164
  Rationalization, 164
  The Admission or Confession, 165
FOLLOWING THE INTERROGATION, 166
  Special Considerations, 166
LAW ENFORCEMENT AND THE PRIVATE SECTOR DIFFERENCES, 167
  The Interview, 167
  Government – Law Enforcement, 167
  Private Sector, 167
  The Interrogation, 168

Chapter 6   Written And Recorded Statements, 175
INTRODUCTION, 176
MINDSET, 176
PREPARATIONS, 178
  Pre-Interview, 180
  Appearance, 181
  Decorum, 181
  Arrival at Location, 182
INTERVIEW, 183
WRITTEN STATEMENT, 185
COMPLETION, 187
POST STATEMENT, 187
TAPE OR NOT TO TAPE, 188

Chapter 7   Surveillance, 191
INTRODUCTION TO SURVEILLANCE, 192
  Definition, 192
  Surveillance Beginnings, 194
TYPES OF CLIENTS: INVESTIGATION IN THE 21ST CENTURY, 195
  Insurance Companies, 195
  Individuals, 196
  Businesses, 197
SKILLS, TECHNIQUES, AND METHODS, 197
  Required Skills, 197
  Private Sector, 197
  Methods, 198
QUALIFICATIONS & OPPORTUNITIES, 198
  Field Agents, 198
GAINING EXPERIENCE: LESSONS LEARNED, 199
APPEARANCES, 200
  Vehicle, 200
  Subject Appearance, 203
  Personal Appearance, 204
TOOLS OF THE TRADE, 205
  Parting Thoughts, 207
  Location, 209
CASE ASSIGNMENT, 210

Chapter 8   Law and Ethics, 213
INTRODUCTION, 214
BILL OF RIGHTS, 215
FEDERAL LAW, 217
RELEVANT FEDERAL ACTS, 217
  Freedom of Information Act, 217
  Privacy Act, 218
  Fair Credit Reporting Act (FCRA), 221
  Gramm-Leach-Bliley Financial Privacy Act (GLB), 222

FEDERAL WORKERS' COMPENSATION, 222
  Federal Employee Compensation Act, 222
  Non-government Federal Workers' Compensation, 222
  Federal Employers Liability Act, 222
  Jones Act of 1920, 223
  Longshore and Harbor Workers Compensation Act, 223
MAIL TAMPERING, 223
STATE LAWS, 225
  Penal Codes, 225
  Eavesdropping and Wire Tapping, 225
  Arizona, 226
  California, 227
  Texas, 227
  Florida, 228
ETHICS, 229
  Merriam-Webster, 230
  Business Ethics, 231
NALI CODE OF ETHICS, 236
RESPONSIBILITIES, 240

Chapter 9   Organization of a Private Investigation Firm, 243

SELECTING THE PATH, 244
  Choosing the Right Path, 244
  Keeping the Lights On; Paying the Bills, 244
COMMON AREAS OF PRACTICE, 245
  Workers' Compensation Insurance, 245
  Personal Injury/Wrongful Death, 246
  Criminal Defense, 248
  Domestic Cases, 249
  Financial Investigations, 250
  Medical Malpractice, 252
  Information Services, 252
  Information Security and Computer Forensics, 254
  Technical Counter Surveillance Measures (T.C.S.M.), 255
BUSINESS INFRASTRUCTURE, 256
  The Office, 257
  Support Staff, 257
  Equipment, 258
  Insurance, 259
  Getting Business, 259
  Your First Client, 266

Chapter 1

The History of Private Investigations

OVERVIEW

Public law enforcement history alludes that private investigators evolved from the police ranks. Historically some degree of rivalry exists among private investigators and law enforcement investigators. However, much of this animosity has waned over the years with the increasing professionalism of both groups.

History reveals that the first "investigators" in America (and the world) were in fact civilians; filling the void before police investigators became established. This chapter will highlight three of the more prolific early private detectives. We will look at the influence private investigators had on modern day policing and on fictional literature.

CHAPTER OBJECTIVES

1. Identify the reasons private investigators came into being.

2. Describe the evolution of private investigations in conjunction with public investigators.

3. Recognize the influence and roles these early private detectives have on contemporary private investigators today.

4. Identify where private investigative work is heading.

Blade stepped out into the damp L.A. night air. He got what he came for; the answers to why his partner had been rubbed out, who sent the dame, and who was still out to get him. Across the alley he watched an amber glow fall to the curb as the cabbie tossed and crushed out a cigarette. The files he had "borrowed" from Logan's office jabbed him in the rib, but it was the jab in his lower back that caused him concern.

"Mind your own business Bub. This is your first and last warning. Stop snooping around Fat Tony's penthouse" whispered the voice behind Blade. "You tell your client; Fat Tony's wife that he ain't fooling around, he's a 'legit business man who just works late hours." With each syllable Blade felt the gun thrust repeatedly into his back, pounding the message home.

The term private investigator often conjures up images of dark shadowy figures lurking in darkness, sneaking into people's private lives and spying on unfaithful spouses. There are plenty of movies and literature on the subject. Let's face it; stories of private detectives have captured the imagination since Edgar Allan Poe penned *The Murders in the Rue Morgue* in 1841. Poe, considered to be the father of detective fiction, is credited with introducing the first fictional private detective, Augueste C. Dupin. We will come back to Poe and his fictional private investigator, but first let's take look at the relationships existing in the real world of private investigations.

TERMINOLOGY

The term 'private investigator' can be broken down into its Latin origins. The term 'private' comes from the Latin 'privatus' or 'privus'. These roughly translate to mean *'one person, single; not in public being'*. The term 'investigate' can be broken down into the terms 'vest, vestige or vestigium' which loosely translate as*: to endow with power and authority; footprint, mark, sign, track, trace, to search after.* Private Investigators are employed to track down leads, search after clues. The private investigator searches to uncover information, data and facts through methodical measures, and then organizes and reports the findings.

Throughout this text the terms private investigator, P.I., private detective, detective, professional investigator, agent, operative, and the like will be interchanged. They all mean the same thing; a private citizen who conducts investigations for hire. Other familiar and colorful terms for private investigators are; gumshoe, sleuth, Dick Tracy, private dick, shamus, Sherlock, elbow, fly-cop, and private eye. Each of these terms has interesting origins behind them, yet the most familiar is the term *private eye.* Private eye has been credited to the late Allan Pinkerton, often referred to as America's Father of Private Investigations. In this chapter we will learn more about the colorful Mr. Pinkerton.

HISTORY OF PRIVATE INVESTIGATIONS

Filling the Void

Before there were government agents and police detectives, there were private eyes. Private detectives filled the void between the police and federal government agencies. Early American and European history reveal that sheriffs and police officer's didn't focus on 'detecting' crimes. They usually acted only when there was an arrest to be made. If crime victim desired to pursue a lawbreaker they had to hire a 'thief taker' who charged for such services.

Henry Fielding

In mid-eighteenth century England, crime and public disorder had spiraled out of control. Brothers and magistrates; John and Henry Fielding, took it upon themselves to address the problem. They created a team of "thief takers" consisting of paid citizens who served writs, conducted detective work, and arrested lawbreakers. They utilized intelligence to aid in tracking and capturing ruthless gangs of thieves that plagued London. Working out of offices on Bow Street, they became known as the Bow Street Runners. They quickly earned a reputation throughout the country as being honest and efficient.

Early nineteenth century America was under the "constable and watch system" which was carried over from England. This "system" was comprised of volunteer private citizens who patrolled the city at night. During the daytime a constable provided similar services for a fee. Most citizens could not be bothered with performing their night watch duty, and paid others to fill in.

Those willing to conduct night watch were usually men who were not employable elsewhere. An untoward effect of this practice was a night-watch typically comprised of men who slept and drank on the job. In worst case scenarios these misfits either ran when confronted by criminals or took bribes to look the other way.

It was not until 1853, with a population over half a million, that New York City established its first official police department. Chicago formalized its nine-man police force into a full fledged 80 man department in 1855. A year later Philadelphia established their department, followed by Boston in 1859.

These early police departments had limited jurisdiction and were only able to address crimes in their own cities. Therefore, smaller villages, towns, and country-sides were left with sheriff departments, or nothing.

There was nothing to unify the different city police departments and sheriffs' offices. Not only did the agencies have varying criminal codes, but there were confusing boundaries and the occasional jurisdictional rivalry. This made apprehension of intercity and/or interstate criminals almost impossible and the savvy criminals took advantage of these weaknesses. Since an agency's authority ended at a city, county or state line, train robberies were especially appealing and lucrative for thieves.

Citizens who desired their stolen goods back, to be reunited with missing loved ones, etc., turned to private detective agencies for help. Wanting to protect passengers and valuable cargo, train companies, and bank transports relied on private investigation companies to fill the void left by government law enforcement. Private detective agencies provided investigative services as well as security protection. Allen Pinkerton was one of the many who was able to capitalize on this need.

In the 1860's the federal government found itself in the need of private detectives. During the Civil War, spies ran rampant between Union and Confederate armies. In order to combat the problem President

Lincoln authorized a covert service of spies to report on Confederate war plans. Who better for gathering intelligence and infiltrating opposing camps than private investigators? Pinkerton, again, made his mark by creating and running this organization for the President. This covert service of spies became the U.S. Secret Service.

Civil War (Pinkerton; left, Lincoln; center)

The federal government only stepped into law enforcement around 1870, when it created the Department of Justice. Even then the Department of Justice appropriated funds to hire private detectives in order to investigate federal crimes.[1]

Theodore Roosevelt became President of the United States in 1901; four years later, he appointed Charles Bonaparte (grandnephew of Napoleon) to be Attorney General. Roosevelt and Bonaparte both Progressives, shared the conviction that efficiency and expertise, not political connections, should determine who could best serve in government.[2]

In 1907, the Department of Justice most frequently called upon Secret Service "operatives" to conduct investigations. These men were well-trained, dedicated — and expensive. Moreover, they reported to the Chief of the Secret Service not to Attorney General Bonaparte. This situation frustrated Bonaparte, who wanted complete control of investigations under his jurisdiction. Congress provided the impetus for Bonaparte to acquire his own force. On May 27, 1908, it enacted a law preventing the Department of Justice from engaging Secret Service operatives.[3]

President Roosevelt
source Library of Congress

The following month, Attorney General Bonaparte appointed a force of Special Agents within the Department of Justice. Accordingly, ten former Secret Service employees and a number of Department of Justice peonage (i.e., compulsory servitude) investigators became Special Agents of the Department of Justice. On July 26, 1908, Bonaparte ordered them to report to Chief Examiner Stanley W. Finch. This action is celebrated as the beginning of the FBI.[4]

Both Attorney General Bonaparte and President Theodore Roosevelt completed their terms in March 1909, and recommended that the (existing) force of 34 agents become a permanent part of the Department of Justice. Attorney General George Wickersham, Bonaparte's successor, named the force the Bureau of Investigation on March 16, 1909. At that time, the title of Chief Examiner was changed to Chief of the Bureau of Investigation.[5]

As the federal government increased its investigative departments and personnel, the need for private detectives began to wane. At one point the federal government officially attempted to exclude private detectives from government investigations. However, it was not a smooth transition as noted in a January, 1909 letter from Attorney General Bonaparte to President Roosevelt. The following is an excerpt from that letter:

> *It is true that...other Executive Departments are supplied with what may be fairly called detective agencies for certain limited purposes, as, for example, the punishment of counterfeiting or frauds upon the revenue, of offenses against the postal laws, and of violations of various penal statutes; but a large and increasing*

residuum of cases exists in which the Department of Justice is obliged by law, and expected as a result of custom, to furnish such services itself; and by a curious anomaly, no specific provision has been made by law to enable it to discharge these difficulties. This is more singular since by the act approved March 3, 1893, (27 Stat., 591) it is provided that "hereafter no employee of the Pinkerton Detective Agency, or similar agency, shall be employed in any Government service or by any officer of the District of Colombia:" so that the law expressly forbids this Department to employ a trained detective from any responsible private agency and yet has made no express provision for any public agency of the like character to render the same indispensable service.[6]

Today, most Americans take for granted that our country needs a federal investigative service, yet in 1908, the establishment of this kind of agency at a national level was highly controversial. The U.S. Constitution is based on "federalism:" a national government with jurisdiction over matters that crossed boundaries, like interstate commerce, and foreign affairs, with all other powers reserved to the states. Through the 1800s, Americans usually looked to cities, counties, and states to fulfill most government responsibilities. However, by the 20th century, increased ease in transportation and communications created a climate of opinion favorable to the federal government establishing a strong investigative tradition.

This change signaled a significant decline of the prominent role private investigators played in government investigations. However, those in the private detective business just reinvented themselves by finding a new need to fill.

Railroad, mining, banks, and other companies had plenty of troubles that kept private investigators in business. Allan Pinkerton's Agency, on behalf of the railroads, was by then embroiled in a battle with the infamous Wild Bunch bandits — Butch Cassidy and the Sundance Kid.

AMERICA'S PRIVATE EYES

Allan Pinkerton (1819-1884)

Allan Pinkerton
source Library of Congress

Often referred to as "America's First Private Eye" Allan Pinkerton made his mark in history when he opened the Pinkerton National Detective Agency in 1850. The Pinkerton Agency logo depicts an open eye, possibly inspired by the "All Seeing Eye" on The Great Seal of the United States found on the one dollar bill. Under Pinkerton's "all-seeing eye" is the phrase "We Never Sleep". It is said that Pinkerton's distinctive logo inspired the term private eye.

The Great Seal

Allan Pinkerton was born in Glasgow, Scotland in 1819. His father, a police sergeant, died from work related injuries when Allan was a boy. At a young age Allan began work as a cooper (barrel maker). Times were tough, not just for the Pinkerton's, but for all laborers at the time. He became actively involved in the Chartist Labor Movement which represented the exploited worker. The movement sought to make changes through peaceful means, such as organizing strikes, but often resorted to violence. In 1842, when a friend tipped him off that he was to be arrested for his involvement in the Labor Movement, Allan Pinkerton fled to the United States with his new bride, Joan.

As with any 'larger-than-life' figure, Pinkerton's history varies among historians. One particularly interesting story states how the couple was to have left days earlier for their escape to America. But Joan insisted they wait until a hat she ordered would be ready. Pinkerton fortuitously indulged her and traded their ship passage for a later departure. Joan's infinity for hats saved their lives, as the ship they had originally planned to travel on tragically sank.

Their luck on the second ship was only a slight better. Shipwrecked, the couple and other survivors managed to wash up in Canada. Upon reaching dry land they were met, not by rescuers, but by marauders. Other than the clothes on their backs, the newlywed Pinkerton's had just one possession, Joan's wedding ring, which they were forced to hand over.

The determined Pinkerton's headed for Chicago and a new life. Once settled in Dundee Illinois, just outside of Chicago, Pinkerton set up a cooper's shop near the Fox River. He may not have been planning a career in investigations, but when he came across a band of criminals his career path took a new course. In search of wood for his barrels, Pinkerton rowed to a small uninhabited island where he detected signs that the island was being used by counterfeiters.

Later, Pinkerton returned to the island and assisted the Kane County Sheriff in apprehending the counterfeiters. This led to public accolades and his first law enforcement appointment as deputy sheriff for Kane County. Pinkerton worked briefly for Kane County before taking a job in Chicago in 1846, as assistant to the Cook County Sheriff. Impressed by his success as a detective, the U.S. Postal Service employed him as a special agent. It wasn't long after, that Chicago's police force came calling.

Qwik-Tip
Pinkerton was an abolitionist (activist against slavery). His coopers shop functioned as a "station" for escaped slaves traveling the Underground Railroad to freedom in the North.

Chicago was experiencing an industrial boom in the late 1840's with the arrival of the railroad. The sleepy frontier town quickly became a hub for the transport of agricultural and manufactured goods between the East and West. Iron mills, coal mines and other industries flourished with help of the railroad.

Along with progress came opportunists and criminals. Pickpockets, horse thieves, rapists, burglars, bandits, and ruthless thugs ran amuck in the city. April showers in Chicago not only brought out May flowers, but bodies as well. Bloated bodies of crime victims washed up in the Chicago River bog during the spring floods.

Young Officer Pinkerton was among the nine men sworn to protect the thirty-something-thousand population of Chicago. Most of the cops steered clear of the dangerous and corrupt areas of the city, but not Pinkerton. He feared no man and walked a no-nonsense beat, taking no slack, bribes or grief from anyone. It has been said he'd quicker swing his billy club than tolerate an insult. Along with his tough demeanor he had developed keen skills of observation. Pinkerton was mentally savvy and he could get a suspect to unwittingly divulge his guilt. It was not surprising then, that Allan Pinkerton became Chicago's first official detective in 1850.

Later that same year Allan Pinkerton set out on his own and opened his own detective agency; Pinkerton's National Detective Agency. A man of incorruptible principles, Pinkerton transferred those principals to his own agency. He established a Code of Ethics for his agents; setting firm boundaries for behavior. Besides not indulging in liquor or cigarettes, they were not to accept rewards, bribes or gratuities.

Already having established a name for himself as a successful detective, it didn't take him long to build up his private business. Frustrated with the robberies of their gold transports, the Chicago Union, Rock Island, Illinois Central and Galena railroads hired Pinkerton and his men to protect their trains. It was during this time that Pinkerton befriended two of Illinois Central railroad's employees; George McClellan (chief engineer) and Abraham Lincoln (attorney).

A few years later, in 1861, Pinkerton and his team discovered a plot to assassinate the newly elected President Lincoln. Allan Pinkerton contacted his old friend and warned him of the danger. Although the vast majority of history books credit Allan Pinkerton with foiling the assassination plot, much of the credit is due to the resourceful work of his agents. One agent in particular was Kate Warne.

Abe Lincoln Lawyer

Kate Warne: First Female Private Investigator

Considering the role women played in the work force at the time, Pinkerton assumed the young attractive widow who entered his office was seeking a clerical job. To his surprise, the interview took an unexpected turn when Kate Warne extolled her qualities outlining why she would make an effective private investigator.

Kate didn't back down when Pinkerton tried to explain he didn't employ female operatives. It was simply unheard of at the time. Police departments did not employ females. In fact it would be another 35 years before police departments began hiring women, and another 12 years after that before there was a female police detective. Impressed with her determination, Pinkerton gave Kate a chance. He disregarded the sexist norms of the times, and in 1856 she became the first known female private investigator.

Kate's abilities impressed Pinkerton so much that in 1860 he hired more female operatives. Kate was appointed to supervise and train this all-female detective unit. Kate and her operatives were able to gain access to people and places that the male agents could not. This team was the first known to operate undercover in assumed roles. The women often befriended the girlfriends and wives of criminal suspects to gain inside information. She and the other women sometimes charmed the suspects under their investigations into bragging about their criminal deeds.

Kate was part of Pinkerton's team that discovered a plot to assassinate newly elected President Abraham Lincoln. It was public knowledge that Mr. Lincoln and his family were traveling by train from Springfield, Illinois to Washington D.C. The assassins' plan was to keep Lincoln from reaching D.C. for his March 4th inauguration. They planned to kill Lincoln in Baltimore, on February 22, 1861, to stop his inauguration as President.

The night before Lincoln's train was to leave for Baltimore, Kate and Pinkerton had a covert meeting with him in Harrisburg Pennsylvania. They arranged for Lincoln's family and entourage to continue with their trip to Baltimore the next morning as planned. In the mean time, in an elaborate undercover operation, Kate and Pinkerton slipped Lincoln out of Harrisburg under the cover of darkness.

Kate procured transportation, disguises, and passage for a late night train out of Harrisburg to Baltimore. To disguise the gangly 6 foot 4 tall Lincoln, she had him stoop over with a cane and wrapped a shawl around him. Per Kate's request, a train porter left the rear door unlocked, providing covert access to the sleeping quarters. She laid the ground work for the deception by telling the porter it would help assist her in boarding her "invalid" brother onto the train.

Armed with a loaded pistol, Kate and several other trusted Pinkerton operatives occupied the last three sleeper compartments surrounding Lincoln. Allan Pinkerton himself took a position on the rear platform, keeping a vigilant watch. The plan was a success. President Lincoln arrived safely in Washington D.C. early the next morning as his family and entourage were just arriving in Baltimore.

The Southern enemy agent sympathizers waiting in Baltimore were sorely disappointed to say the least, when to their surprise they did not see Mr. Lincoln step off the train. Lincoln's family continued on to Washington with out further incident.

Later that same day Lincoln summoned Pinkerton's protective force so he could personally thank his guardians. The grateful Mr. Lincoln personally conveyed his appreciation and gratitude to the skillful and charming Kate Warne; who had been instrumental in saving his life and his presidency.

When Civil war broke out in April that same year, President Lincoln, occupied with the responsibilities of preserving the Union, worried about the reported saturation of Confederate spies in Washington D.C. He again sought out Pinkerton and asked him to organize a secret service of spies for the Union.

Pinkerton again called on his top operative Kate Warne. Kate created a Southern Belle identity and used her skills of deception to enable her to infiltrate the social circles of the Washington DC elite. Kate arranged to get herself invited into the parlors of D.C. families who were suspected of being Southern State sympathizers. In addition to her investigations of the Confederate sympathizers in D.C., she spent time in the South garnering secrets from the girlfriends and wives of Confederate soldiers. She was a natural at the game of espionage and gained crucial information regarding the Confederate army's plans and spy networks.

Kate's contributions, talent, and dedication made their mark on Allan Pinkerton, her leader and mentor; who was at the bedside of his loyal agent during her last hours. In 1868, Kate Warne, the first female detective, died at the young age of 35 from pneumonia. Because she was widowed at a young age, and had no children or family of her own Allan Pinkerton gave her a resting place in his family plot at the Graceland Cemetery, in Chicago.

During his Civil War service, Pinkerton worked closely under his old associate from the railroad; George McClellan. McClellan, had become General and commander of the Union Army and selected Allan Pinkerton as his counterintelligence chief.

Although General McClellan had achieved great success early in the war, President Lincoln grew frustrated with him. McClellan's continual reluctance to mount swift attacks on the Confederate Army was drawing criticism within political and military circles. In one case McClellan reported the number of Confederate troops to be around 115,000 and would not move until he had reinforcements. Despite urging from Lincoln's administration during the end of 1861 and the early part of 1862, McClellan would not attack.

Generals McClellan and Ambrose Burnside

It was later discovered that McClellan's figures were greatly exaggerated and the enemy forces were only about 35,000 in number. Through out the war McClellan used the excuse of being outnumbered for reasons not to attack. Interestingly, it was Pinkerton who reported these numbers to McClellan. Pinkerton's misinformation could have been due to his reliance on reports from captured soldiers under interrogation. When Lincoln removed McClellan in November 1862, and put General Ambrose Burnside in charge, Pinkerton left Washington. He left behind the foundation for what became the Federal Secret Service.

After the war Pinkerton went back to his detective agency and worked on establishing offices around the country. At the same time coal minors, steel mill workers and other labor groups were establishing unions around the country. Oddly enough, Pinkerton who had been run out of Scotland for fighting on behalf of workers now invested his agency's reputation on blocking labor strikes. The Pinkerton Agency took part in at least seventy labor disputes and opposed over 125,000 strikers between 1866 and 1892. One of their big cases was the infiltration and elimination of the Mollie Maguire's; a ruthless Irish Mafia.

Besides crushing labor unions, Pinkerton and his agents hotly pursed the many outlaw gangs of the day. Some of the bandits Pinkerton (and now his two sons) helped take down list as a 'who's who' of outlaws'. Among them were; the infamous Jessie James-Younger gang; the Wild Bunch's Butch Cassidy and the Sundance Kid; the Burrow Gang; William Randolf; and the Hole-in-the-Wall-Gang.

Jessie James

In his later years, Pinkerton took pen to paper and recounted his adventures. Among his many writings were the books; *The Mollie Maguire's and the Detectives* -1877, *Criminal Reminiscences and Detective Sketches* -1878, *The Spy of the Rebellion* -1883 and *Thirty Years a Detective,* 1884.

It wasn't a bullet or a scuffle with a suspect, but an injury from a fall and subsequent gangrene infection, that took Allan Pinkerton's life in July, 1884. He was 65. After his death, his sons, William and Robert continued the business. They gradually moved the company's focus away from detective work and towards security services. By the 1880's Pinkerton's National Detective Agency had over a dozen offices across the United States, and in 1899; a branch in Canada.

Despite all the glowing accolades Allan Pinkerton and his agents acquired over the years, they received bad press as well. A posse of Pinkerton's men was accused of bombing a home believed to be sheltering the outlaw Jesse James. James wasn't in the home, but his mother was maimed and his brother was killed. Then in 1892, (several years after Allan's death) steel industry mogul, Andrew Carnegie hired the Pinkerton's to put down a workers strike in Homestead Pennsylvania. The conflict ended with many wounded or killed; on both sides. The press lashed out at Carnegie and the Pinkerton's.

Despite these and other damaging accounts, Allan Pinkerton forged the way for private detectives today and earned his place in history as "America's First Private Detective". Pinkerton and his agents were not only America's first *private detectives*, but they are possibly America's first *detectives*. Pinkerton was a pioneer, he employed women, applied techniques such as; undercover (covert) operations, surveillance, shadowing, and use of disguises. He even began a criminal record file, or rogues gallery that included photos of criminals, thus creating the first mug shots. Pinkerton shared his rogues galleries with other law enforcement agencies, including Scotland Yard and the French Surete. The FBI based its Identification Division on Pinkerton's early efforts.

Pinkerton Strike Breakers
source Library of Congress

Upon the death of Allan's great-grandson Robert II in 1967, the company became a corporation. In 1999 the Pinkerton Corporation merged with Swedish based Securitas, the world's largest security provider. Soon after acquiring Pinkerton, Securitas purchased another legendary American detective agency; The William J. Burns International.

The Securitas group of companies now specializes in security for domestic alarm services and cash-in-transit operations. They employ over 210,000 employees spread over 30 countries.

William J. Burns (1861-1932)

William J. Burns

The acquisitions that put the William J. Burns International Detective Agency under the same roof with the Pinkerton Corporation must have had William Burns rolling in his grave. The Pinkerton Agency was not just a competitor; they were Burns' arch rival. When Burns opened his detective agency in 1909 he went toe-to-toe against Allan Pinkerton's two sons, William and Robert.

Burns was thought to detest William and Robert Pinkerton. In spite of his disdain for the brothers, Burns was shrewd enough to recognize Allan Pinkerton's ingenuity and mirror its success by setting up headquarters in Chicago and New York as Pinkerton had done. Soon Burns even went so far as sway one of the Pinkerton's most lucrative security service contracts out from under them.

Providing security services became the mainstay for many private investigative firms by the turn of the century. As public law enforcement was attempting to catch up with crime fighting and prevention methods, the private police and/or detectives were finding themselves shut of criminal investigations.

One year before Burns opened his agency, Attorney General Charles Bonaparte created a force of Special Agents under direction of President Theodore Roosevelt. The Special Agents were former Department of Justice Secret Service men; the forerunner of what was to become the

FBI. As the federal government took on larger criminal investigative role the private agencies had to adapt to new markets.

While the Pinkerton boys were being antagonistic; Burns quickly created a larger than life image of himself. Burns had already become quite well-known for his earlier achievements in the Secret Service. In one particularly celebrated case, President Theodore Roosevelt personally selected Burns and government lawyer, Francis J. Henry to San Francisco to investigate charges of political corruption in the mayoral office.

Burns made big news for the Secret Service with his investigation of San Francisco Mayor Eugene Schmitz. It seems that Schmitz was engaged in unscrupulous business practices with underworld figures. Graft, extortion and bribes were rampant.

The investigation was temporarily stalled due to the great earthquake of 1906. The corrupt Mayor and his underworld connections soon took advantage of the earthquake. They rigged contracts with the utilities, transportation and construction companies to their financial gain. Burns wasn't stalled for long; and his exhaustive investigation lead to several hundred indictments, including the corrupt Mayor. Schmitz was later convicted and sent to San Quentin.

William Burns received many public accolades and has been called "the greatest detective America has ever produced". He has even been compared to the great Sherlock Holmes. This remarkable reputation was not lost on the Mayor of Los Angeles. It was the William J. Burns Detective Agency that Mayor Alexander called on to investigate the bombing of the L.A. Times building.

On October 1st 1910, a bomb made of dynamite destroyed the home of Harrison Gray Otis and another ripped through the L.A. Times building. Many newspaper workers were injured and 21 were killed. The owner of the paper, Harrison Gray Otis, was an outspoken conservative and his anti-union stance made him and his paper a target.

From previous investigations involving the use of dynamite against anti-union businesses, Burns knew to turn his attention to the McNamara brothers. James McNamara was associated with the Typographical Union and Joseph with the International Union of Bridge and Structural Workers. Burns was able to solve the crime and bring the perpetrators to justice. For his troubles he received the sum of $100,000 (just shy of $2 million in today's dollars).

A combination of good casework and an instinct for publicity propelled Mr. Burns into an international celebrity. His exploits made national news, the gossip columns of New York newspapers, and the pages of detective magazines; in which he published "true" crime stories based on his exploits. Well qualified to direct the Bureau, and friends with Warren Harding's Attorney General, Harry M. Daugherty; Burns was appointed as the Director of the Bureau of Investigation on August 22, 1921.[6]

William J. Burns

Under Mr. Burns, the Bureau shrank from its 1920 high of 1,127 personnel to around 600 three years later. Because of his role in the Teapot Dome Scandal, Burns resigned in 1924 at the request of Attorney General Harlan Fiske Stone. This scandal involved the secret leasing of naval oil reserve lands to private companies. This wasn't the first scandal Burns had been connected with. In fact he had engaged in dubious practices while running his own agency and even during his time with the Secret Service.

Despite his some what questionable image, William J. Burns remained popular and successful. Mr. Burns retired to Florida and for several years published detective and mystery stories based on his long career.[8] Even after his death in 1932, his image thrived through a 1960's Television series *International Detective* starring Arthur Fleming. The nearly 40 episodes were taken from the files of the William J. Burns Detective agency.

THE WORLD'S FIRST PRIVATE EYE

The French Detective: Eugene Francois Vidocq (1775-1857)

This is another famous private eye and whose exploits in Europe precede Burns and Pinkerton. In the early 1830's, nearly seventeen years before Pinkerton set up shop as America's first private eye, Eugene Francois Vidocq had established Le Bureau des Renseignements (Office of Intelligence) the first private detective firm. Vidocq is considered to be France's and the "world's" first private eye.

Prior to opening his own agency, Vidocq had a most impressive career as a police detective. However, he did not start out on the right side of the law, and unlike the socially principled Pinkerton; Vidocq began his life as a criminal. Stories of swashbuckling duels, pirating, confidence games, forgeries, and ingenious prison escapes color the early years of Vidocq's life. In efforts to elude police he became a master of disguise. In the course of one escape he successfully posed as a nun.

Most of the information about Vidocq's earlier life comes from his ghost-written biography. According to it, Vidocq was born in Arras, France in July 23, 1775. His father was a baker.[9]

At the age of 14 he allegedly accidentally killed his fencing instructor and decided to skip town. He planned to sail to the Americas, but lost his money to an unscrupulous actress. He ended up joining the Bourbon Regiment a year later.[10]

He was hardly a model soldier. He later claimed that he fought 15 duels and received numerous reprimands. Even during the war against Austria he continued dueling, despite this he still arose to a rank of grenadier corporal. In 1792, when a sergeant major refused a duel with him, he hit him. Striking a superior officer could have led to a death sentence so he deserted and moved back to Arras.[11]

The French Revolution was already in the full swing. Vidocq claimed that he saved two noblewomen from a guillotine in Arras, but was captured and faced the same fate. His father got him out by asking the Chevalier family to help. Vidocq fell in love with their daughter Louise and married her when she falsely claimed she was pregnant.

When he found out that Louise was having an affair with an officer, he left for Brussels. He acquired a false passport with the name of Rousseau. In Belgium he courted an older baroness and joined a band of raiders. He left later with a parting gift of 15,000 gold francs. [12]

Vidocq moved to Paris where he ended up spending all his money on loose women. He became a bandit and was arrested many times but always managed to escape. Once he tried to forge a pardon to a cellmate who had been sentenced to death. He also dabbled in smuggling. When he gave himself up to clear the name of a guard, he was arrested and sentenced to eight years of hard labor. When he was transferred to Brest for the use in galleys, he escaped again, this time using a disguise. [13]

It was this experience and understanding of crime that made Vidocq a natural in criminal investigation. Who better to catch a thief than a thief? Vidocq convinced la Préfecture de Police de Paris (Paris P.D.) that he could detect and catch the thieves and rogues that had eluded them. In 1809 he went to work for the police as an undercover informant in a Paris prison. After proving his skills, officials covertly orchestrated his escape from prison.

Believing he really was a fugitive, the rogues of Paris accepted Vidocq as one of their own. He began employing several other former criminals to work as informants and operatives. In 1811 his group of "detectives" became *la Sûreté*, (criminal investigation division) and Vidocq was appointed chief. In 1817 he had a hand in 811 arrests, including 15 assassins and 38 fences. His annual income was 5,000 francs, but he also worked as a private investigator for a fee. [14]

Not all the police approved of his methods however, and bitter rivalry developed. In 1832 he was obliged to resign because of a charge that he instigated a crime through an intermediary for a sole purpose of getting credit for solving it. He then set up a paper manufacturing and printing company in Saint-Mandé (again hiring ex-criminals to work for him). [15]

In 1833 he founded the first known private detective agency, Le bureau des renseignments (Office of Intelligence) and again, hired ex-cons. Official law enforcement tried many times to shut it down. In 1842 police arrested him in suspicion of unlawful imprisonment and taking money on false pretenses after he had solved an embezzling case. Vidocq later suspected that it had been a set-up. He was sentenced for five years with a 3,000-franc fine but the Court of Appeals released him.[16]

Vidocq may not be the first or only person to bear the title "father of criminalistics", but he was the first formalize the use of criminalistics in police work. Vidocq is credited with having introduced record-keeping (rap sheets), criminology, and ballistics to criminal investigation. He made the first plaster casts of shoe impressions. He created indelible ink and unalterable bond paper with his printing company. His form of anthropometrics is still partially used by French police. He is also credited for philanthropic pursuits – he claimed he never informed on anyone who had stolen for real need.[17] In addition he created the first credit bureau. Some historians acknowledge Vidocq with conducting the first sting-operations and inventing plainclothes police work. Crime scene preservation was a concept that Vidocq envisioned and implemented.

INFLUENCE OF FICTION ON PRIVATE EYES AND PRIVATE EYES ON FICTION

One might wonder how someone as remarkable as Vidocq; who revolutionized criminal investigations has little to no name recognition. Although Vidocq is not a household name, the characters inspired by him are. In the beginning of this chapter we mentioned how Edgar Allen Poe introduction the first fictional private eye, Augueste C. Dupin in *The Murders in the Rue Morgue* in 1841. It seems that Poe's inspiration for the ingenious detective Dupin came from the tales of Vidocq. When Poe was six he was sent to London to study. During these years (1815-1820) Vidocq most likely was a household name in Europe and Poe took note. Perhaps he even studied *Memoires de Vidocq,* published in 1827.

Memoires de Vidocq (The Memoirs of Vidocq) was a best-seller in Europe and the first of several successful books written by Vidocq. Although Vidocq toted them as factual accounts of his triumphant career as a criminal investigator, it is apparent that he, like Pinkerton and Burns, was a master at self-promotion and publicity. The Memoirs recount embroidered tales of extraordinary methods of detection and reasoning performed by Vidocq to the chagrin of murders and evil villains. Some people have speculated that Vidocq did not write all of the texts, and that he employed the services of expert ghost writers.

Whatever the case these brilliant and lively tales inspired other writers besides Poe.

Definitely a household name is that of Sherlock Holmes. Sir Arthur Conan Doyle presented Holmes to the literary world a mere twelve years after Vidocq's death. Sherlock Holmes is depicted as the master of disguise and scientific analysis; skills well noted as those of Vidocq. The fictional Holmes uses his contacts with shady characters to get a line on his criminal target; much like the criminal network Vidocq employed. French authors Victor Hugo and Honore Balzac, both based characters on Vidocq. Hugo with *Les Miserables* and Balzac with Pere Goriot. Even Charles Dickens created characters inspired by Vidocq. Herman Melville's Moby Dick was motivated in part on Vidocq. "The French novelist Honore de Balzac was moved to invent the villainous Vautrin in Comedie Humaine (The Human Comedy), after befriending the famous French detective and studying his ways".

From Fact to Fiction to Future

In this chapter we covered the facts about some of the first true private detectives; Pinkerton, Burns and Vidocq. We gave mention to the impact these real life private detectives had on fiction and non-fictional literature. Society's image of private investigators has been based much on fictional literature and Hollywood portrayals. The role of the private investigator has evolved through time being shaped by the needs and expectations of society. Today's private investigators handle cases far different than the days of old.

The following is an excerpt from an article by Richard Lindberg in 1999. It was written during the time he was employed by Search International, a private investigations firm in Schaumburg Illinois. Richard Lindberg is a lifelong Chicagoan, an author, journalist, and research historian who has written and published eleven books dealing with aspects of city history, politics, criminal justice, sports, and ethnicity. For the full text and other engaging stories visit www.richardlindberg.net

Gum Shoes and "Hard Boiled" Private Eyes: The P.I. in Fact and Fiction[18]

By the turn-of-the-last century, the reckless and daring exploits of the men who pursued the Molly McGuires and Jesse James stirred the imagination of the American reading public. The real-life detectives fueled a cottage industry that traded upon a growing fascination with the sensationalized aspects of true crime and the men who brought these malefactors to justice.

The famous "dime novels" and "penny dreadfuls"(as they were commonly known in England), enjoyed immense popularity between the Civil War and World War I. Increased mechanization of printing made it possible to cheaply produce printed matter for the masses, and distribute these publications to newsstands, cigar stores, barbershops, and dry goods emporiums nationwide.

Aimed at working class youth, the dime novels introduced a larger than life array of western heroes, outlaws, and fictional detectives like the heroic Nick Carter to the popular reading genre. Said to have been created by John Russell Coryell, the amateur sleuth was America's answer to the polished and refined Sherlock Holmes, an earlier creation of novelist Sir Arthur Conan Doyle, and introduced to the British public in pages of Beeton's Christmas Annual in 1887.

Beginning in 1891, the popular adventures of the refined and intractable British detective, based on Doyle's recollections of Dr. Joseph Bell of the Edinburgh Infirmary, began attracting worldwide attention after his debut in the Strand Magazine.

Nick Carter, a defender of the law and upholder of virtue in nearly 1,000 stories hatched in the fertile imagination of Coryell and various other authors, was introduced in 1895. Nick Carter was the subject of an early silent film in 1908. Thomas Carrigan, Walter Pidgeon, Eddie Constantine, and Robert Conrad have all portrayed the great New York detective at one time or another.

The success of Beadle's New York Dime Library, and other competing companies churning out formula plots laden with intrigue and morality messages, slowly waned. By the 1920s, the Police Gazette and slick mass-marketed magazines like the Black Mask (published by H.L. Mencken and George Jean Nathan as a means of generating revenue for their more "literary" endeavors) ushered in the modern era of pulp fiction, forever changing societal notions concerning the work of the private detective.

Four years after the Black Mask first appeared on newsstands in 1920, publisher Bernarr Macfadden brought out True Detective, arguably the most successful crime and detection magazine of its kind. Featuring "clever, brainy, and brave men," invented by hack writers and famous newspaper reporters like Edward Radin, Alan Hynd, and John Barlow Martin, the stories were both shocking and sensational, and at times, sexually lurid.

Article 1.1 Gum Shoes and "Hard Boiled" Private Eyes: The P.I. in Fact and Fiction (Cont.)

True Detective spawned dozens of second and third-rate imitators like Confidential Detective, Daring Detective, Shocking Detective, and True Police Cases, but none of them measured up to the higher literary standards of the Black Mask, featuring the work of Erle Stanley Gardner, Raymond Chandler, S.S. Van Dine, and Dashiell Hammett, or the gritty black and white realism of Macfadden's publication.

The pulp magazines tended to glamorize the work of the P.I. Unlike the cautionary tales imparted to impressionable youth about the wages of sin in the earlier dime novel detective stories, the twentieth century P.I. exhibited a coldly-detached cynicism as he battled fictional criminals based in part on real life murders, forgeries, con-games, embezzlements, and strong-arm robberies reported in the daily newspapers.

The new detectives were often at wits end trying to make a go of it in a shabby back-street office; their gin flasks concealed in the top drawer of a roll-down desk parked along side a holstered .44. More often than not, a betraying femme fatale with underworld connections and a mysterious past shook the P.I.'s confidence.

By the 1930s, the private eye had become society's consummate loner, a battered world-weary cynic plying his trade in a smoke and shadows world of duplicitous dames, resentful cops, and double-crossing scoundrels of the worst stripe.

The boozy, skirt-chasing fictional P.I.s were often mirror reflections of their creators. Chandler, his early years awash in disillusionment and literary failure, was an alcoholic long before he invented the brooding P.I., Philip Marlowe. Likewise, Dashiell Hammett was employed by a Baltimore brokerage firm in a dead-end job before joining the Pinkertons as an agent specializing in surveillance work. Hammett's real-life experiences formed the premise of dozens of short stories and novels, but his heavy drinking bouts and a disruptive personal life diminished his productivity and output in later years.

The literary noir technique, elevated to an art form by Chandler ("The Big Sleep"), Hammett ("The Maltese Falcon"), Mickey Spillane ("I The Jury") and James M. Cain ("The Postman Always Rings Twice"), is known by a catch-all phrase, "hard-boiled" detective fiction, for the edgy demeanor of its central protagonists. The genre has never faded from popular view, and the recent contributions of Elmore Leonard, Robert Parker and Eugene "Guy" Izzi, supply fresh leads and darkly humorous insights to the character of the fictional private eye.

As entertaining and compelling as detective fiction has remained over the years, it bears no striking resemblance to the day to day casework of the modern investigator caught up in the information age world of data base retrieval and high-end technology. Innovation has rendered much of what the old-fashioned P.I. used to do, as obsolete.

Fifty years ago, matrimonial investigation was a core business for the smaller P.I. firms. The surveillance of cheating husbands and wives and the results obtained was a high-stakes, make or break issue in pending divorce litigation. Proving adultery in court often resulted in the forfeiture of up to 80% of the philanderer's assets.

The era of the cynical P.I. spying on errant spouses in sleazy motel rooms has passed. It is a modern casualty of no-fault divorce, changing societal perceptions, and increased professionalism within the industry. The new arena of domestic investigation and undercover work involves asset searches prior to, or following a divorce action, and child custody and parental abduction cases.

The modern investigator is much more likely to be involved in assisting companies with their due diligence requirements; qualifying business partners through background checks; asset location; pre-employment background screening; investigating bogus workmen's compensation claims, investment frauds, financial crimes, trademark infringement, product diversion, security surveys, and high-tech surveillance to verify personal injury claims.

The single most important emerging industry trend nowadays is Competitive Intelligence (CI), the gathering and analysis of highly specific information to assist modern corporations as they look to expand their business across domestic and international borders.

After World War II, a time when the American intelligence gathering community was forced to downsize, many out-of-work agents gravitated into the private sector where large, multi-national corporations found their skills to be of particular use. This incongruous, odd assortment of tricksters, former O.S.S. operatives, black operations specialists and code breakers now employed in the private sector helped level the playing field for American business who lagged far behind their Japanese counterparts in the field of Competitive Intelligence.

There is a growing recognition among CEOs and CFOs for the necessity of dedicated Competitive Intelligence units within their corporate culture. Many savvy Fortune 500 companies already have these units in place; assessing a competitor's sales, and marketing and financial data. By the second decade of the Millennium, they will be as common as loss prevention/security units are today.

The demand for detailed information from CI specialists requires that the specialists bring to the table broad analytical skills, problem solving, and an awareness of evolving business conditions. Valuable insights are often gained from the Internet, on-line information providers like LEXIS-NEXIS, CDB-Infotek, Dialog, Dow Jones, Dun & Bradstreet, skilled interviewing technique, and an ability to strike at hidden truths through a vortex of numbing facts and figures. Gaining sight, insight, and solutions by penetrating this myriad of seemingly disparate information is a

SUMMARY

Amazingly, some of the exploits of real life detectives have been as insightful, exciting, and mysterious as their fictional counterparts. Much of today's criminal investigative techniques and crime scene procedures are due to private investigators, namely; Pinkerton, Burns, and Vidocq. However, we gain most of our knowledge about their adventures from books they authored. It's fair to say egos may have embellished the accounts. In following chapters we will find how modern private investigations have evolved and how some investigative techniques of old still influence private investigators today.

DISCUSSION QUESTIONS

1. Kate Warne had an advantage over her male counterparts in certain situations. Do you think there are situations today that a female private investigator may have an advantage? What would they be? What advantages would a male and female investigative team have?

2. Were you surprised to discover that modern day criminalistic methods such as; mug shots, criminal records, plaster cast impressions, and undercover work were pioneered by private investigators? Why or why not?

3. Noting the changes in the private investigative field, where do you see profession heading? What skills or special training will be needed?

END NOTES

1   FBI. *History of the FBI, Origins: 1908 – 1910.* Retrieved May 25, 2005, at http://www.fbi.gov/libref/historic/history/origins.htm

2–5 Ibid

6   FBI. FBI History. Historical Documents from the Bureau's Founding: *Letter, Bonaparte to President Roosevelt, 1/14/1909.* Retrieved May 25, 2005, at http://www.fbi.gov/libref/historic/history/historic_doc/doc1909jan.htm

7   FBI. *History of the FBI, Origins: 1908 – 1910.* Retrieved May 25, 2005, at http://www.fbi.gov/libref/historic/history/origins.htm

8   Ibid

9   From Wikipedia, the free encyclopedia. Eugène François Vidocq. Copyright (C) 2000,2001,2002 Free Software Foundation, Inc.59 Temple Place, Suite 330, Boston, MA 02111-1307 USA Everyone is permitted to copy and distribute verbatim copies of this license document, but changing it is not allowed.

10–17 Ibid

18 Lindberg, Richard. (1999). *Cloaks and Daggers and Thief Takers: A Concise History of Private Detection.* Retrieved December 24, 2004, from http://richardlindberg.net Copyright Richard Lindberg reprinted with permission.

Chapter 2

Career Fields For Private Investigators

OVERVIEW

In the first chapter we ended with how fictional literature on the private investigators and private investigators that influenced literature. This chapter continues the "myth vs. reality" theme in private investigations and will address the many facets of investigation work, making distinctions between work in the public and private sectors. We will cover the various clients and types of cases one can expect to encounter in the private sector and methods for meeting the client's needs. Career fields related to private investigations are touched upon. Future employment outlook and financial estimates are provided as well.

CHAPTER OBJECTIVES

1. Myths will be replaced by facts and accounts of actual cases.

2. Recognize the roles played by professional investigators in society today.

3. Discover who hires private investigators and the financial prospects they can expect.

4. Necessary skills needed for success will be identified.

5. Examine occupations related to private investigations

From the Files of Diane Evans

It just doesn't seem right to discuss private investigators without at least a mention of one of the best known fictional ones. The longest running television series from 1957-1966, was "Perry Mason". It was one of the first to portray an attorney-at-work, and more importantly his investigator, (drum roll) Paul Drake, played by actor William Holden. For years I've lived in the shadow of Paul Drake, the fictional investigator for fictional lawyer, Perry Mason and Della Street his woman-of-all-trades. The Mason character was actually created 20 years earlier by author Earle Stanley Garner, yet it was actor Raymond Burr who brought Perry and his friend, Paul, into our living rooms each week.

Perry was a criminal defense lawyer and each week he was in trial getting his innocent client free and usually a confession from the guilty party. It was definitely a formula production, yet we kept watching as Perry confidently and competently cross-examined opposing witnesses, analyzed evidence with out ever getting his feathers ruffled.

The weekly hero was actually Paul, in virtually every show the always smooth and unflappable, Paul would appear in the courtroom at the last minute presenting the surprise mystery witness! This witness both testified, and won the case for Perry's client or his mere presence in the courtroom was enough for the guilty party to succumb to Perry's pointed probing.

Scripted television shows are more about entertaining than educating, and this one has the dubious honor for widely introducing the public to the misconception of private investigators.

In reality, there are pre-trial hearings and exchanges of information between opposing parties. Both sides have the opportunity to interview and question witnesses in advance of trial. Very few prosecutors would allow a Perry Mason to continue on and on, without an objection. It is a rare occasion, indeed, that a witness brought in at the last moment will be allowed to testify, much less provoke a certain verdict. A trial is built on legal procedures, testimony of experts and eyewitnesses, plus physical evidence, such as, weapons, photos or documents.

Perry Mason did for investigative work what Jack Webb and Dragnet did for police work; simple entertainment nothing more. What we see seeps into our brains, and lacking any contrary knowledge we come to believe what we see. If it has to do with private investigators or legal procedures, don't believe it unless you see it in a documentary, on the History Channel or Court TV.

Screenwriters apparently have little imagination or maybe they think it is a rule, that as soon as some poor guy gets the cuffs slapped on him the arresting officer begins "You have the right to remain silent…" In actuality, an arrestee is Mirandized (read his rights) only before questioning. These are what I laughingly refer to as "TV codes."

Since Paul Drake, the public has had the opportunity to become acquainted with Jim Rockford, Magnum P.I., Dan Tana, and dozens of other "P.I.s" who were much more radical than our legal investigator, Paul. Those other guys & gals were always getting into shooting matches, car chases, and romantic situations with clients and each other. Uh, not one of any of those things ever happened in my experience of 20 years in private investigation.

Ethics check: I have yet to meet the client who would pay enough for me to be willing to risk losing my limbs, life, license, and livelihood or worse land myself in jail. This is not to say that every investigator in the business has the same good sense. The former 'investigator to stars' Anthony Pellicano is in prison for his illegal activites and will likely faces additional charges of wiretapping. I know of a few investigators who did commit illegal acts and made a lot of money doing so until they were caught. How much can one spend in the prison commissary? Does the trite phrase "no brainer" come to mind?

As if there weren't already enough misconceptions about private investigators, a few years ago the broadcast media presented the bomb "Snoops" about a female investigator whose ethics were of no concern. Legal or illegal, it apparently didn't matter to her. As an industry, we cringed at the thought of being portrayed as being so outrageous, irresponsible, reprehensible, and simply devoid of ethical concerns. We are still working on getting rid of that "gumshoe" image created by writers in the 30's and 40's. Show's like "Snoops" probably did more damage than real life investigators like Pellicano.

The literary field doesn't bring any more realism to what we do as private investigators. I've read all of author Sue Grafton's alphabet series starting with "A is for Alibi" and enjoyed them all, yet I can't say I learned anything from any of them.

Grafton's pragmatic character; the ex-cop, former insurance investigator, and now licensed private investigator, Kinsey Millhone, is fun, quirky, and likeable. Yet, she is always in trouble and faced with danger tripping over dead bodies while performing research or verifying a street address. There are great authors with great imaginations, but because they are good storytellers, that is why their works sell as fiction.

So now that you have an idea of what private investigations isn't, I'll let you in on the real deal from my own 20 years experience. Investigators, whether law enforcement, private industry, working for law firms or insurance companies, all use similar methods. It is simply the case circumstances and objectives that differ.

Investigating is primarily an information-gathering endeavor. An investigator's job is to discover facts and evidence that will benefit their client or employer's position in a given matter. We gather our facts, statistics, and other evidence, and then commonly prepare a report for our client or superior. The client wants to know what information we found, what it means to their situation, our impressions or evaluations of the case, and our analysis of how reliable a witness may, or may not be.

PUBLIC/GOVERNMENT INVESTIGATIONS

You are already aware that law enforcement and other government agencies have fairly narrow goals. Police departments will investigate alleged crimes. Detectives and investigators work to determine if a crime was actually committed. If so, they will eliminate suspects until they find the most likely one, then gather evidence to turn over a suspect to the district attorney for prosecution.

The local District Attorney's office will take and analyze the police reports. The D.A. may have their own investigators delve further into the matter; before deciding if they have enough evidence to prosecute.

Department or Bureaus of Motor Vehicles, Professional Licensing, Public Assistance, all have investigators who look into possible frauds, forgeries, thefts or other violations of law concerning their agency. Actions may be brought for disciplinary actions of employees and/or criminal charges for others. Police Departments have their own Internal Affairs divisions that investigate suspicions or allegations against other officers.

Every government department or agency has investigators to look into irregularities within that agency. When the matter involves a local law enforcement agency, the state's Attorney General, or possibly the FBI will probe that department.

Government officials have a legal obligation to search for the truth, and are even required to reveal to the accused any evidence pointing to their innocence. Since salaried government employees make each task or inquiry, cost is of little, if any, concern. Their purposes are clear, and their financial resources unrestricted.

Government agencies commonly contract with licensed private investigators to conduct pre-employment background checks and other sensitive investigations for their departments.

CHARACTERISTICS OF PRIVATE INVESTIGATIONS WORK

Private detectives and investigators use many means to determine the facts in a variety of matters. To determine the whereabouts of persons and/or evidence, they may use various types of surveillance or searches. To verify facts, such as an individual's place of employment or income, they may make phone calls or visit a subject's workplace. In other cases, especially those involving missing persons and background checks, investigators interview people to gather as much information as possible about the individual. In all cases, private detectives and investigators assist attorneys, businesses, and the public with a variety of legal, financial, and personal problems.

Private detectives and investigators offer many services, including executive, corporate, and celebrity protection; pre-employment verification; and individual background profiles. They also provide assistance in civil liability and personal injury cases, insurance claims and fraud, child custody, and protection cases, and premarital screening. Increasingly, they are hired to investigate individuals to prove or disprove infidelity.

Most detectives and investigators are trained to perform physical surveillance, often for extended periods of time, in a car or van. They may observe a site, such as the home of a subject, from an inconspicuous location. The surveillance continues using tools such as; still and video cameras, binoculars, and a cell phone, until the budget is exhausted or desired evidence is obtained. They also may perform computer database searches, or work with someone who does. Computers allow detectives and investigators to quickly obtain massive amounts of information on individuals' prior arrests, convictions, and civil legal judgments; telephone numbers; motor vehicle registrations; association, and club memberships; and other matters.

The duties of private detectives and investigators depend on the needs of their client. In cases for employers involving workers' fraudulent compensation claims, for example, investigators may carry out long-term covert observation of subjects. If an investigator observes a subject performing an activity that contradicts injuries stated in a workers' compensation claim, the investigator would take video or still photographs to document the activity and report it to the client.

[For more information, see Bureau of Labor Statistics. Office of Occupational Statistics and Employment Projections.
http://www.bls.gov.OCO]

WORKING CONDITIONS

Be forewarned, the first few years in the field will be financially tight, especially when working under some one else's license and/or when you start your own agency. This is an industry were one must pay their dues before reaping monetary gains.

Private detectives and investigators often work irregular hours because of the need to conduct surveillance and contact people who are not available during normal working hours. Early morning, evening, weekend, and holiday work is common.

Many detectives and investigators spend time away from their offices conducting interviews or doing surveillance, but some work in their office most of the day conducting computer searches and making phone calls. Those who have their own agencies and employ other investigators may work primarily in an office and have normal business hours.

When working on a case away from the office, the environment might range from plush boardrooms to seedy bars. Store and hotel detectives work in the businesses that they protect. Investigators generally work alone, but they sometimes work with others during surveillance or when following a subject in order to avoid detection by the subject.

Some of the work involves confrontation, so the job can be stressful and dangerous. Some situations call for the investigator to be armed, such as certain bodyguard assignments for corporate or celebrity clients. The appropriate authority must license detectives and investigators who carry handguns. In most cases, however, a weapon is not necessary because the purpose of their work is gathering information and not law enforcement or criminal apprehension. Owners of investigative agencies have the added stress of having to deal with demanding and sometimes distraught clients.

From the Files of Douglas Crewse

> Being a Certified Fraud examiner, I do a lot of fraud and civil litigation investigations and consultation. What is fun and challenging is trying to keep up with the ingenious ways people commit fraud and keeping up with the civil litigation issues.
>
> Just like any job, drudgery takes its toll. However, I find that reviewing a vast amount of documents, that by creating databases, charts, graphs, and other visual aids takes the drudgery out the equation. This also helps in the presentation to the client, acts as guidelines in trials, and depositions.

INVESTIGATOR LICENSING, EDUCATION AND TRAINING

Licensing

Chances are when you begin a career in private investigations you will work under some else's license as an investigator employee/intern until you learn the ropes (pay your dues) and can get your own license. Most states require private investigators to be licensed. Licensing requirements in each state varies. Some require applicants pass a written exam, be insured, and provide documentation of a prescribed number of investigative hours under supervision of licensed P.I., or have been a sworn law enforcement officer. Almost all states deny convicted felons private investigator licenses.

A growing number of states are enacting mandatory training programs for private detectives and investigators. Some States have few requirements, and at the time of this writing, 6 States: Alabama, Alaska, Colorado, Idaho, Mississippi, and South Dakota, have no statewide licensing requirements. However, other states have stringent regulations. For example, the Bureau of Security and Investigative Services (BSIS) of the California Department of Consumer Affairs requires private investigators to be 18 years of age or older; have a combination of education in police science, criminal law, or justice, or experience equaling 3 years (6,000 hours) of investigative experience. An applicant must pass an evaluation by the Federal Department of Justice and a criminal history background check. They must receive a qualifying score on a 2-hour, 150 question written examination covering laws and regulations. There are additional requirements for a firearms permit.

California issues licenses to conduct an investigation business to sole proprietors, partnerships, and corporations. As a requirement for licensing, each entity must have an actual breathing person acting as a Qualified Manager. The QM can be an owner, partner, officer or employee of the licensee, and must reside in California.

Laws vary greatly from state to state. Some states issue one license that includes private investigators and security guards; others don't allow private investigators to do executive protection aka (also known as) bodyguard. Some states have no state regulation and rely on local governments to legitimize a firm; others have no regulation. California, for example, does not allow its private investigators to stand guard positions.

Florida has various classes of licenses. There is one for a private investigation agency and another for a branch office. Individuals can be licensed as a "Manager" of a private investigation agency, private investigator, and private investigator intern. Candidates must be 18 years of age, have a legal right to work in the United States, have no disqualifying criminal history, be of good moral character, and have no disqualifying history of mental illness or alcohol or controlled substance abuse.

For an agency license in Arizona the Qualifying Party must be at least 21 years of age with 6,000 hours of qualifying experience. No test is required, yet a $2,500 bond is.

Nevada has some fairly stringent requirements, which one might imagine is fallout from attempting to keep the gaming industry above board. Nevada requires 6,000 hours experience, passing of a qualifying examination, and extensive background investigation.

In most states a private investigator is defined as any individual or agency that, for consideration, advertises as providing or performs the following activities:

- Subcontracting with the government to determine crimes or wrongs done or threatened against the United States
- Determining the identity, habits, conduct, movements, whereabouts, affiliations, associations, transactions, reputation or character of any society, person, or group of persons
- The credibility of witnesses or other persons

- The whereabouts of missing persons, owners of abandoned or escheated property, or heirs to estates
- The location or recovery of lost or stolen property
- The causes or origin of fires, libels, slanders, losses, accidents, damage, or injuries to real or personal property
- Securing evidence to be used before investigating committees or boards of award or arbitration or trial of civil or criminal cases

Each state that requires licensing for private investigators also has exemptions for those who conduct similar work for government agencies, insurance companies, and other legal and business concerns. The following are commonly exempt:

- Those exclusively using public records
- Government employees
- Law firms in their matters
- Private employers concerning their own matters
- Employees of licensed investigators

Education and Training

There are no formal education requirements for most private detective and investigator jobs, although many private detectives have college degrees. Private detectives and investigators typically have previous experience in other occupations. Some work initially for insurance or collections companies or in the private security industry. Many investigators enter the field after serving in law enforcement, the military, government auditing, and investigative positions, or federal intelligence jobs.

Former law enforcement officers, military investigators, and government agents often become private detectives or investigators as a second career because they are frequently able to retire after 20 years of service. Others enter from such diverse fields as finance, accounting, commercial credit, investigative reporting, insurance, and law. These individuals often can apply their prior work experience in a related investigative specialty. A few enter the occupation directly after graduation from college, generally with associate or bachelor's degrees in criminal justice or police science.

Training in subjects such as criminal justice is helpful to aspiring private detectives and investigators. Most corporate investigators must have a bachelor's degree, preferably in a business-related field. Some corporate investigators have master's degrees in business administration or law, while others are certified public accountants. Corporate investigators hired by large companies may receive formal training from their employers on business practices, management structure, and various finance-related topics. The screening process for potential employees typically includes a background check of criminal history.

Some investigators receive certification from professional organizations to demonstrate competency in a field. For example, the National Association of Legal Investigators (NALI) confers the Certified Legal Investigator (CLI) designation to licensed investigators who devote a majority of their practice to negligence or criminal defense investigations. In order to receive the designation, applicants must satisfy experience, educational, and continuing training requirements, and must pass written and oral exams administered by the NALI. [13]

ASIS International is one of the leaders in the field of professional security organizations. ASIS is devoted to raising the efficiency and productivity of security professionals by developing educational programs and materials that address broad security concerns. In 2002, ASIS and their Professional Certification Board began a Professional Certified Investigator (PCI) certification program.

EMPLOYMENT OPPORTUNITIES

Many private detective agencies are small, with little room for advancement. Usually there are no defined ranks or steps, so advancement takes the form of increases in salary and assignment status. Many detectives and investigators work for detective agencies at the beginning of their careers and, after a few years, start their own firms. Corporate and legal investigators may rise to supervisor or manager of the security or investigations department.

From the Files of Diane Evans

> There are many huge licensed firms that have offices across the country. My experience is that for the most part, we are a bunch of loners and choose to perform cases ourselves; then call in another professional when we need a hand. Examples of this can be found in this chapter under "General Investigations: Calls for Diversity".

Once you get your own private investigator license, the employment opportunities expand. Of course you can still choose to work under an employer's license or as an in-house investigator if you don't want the liabilities of running your own agency. A large number of licensed private investigators prefer work solo or team up with another partner. Some prefer to contract with government or private companies rather than deal with customers that walk-in off the streets. Some private companies that hire private investigators are casinos, bank, and financial corporations, hotels, and resorts, and railroads.

What P.I.'s Do and Who They Do It For: Areas of Specialization

Figure 2.1 Who PI's Work For and What They Do

GENERAL INVESTIGATIONS	EMPLOYER -BUSINESS	LEGAL	INDIVIDUAL
locate persons	workers' compensation	locate witnesses	locate family members
asset searches	insurance fraud	interview & statements	locate adoptive child/parents
Pre-marital background	aoe/coe	evaluate witness or evidence	Collect judgments
process server	federal workers' comp	crime scene analysis	elder abuse
computer research	pre-employment background	criminal defense	mentally impaired clients
	loss prevention	civil case preparation	never can tell
	retail integrity		
	industrial undercover		
	sexual harassment		

Private detectives and investigators often specialize. Those who focus on intellectual property theft, for example, investigate, and document acts of piracy, help clients stop the illegal activity, and provide intelligence for prosecution and civil action. Other investigators specialize in developing financial profiles and asset searches. Their reports reflect information gathered through interviews, investigation, and surveillance, and research, including review of public documents. The following areas of investigation are just a small sampling of what private investigators do.

Insurance Investigations

Insurance companies are in businesses to make a profit, usually for stockholders. One exorbitant cost of doing business is the billions of dollars in premiums being paid out to satisfy false or inflated claims. In the state of Connecticut, it is estimated insurance fraud costs the average family over $1,800 a year in premiums. Connecticut's Insurance Department places the statewide cost to consumers to be as much as $1.9 billion annually. According to the Erie Indemnity Company of Pennsylvania, the cost of insurance fraud across the nation is estimated around $96.8 billion annually.

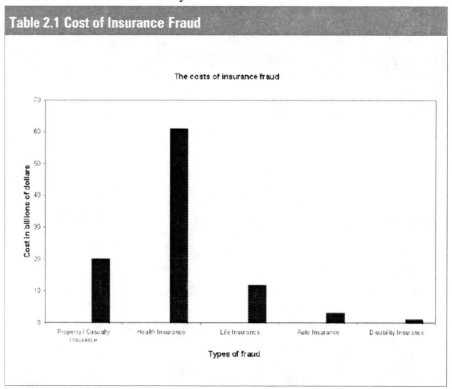

Table 2.1 Cost of Insurance Fraud

Homeowners insurance is a common target for false and or inflated claims. Homes are burglarized so frequently that some police departments have begun taking reports over the phone. Clues and leads are usually scarce, resulting in unsuccessful investigations and arrests. It is rare for the stolen items to be recovered and returned to the owner. For some people the temptation to make a profit from their loss is too great. When filing their report with the police they may exaggerate how many gold coins and pieces of jewelry were taken. Some people flat out stage their own burglary in an attempt to profit.

Insurance adjusters know that some claims will cost more to litigate, than to simply settle out-of-court for several thousand dollars. Auto insurance companies know this better than anyone. There are people who stage traffic accidents and work with networks of unethical law firms, doctor's offices, physical therapy clinics, and chiropractors in order to cash in on insurance payments. This is big business in most major cities and those of us who play by the rules get to make up the difference to the insurance companies.

From the Files of Diane Evans

I know a couple that were burglarized while they were sleeping and only a VCR was taken. They discussed filing an insurance claim for additional items; then decided against it. It's a good thing too, because when the homeowners called to report the burglary and theft of their VCR, the burglary detectives told them that the cable had been cut with their own kitchen knife. Apparently one particular burglar had been working the same neighborhood and only took VCR's. In addition, he always used the victims own kitchen knife to cut the cable that was true in this case, as well.

Workers' Compensation fraud is rampant. Injured workers claim non-work injuries as being on-the job and/or continue treatment when fully recovered. Uninjured workers may feign injury after being invited into a network of unethical professionals who will prepare fraudulent reports and invoices for thousands of dollars of treatments while putting a few hundred dollars in the patient's pocket. There are plenty of "free lancers" who were legitimately injured, yet continue to complain of persistent pain long past the time when they have returned to their weekly softball game.

There is plenty of work for insurance investigators who take reports, speak with witnesses, conduct research and/or conduct surveillance of a claimant's activities. It is not unusual for a field investigator to see an "injury victim" hobble into a doctor's office using a cane or crutches, struggle back to their vehicle only to go home, then pick up their clubs to play a round of golf.

Others may be collecting disability payments from an insurance company while still working on another job, unbeknownst to the insurer. Whether an insured files a totally false claim or simply exaggerates his losses, he has committed a crime. The insurance company goal may simply be to be able to decline further payments, or in other instances may wish to prosecute the fraudulent claimant to the extent of the law, and seek restitution. If more companies did that there would be much less fraud.

Insurance companies may hire their own in-house investigators to investigate claims, in which case each employee is salaried and is assigned a certain amount of cases to investigate. He or she is not necessarily limited to a specific dollar amount for each case.

From the Files of Susan Ford-Baltazar

Following a four-year stint in U.S. Army Counterintelligence, I began working in the private the sector as an investigator in 1990. I have had the opportunity to work for small private investigations agencies, and in the special investigations units for two insurance carriers. One was arson investigation, the other, workers' compensation fraud investigations.

One of the benefits I have found to being an in-house investigator is that my employer's clients are more helpful and cooperative than those of the insurance carriers who hire outside investigators to work on their cases. They generally seem to have an open attitude about sharing information and documents. When I would go to similar clients as an outside investigator working for their insurance carrier, I didn't get this open attitude. When working as an in-house investigator, it is as almost as if the client sees all of us as part of team, working for a common goal (them not being victimized by fraudulent claims), rather than me just being an outsider sent by their insurance carrier.

Another benefit of being employed by a corporation, besides a steady salary, is the perks. These can include a company provided vehicle (including gas and insurance), laptop computer, cell phone, company credit card for expenses, desk and office space, and things such as group medical insurance and 401K plans. Oh, and vacation pay!

There is a down side too of course. There goes a lot of your flexibility when it comes to picking and choosing when and what cases you want to work. And for many investigators, it's that freedom to "do your own thing" that is the addiction to this field of work.

Insurance or other companies may directly sub-contract with independent investigators who are in business for themselves. An insurance adjuster or claims processor will ordinarily assign the private investigator a particular case and set a limit for time and/or funds that can be expended. This limitation of time sometimes reduces the ability of the investigator to get the information.

Corporate Investigations

Corporate investigators conduct internal and external investigations for corporations other than investigative firms. With internal investigations, they may investigate drug use in the workplace, ensure that expense accounts are not abused, or determine if employees are stealing merchandise or information. External investigations typically prevent criminal schemes originating outside the corporation, such as theft of company assets through fraudulent billing of products by suppliers.

Large companies will have their own in-house investigators who are rarely required to be licensed, as long as each is a direct employee of the company. These employees may work on internal fraud and employment related matters, plus tracking down customers who skipped out owing the company money.

Financial Investigations

Financial investigators may be hired to develop confidential financial profiles of individuals or companies who are prospective parties to large financial transactions. They often are Certified Public Accountants (CPAs) and work closely with investment bankers and accountants. They search for assets in order to recover damages awarded by a court in fraud or theft cases.

Bank of America, Citibank, Chase Manhattan, and all the other banks have employees who locate customers who have defaulted on loans. Banks will background potential investors to be assured of the individual's financial ability and reliability. Pre-employment background investigations are in high demand.

Loss Prevention and Security

Detectives who work for retail stores or hotels are responsible for loss control and asset protection. Store detectives, also known as loss prevention agents, safeguard the assets of retail stores by apprehending anyone attempting to steal merchandise or destroy store property. They prevent theft by shoplifters, vendor representatives, delivery personnel, and even store employees. Store detectives also conduct periodic inspections of stock areas, dressing rooms, and restrooms, and sometimes assist in opening and closing the store. They may prepare loss prevention and security reports for management and testify in court against persons they apprehend. Hotel detectives protect guests of the establishment from theft of their belongings and preserve order in hotel restaurants and bars. They also may keep undesirable individuals, such as known thieves, off the premises.

Retail stores such as Target, Sears, and JC Penney have their own staff of "loss prevention" employees who detect shoplifters and investigate employee theft, or those investigations may be assigned to independent professional investigators.

Bars, fine restaurants and even fast food franchises hire observers to come in and pose as customers. Not a bad job in most cases. You get free food and drink AND get paid to consume it. Even the public utilities, cable services, etc. have a need to investigate fraud and theft of their services.

Legal Investigators

An individual employed by law offices works on behalf of his or her employer/client. These workers can legally locate and interview witnesses, conduct background investigations of clients or witnesses under their employer's supervision. Direct employees may have other tasks such as preparing legal documents and/or making court filings; yet usually, can do everything a private independent investigator can do. Lawyers may depend on, and subcontract with licensed private investigators on a per-case basis.

Law firms generally cannot contract to conduct investigations unrelated to a legal case, for which they have been retained.

Legal investigators are employed equally between civil and criminal practices working with the attorney for the plaintiff, respondent or defendant's attorney. Legal investigators frequently take part in trial preparation as fundamental members of the trial team by gathering data regarding the parties to litigation and putting together discovery and reports. They locate witnesses, serve legal documents, interview police, and prospective witnesses, take photographs, testify in court, and gather and review evidence.

It should be noted that every state has different rules regarding the licensing status of these types of investigators. In some situations the legal investigator is referred to as a paralegal.

> **Qwik-Tip**
> Just in case you were wondering there is usually no difference between investigator and detective. In this country "detective" is more old school and most of us refer to ourselves as a "private investigator". To call oneself a private investigator may require licensing in that state.

Charities

Amazingly enough, large philanthropic organizations and universities have employees who conduct investigation into well-off community members to see whom has the ability to make a contribution to their organization or cause. They analyze the contributor's financial background to see in what amount the charity should make a request.

Nursing Home Abuse Investigations

American's are living longer and the number of elderly in the U.S. is growing at a rapid rate. As a result of this geriatric boom, nursing homes are experiencing a huge increase in resident population. Along with the increase in population comes increase in profits, in fact, the nursing home business has become a multi-billion dollar industry. Unfortunately some are driven purely by profit and rather than the morality of offering quality care.

Negligence and abuse may have always occurred on some level, but now because of the sheer volume is has become the focus of state and federal scrutiny. New legislation has been introduced to combat abuse and protect the elderly. Elderly victims and their families can take legal action to gain compensation for their injuries and loss. Litigation of these cases is becoming a big business causing a need for private investigators specialized in elder abuse.

Government Contract Investigations

A private investigator can contract to do work for government agencies. Government agencies typically have their own investigators or special agent in charge (SAC) but often need to hire outside support for financial, subject expertise, staffing or additional reasons. Federal, state, and county government agencies utilize investigators for a variety of departments and investigations.

State and County Agencies

You have a right to remain silent. You have the right to an attorney, if you cannot afford an attorney one will be appointed to you at government expense.

In addition to the courts appointing attorneys to indigent defendants, many also appoint private investigators to aid in defense as well. Typically the county public defenders office that may have their own in-house defense investigators will represent those who cannot afford an attorney. Due to insufficient staff or conflicts of interest, the public defenders (PD) office may not be able to provide representation to all defendants. In these cases the court appoints the case to a contract defense department. The county's contract defense department selects from a pool of pre-qualified attorneys and private investigators.

 From the Files of Diane Evans

> Only once did I accept a criminal defense investigator assignment from a defendant who was representing himself. I spoke with the defendant from and jail and he gave me his name, and told me about the case. It was one that had been publicized a few years before and I recalled my thoughts about. It seems a young woman did not return from "spring break" and after her disappearance her apartment had been burglarized. I was fairly sure of her fate.
>
> The case was slow to come tighter and the first break came when her vehicle was finally found in Fresno California. Strangely her car had been sold to a dealer, then to an individual who reports it stolen. Then someone 'finds' the vehicle and unknowingly takes it back to the dealer who sold it before, the police got their first lead.

With a lot more legwork the police identify two suspects who were husband and wife. Yet, they could not be found. At one point it seems the police were just an egg roll away. After the aired on television's "America's Most Wanted" numerous phone calls came in and police were given an address. When they arrived and entered the house police found only some lukewarm Chinese food. Apparently the couple was preparing to watch the show when they heard their own names and shall we say 'split' before the police arrived. It was their second television appearance that did them in. They missed the show this time and police were waiting for them when they arrived home from shopping.

My client, the husband, was representing himself (pro-per) while his wife had counsel and an investigator with which I was acquainted. It was a mistake on the defendant's part, because they both accused the other of being the shooter, which made it easy for the prosecutor. The wife, being the smarter of the two, accepted a plea bargain rather than face a death sentence.

The husband decided to go to trial on his own. Criminals always think they are so smart and can wiggle their way around anything or anybody. It doesn't occur to them that someone else was smarter and put them in jail. He wasted a lot of time and court appointed money sending his court runners, and by this time investigators, after dead end leads and imaginary witnesses. I finally dropped out and let another investigator take over who drove all over southern Arizona with running down dead end streets.

He had no idea how to handle himself at trial and was more interested in proving to his witnesses that he knew more than they did. He became hostile with his own witnesses and more than once tried to cross-examine people who were supposed to be on his side.

He is now on death row in San Quentin. He has his own television, computer, website, and social life. He gets along with the whole population including the correctional officers. I believe he did not think there was anyway he could get out the situation he was in, and decided to have some fun trying his own case. I guess it would beat sitting in a county jail waiting for trial.

An example of how the private investigator/public defender system works is seen with Sacramento County's conflict overload cases. Sacramento County, California has chosen to provide secondary (conflict overload) representation through a county Conflict Defender office (Conflict Criminal Defenders or CCD). At the time of this writing the CCD is directed by Executive Director Fern Laethem, and supported by a staff of county employees. Independent contractor attorneys are members of the Bar Association Indigent Defense Panel, and are assigned to cases by the Executive Director of CCD provide legal representation.

Executive Director Laethem explains that the contracted attorneys can choose a private investigator from the CCD qualified panel. In some cases the contract investigator will be assigned by the CCD to work for the defendant directly in what is called a "pro-per" case. Because the direction of the investigation will be coming from a defendant who typically is not an expert in the law; these cases can be challenging for the investigator.

The CCD has provided guidelines to assist the investigator and the defendant on how to handle these cases. A following Figure outlines the policies and procedures for Sacramento County. Keep in mind that these guidelines written by Executive Director Laethem are specific to the County of Sacramento. It is suggested that research the court appointed investigator practices in your area.

Fig 2.2 Sacramento (CA) County Sample Policy

POLICY AND PROCEDURE FOR IN-CUSTODY IN PRO PER DEFENDANTS & INVESTIGATORS ASSIGNED TO IN-CUSTODY IN PRO PER DEFENDANT CASES

A. Introduction

One of the responsibilities of Conflict Criminal Defenders (CCD), by court order, is to provide defendants who are "In pro-per" with qualified CCD approved criminal defense investigators. The investigators responsibility is to assist a pro-per defendant in the investigation of his/her criminal case.

The Executive Director or Deputy Director of Conflict Criminal Defenders will assign the investigator from Conflict Criminal Defenders list of qualified panel investigators. Investigator assignments are made using the following criteria:
- Court order.
- Investigative needs of the pro-per defendant.
- Case specific investigator qualifications;

B. Purpose of Policy and Procedures

The purpose of these policies and procedures is:
- To provide written guidelines to investigators and pro-per defendants on the use of investigators in court appointed cases.
- To provide the court appointed investigators with written policy and procedures when dealing with defendants who choose to represent themselves.

C. Investigator Guidelines

1. Investigators shall:
- Provide the same level of investigative services to a pro-per defendant as would be provided to an attorney.
- Provide only investigative tasks pre-approved by CCD or the Court.

Fig 2.2 Sacramento (CA) County Sample Policy (Cont.)

- Follow jail rules and procedures when dealing with in pro-per defendants.
- Read, understand, and follow, Penal Code Section 1054.2, pertaining to disclosure of victims or witness addresses or phone numbers.
- Have the Director or Chief Investigator review for procedural correctness pleadings and subpoenas prepared by the in pro-per defendant, prior to service by the investigator.

2. Investigators shall not:
- Provide legal advice to an in pro-per defendant.
- Provide any items that violate jail policy, procedure, or guidelines.
- Prepare or provide any legal document not approved by the Court or Conflict
- Criminal Defenders;
- Provide any service other then investigative tasks approved by the Court or
- Conflict Criminal Defenders;
- Provide any contraband as defined in the "Inmate Handbook".
- Provide any advice or opinion to a pro-per defendant that could be construed as directing the investigation;

Any violation or allegation of a violation of these rules will be fully investigated and appropriate action taken, up to and including removal from Conflict Criminal Defenders list of approved investigators, which can result in the loss of investigative privileges.

D. In Pro per Defendant Guidelines

1. In Pro-per defendants shall:
- Obtain a Court appointed investigator when the court appoints and notifies
- Conflict Criminal Defenders of the appointment.
- Read and agree to follow the polices and procedures herein.
- Provide to Conflict Criminal Defenders a written request of investigative needs and tasks to be completed by the investigator. There are no automatic authorizations of investigative funds for in-pro-per defendants.
- Direct the investigation pertaining to the pending charges for which the investigator was appointed.
- Obtain all legal materials and legal books through the jail law library.

2. In Pro-per defendant shall not:
- Request the investigator to perform any task that is not pre-approved by the Court or Conflict Criminal Defenders.
- Request the investigator provide contraband materials or non-investigative items. Some examples of non-investigative requests are:

Fig 2.2 Sacramento (CA) County Sample Policy (Cont.)

1. To communicate messages to outside persons not pertaining to approved investigative tasks.

2. To deliver mail or written communication not pertaining to approved investigative tasks.

3. To obtain food, stamps, pens, pencils, file folders, legal materials, books or any other items that are considered to be contraband as set forth in the "Mail Jail Inmate Handbook" provide to the inmate by the jail.

4. To do anything that violates jail security procedures.

Any violation or allegation of a violation of these rules by in pro-per defendants will be fully investigated and appropriate action taken including reporting the violation to the Court.

Reprinted with permission of Fern Leathem Sacramento County Conflict Defender Office www.ppaccd.saccounty.net

As of July 2004, private investigators contracting with the County of Sacramento earn between $28 and $45 an hour depending on the level of the charges. In Pima County Arizona a contract investigator can earn $35 an hour.

From the Files of Carol Hawks

During my first job as a private investigator employee, the agency had a contract with the county to perform investigative services for indigent defendants. It might not have been the highest paying work, but there was certainly no lack of cases.

I always fancied that my career in criminal justice would be preventing, detecting, and solving crime. Growing up I thought private investigators solved "whodunits'. Yet there I was, aiding in the defense of suspects charged with major felonies and even murder. Not much of a mystery considering 98 percent of the time our client *was* the one 'whodunit'.

Most of the guys (and gals) that were facing the death penalty had a lengthy violent history. It was difficult at first to sit face-to-face with some of them. A large part of the job was conducting legal visits with the client in jail or prison. If you have considered working as a private investigator in criminal cases, chances are you won't be figuring out 'whodunits' either, and there is a very good chance many of your clients won't be innocent. There are a lot of people who feel they just can't consciously do defense work.

Although criminal defense investigators might not get a lot of respect or pats on the back, I soon found the work rewarding. By doing a through investigation; leaving no stone unturned, we did our part to insure that all the facts were presented. This compels the prosecution to do their job; proving the case beyond a reasonable doubt. Our justice system is an adversarial one, which without the defense, the prosecution would just become persecution.

How does one become qualified to do contract indigent defense investigations? In Pima County, Arizona, one is required to have a current Arizona State private investigator license and experience interviewing and recording witness statements. Additionally it is required that the investigator have at least three years of experience in criminal investigations of complex specialized cases such as, child abuse, fraud, murder, narcotics and sexual assault. Former police or government investigation work qualifies; however, most people work under some one else's license to gain the experience.

Other qualifications Pima County desires are; work experience on indigent defense cases for Pima County, membership in AALPI (Arizona Association of Licensed Private Investigators) and five hours a year of continuing education courses and training. Every county is different, check with your county for requirements and rates.

Some possible contract investigation work can be found with county welfare departments, and child support departments. State Agencies that might offer contract work are; Department of Corporations, Alcohol Control, Department of Motor Vehicles, Department of Transportation, Franchise Tax Board, Fish and Game, State Court Investigator Panel, and the Social Services Department

Federal Contract Work

Federal Agencies sometimes contract with the private sector investigators. The United States Department of Defense has contracted with private investigators to do personnel security investigations for the Defense Security Service. At the end of this chapter an excerpt from a U.S. DOD document describing the purpose and qualifications of contract investigators is provided in the following Figure.

Figure 2.3 U.S. Diplomatic Security Policy

U.S. DEPARTMENT OF STATE DIPLOMATIC SECURITY

UNITED STATES DEPARTMENT OF STATE BUREAU OF DIPLOMATIC SECURITY

12 FAH-3 H-040 INVESTIGATORS UNDER CONTRACT (SPECIAL INVESTIGATORS)

12 FAH-3 H-041 PURPOSE AND AUTHORITY (TL:FOMH-1; 12-4-95)

a. Special investigators, usually referred to as contract investigators (see section 12 FAH-3 H-042), are contract personnel hired to conduct background (personnel) and munitions control investigations. The ASAC or section chief of the appropriate field office normally provides investigative assignments, oversight, and support for special investigators. Special investigators do not serve on protective details and they do not have law enforcement authority.

b. The Bureau of Diplomatic Security (DS) employs contract investigators in circumstances where utilization of special agents is cost prohibitive or when special agents are not available to conduct the investigation. The Field Offices may not utilize contract investigators under any other circumstance except by the express authorization of the Director of DS/DSS/FLD.

c. Contract investigators will conduct investigations for the Department in accordance with subchapter 12 FAM 240.

12 FAH-3 H-042 ADMINISTRATIVE AND PERSONNEL MATTERS
12 FAH-3 H-042.1 Employment (TL:FOMH-1; 12-4-95)

a. The Director of DS/DSS/FLD is the sole hiring authority for contract investigators. Field Offices will use contract investigators on an as-needed basis.

b. DS may consider individuals for employment as contract investigators upon the recommendation of the special agent in charge (SAC) of the region in which they will function upon the approval of the Director of DS/DSS/FLD.

c. Once identified, a contract investigator will perform his or her tasks under the supervision of the SAC of the region to which assigned. SACs will brief all new contract investigators on all relevant policy and administrative matters.

12 FAH-3 H-042.2 Qualifications (TL:FOMH-1; 12-4-95)

a. Individuals must possess the following qualifications to be used as a contract investigator:

(1) Training and extensive experience (minimum of three years) in the field of U.S. Government personnel investigations;

(2) Experience and in-depth knowledge of the technical details involved in collecting, evaluating, and reporting investigative data;

Fig 2.3 U.S. Diplomatic Security Policy (Cont.)

(3) U.S. citizenship and eligibility for a security clearance up to and including SECRET;

(4) Residency in a geographic area where a Field Office requires investigative coverage;

(5) Willingness to travel anywhere in the United States as required;

(6) Healthy enough to withstand the rigors of travel;

(7) Capability to express him- or herself clearly both orally and in writing;

(8) BA or BS from an accredited college or university; and

(9) Ability to personally prepare typed Reports of Investigation that meet DS standards.

b. Only the Director of DS/DSS/FLD may grant exceptions to these standards.

12 FAH-3 H-043.2 Conducting Investigations
12 FAH-3 H-043.2-1 Personnel Investigations
(TL:FOMH-1; 12-4-95)

Contract investigators will conduct personnel investigations in order to accomplish the following objectives:

(1) Obtain data from appropriate official records and sources who have personal knowledge for confirming identity and personal history of the subject of investigation;

(2) Establish the continuity of the subject's claimed activities, account for the subject's movements from one place to another;

(3) Provide sufficient data to enable the Department to establish the subject's loyalty to the United States;

(4) Provide sufficient data to enable the Department to establish the subject's general character, integrity, trustworthiness, and overall suitability for employment and/or access to classified information;

(5) Conduct a personal interview of the subject;

(6) Verify the subject's employment and education claims;

(7) Conduct neighborhood inquiries; and

(8) Search records of police and credit organizations.

Source: http://foia.state.gov/masterdocs/12fah03/Fom0040.pdf

General Investigations: Calls for Diversity

Private investigators are asked to perform diverse tasks. The following samples are actual requests made to private investigators for assistance. These should give you some idea of the types of cases in which we become involved. There are few routine or boring days when one works in general investigations. There is no training class that will provide the answers to all the following questions. Much of the work we do is by the 'seat of our pants' and we take our life experience and make it work for us. Ingenuity comes in real handy when you are doing general investigations. Do you have any ideas on how you might approach any of the following requests?

- We are looking for an investigator that specializes in locating insurance policies. Have a widow that is trying to locate polices of deceased spouse.

- I am in need of an English speaking contact with local PD (police department) in Heredia, CostaRica, this is regarding a missing American there.

- I have a client who wants to know if a specific person (Client furnished Name, DOB and SSN) is a member of the Hells Angels. I know this is a rather unusual request and I have no expertise in the field of motorcycle gangs.

- I have a client whom has a child support judgment for past support of approximately $30,000. The government has been unsuccessful in collecting it, and told my client he has not appeared on the work rolls for two years so they are giving up.

- We are assisting a family in locating their son who has a cellular phone on his person at all times and has an outstanding felony warrant for his arrest in the system. Anyone have an idea how this person, once on his cell phone during a call could be located based on triangulation? Is it legal? Can it be done? And of course, How?

- I am working on a wrongful death case where a funeral escort motorcyclist hit a pedestrian who subsequently died. However, the defendant denies working for the escort company and his personal insurance company states he was working, so they won't extend coverage (However, this company won't divulge who the employer was either.) Now I have to prove he was working for XYZ Company in order to add them to the claim.

- Here's one for ya... Is there any relatively simple way to find out if a person has been actively participating in rodeos (steers, horses, bulls, etc.) in California? I already know that the subject is not a PRCA member so that eliminates those but what about amateur events. My only thought is to call every city in So CA that has rodeos and ask.

- Licensed investigator needed for short neighborhood investigation in Atlanta with the objective of determining residency and living conditions of the subject. Several pretext interviews in the area, but no direct contact with subject. Digital photos required of residence vehicles, etc. This should be about a half-day project.

From the Files of Diane Evans

When I was a "newbie" I became the office hero for a few minutes, after a client called willing to pay to find out a certain pre-surgical hospital patient's blood type. Even my boss was stumped. No one had any idea how to approach the case except me, because I have some knowledge of hospitals and stuff.

I didn't tell my co-workers how I managed to get the information, but I will tell you it was simply common sense I knew the patient was scheduled for surgery, and as a usual procedure the hospital blood bank would have blood "typed and cross-matched" in anticipation. That was all I needed. (FYI-Privacy laws are now in effect making that patient information confidential.)

If the case involved a restaurant or hotel, I'd be looking for someone who has experience in those fields. I'm afraid I wouldn't be of much help on a construction site accident, because that is not part of my experience or training.

Types of Cases

We have a rather long list of some of the types of matter in which private investigators may be called upon to conduct. Certain types of cases tend to come from particular types of clients. We will begin with tasks assumed by entry-level positions.

Figure 2.4 Entry Level Positions

Entry Level Positions	
In House Investigator	Field Investigator
Case file preparation	Court runs
Record searching	Document retrieval
Computer searches	Begin pretexts
Document research	Activity checks
Order lunch	Stakeout
Answering phones	Integrity and honesty shops
Filing	Buy counterfeit goods
Finding lost files	Pick up lunch
Locate persons	Sub-rosa surveillance
Begin to learn the business end	aoe/coe

With sufficient training and experience investigators may specialize in any number of areas. This list is by no means exhaustive; the areas of specialization for private investigators are vast.

Figure 2.5 Specialized Areas of Investigation

Forensics – crime scene analysis – computer forensics – Accident reconstruction – email tracing – document examination	**Photography** – still – digital – videography
Homeland Security background checks – security analysis – executive protection – sabotage	**Accidents** – auto vs ped – auto vs auto – train – boating – aircraft
Crimes Against property – vandalism – theft – embezzlement – burglary – arson	**Crimes Against persons** – assault/battery – robbery – extortion – abduction – child stealing – child concealing
Crimes Against Children/Elderly – abuse – abduction – coercion – sexual abuse – child custody – child's & elder's rights	**Legal Pre-trial** – handling/collection – evidence presentation – evidence procedures – process service
White Collar – fraud – embezzlement – patent/trademark – media piracy	**Environmental** – asbestos cases – black lung – toxic materials/waste
Rights Violations – civil – children's – disabled – workplace	**Civil** – wrongful death – personal injury – product liability – medical malpractice

Figure 2.5 Specialized Areas of Investigation (Cont.)	
Criminal Defense	Corporate
– drug trafficking	– federal regulations
– organized crime	– intellectual theft
– gambling/extortion	– undercover
– expert witness testimony	– workplace violence
– DUI	

CAREER OUTLOOK

For private detective and investigator jobs, most employers look for individuals with ingenuity, persistence, and assertiveness. A candidate must not be afraid of confrontation, should communicate well, and should be able to think on his or her feet. Good interviewing and interrogation skills also are important and usually are acquired in earlier careers in law enforcement or other fields. Because the courts often are the ultimate judges of a properly conducted investigation, the investigator must be able to present the facts in a manner a jury will believe.

Private detectives and investigators held about 48,000 jobs in 2002. About a third were self-employed, including many who held a secondary job as a self-employed private detective. Almost a fifth of jobs were found in investigation and security services, including private detective agencies, while another fifth were in department or other general merchandise stores. The rest worked mostly in State and local government; legal services firms, employment services, insurance carriers, and credit intermediation and related activities, including banks and other depository institutions.

Keen competition is expected because private detective and investigator careers attract many qualified people, including relatively young retirees from law enforcement and military careers. Opportunities will be best for entry-level jobs with detective agencies or as store detectives on a part-time basis. Those seeking store detective jobs have the best prospects with large chains and discount stores.

Employment of private detectives and investigators is expected to grow faster than the average for all occupations through 2012. In addition to growth, replacement of those who retire or leave the occupation for other reasons should create many job openings. Increased demand for private detectives and investigators will result from fear of crime, increased litigation, and the need to protect confidential information and property of all kinds. More private investigators also will be needed to assist attorneys working on criminal defense and civil litigation. Growing financial activity worldwide will increase the demand for investigators to control internal and external financial losses, and to monitor competitors and prevent industrial spying.

Financial Prospects

According to a 2002, report by the Bureau of Labor; Median annual earnings of salaried private detectives and investigators were $29,300 in 2002. The middle 50 percent earned between $21,980 and $41,710. The lowest 10 percent earned less than $17,290, and the highest 10 percent earned more than $57,370. In 2002, median annual earnings were $29,030 in investigation and security services, and $22,250 in department stores.

Client fees and employee wages vary greatly across a particular state and with-in a county. Large metropolitan area firms charge more for the same services than a sole proprietor in a small town. Wages and earnings for investigators depend upon the costs associated with doing business. Beginning salaries can range from about $8 to $15 an hour or more depending on an applicants prior skills and/or economy. Small investigative firms have fewer expenses and may charge only $25-35 per hour to get the business. Well-known and larger firms charge $125 or more per hour.

Earnings of private detectives and investigators vary greatly depending on their employer, specialty, and the geographic area in which they work. According to a study by Abbott, Langer & Associates, security/loss prevention directors and vice presidents had a median income of $77,500 per year in 2002; investigators, $39,800; and store detectives, $25,000. In addition to typical benefits, most corporate investigators received profit-sharing plans.

RELATED OCCUPATIONS

Private detectives and investigators often collect information and protect the property and other assets of companies and individuals. Others with related duties include bill and account collectors; claims adjusters, appraisers, examiners, and investigators; police and detectives; and security guards and gaming surveillance officers.

Investigators who specialize in conducting financial profiles and asset searches perform work closely related to that of accountants and auditors and financial analysts and personal finance advisors.

Private Security

The role private investigators play in society is ever evolving. If you recall from the first chapter, Allan Pinkerton was providing his investigative services to the U.S. States Army before there was an official Secret Service or Federal Bureau of Investigations. However, as the U.S. government began to address the need for a federal investigation authority, private investigators started to get shut out of a large part of the business. Pinkerton's sons, along with William J. Burns quickly adapted and re-directed their services to the ever-increasing need for private security officers.

Never in the history of the nation have law enforcement agencies been called upon to fulfill two fundamentally different and competing missions to deter domestic crime while also being engaged in the fight against potentially new and devastating terrorist attacks orchestrated from abroad. Consequently, in this era of heightened need and demand for better security, private security officers are being asked to fill the gap.

Today, private security companies collectively employ nearly two million security officers nationwide. As this moment, security personnel are on duty protecting American businesses, public offices, schools, shopping centers and housing communities. In addition, private security officers are stationed at many of the nation's critical infrastructure sites and facilities including nuclear plants, public utilities, oil pipelines, ports, bridges, tunnels and many other places where our citizens live, work and play.

Bail Enforcement Agents

Bail Enforcement Agents (BEA)'s; more commonly know as bounty hunters. Many in the field are trying to professionalize the image and prefer the title bail enforcement agent. Bail bondsmen hire BEA's to bring in fugitives who have missed their court date. Naturally the fugitive does not want to go to jail and can be elusive and even dangerous to locate and apprehend. Because of the nature of the business many private investigators are very skilled at tracking and locating people. A private investigator that has street smarts and good networking connections can do well side lining in this field.

Again, as with private investigations, each State has specific laws governing licensing of bail enforcement agents. The State of Texas for instance allows a licensed private investigator to contract or be employed by a bail bondsman to bring in fugitives under Occupational Code Sec. 1702.3863. The same goes for the State of Arkansas; H.B. 1163, allows licensed private investigators to locate and arrest fugitives. Florida however, has eliminated free lance bounty hunters and requires all bail enforcement agents be licensed through the State. Some States have eliminated the commercial bail bond industry, such as Illinois and Oregon.

SUMMARY

By now you realize that in addition to these familiar investigations there are bountiful areas in which one can apply their skills. Once you get your own license you can hang your own shingle or contract with a government agency, or work for a bank or other business. In reality anything can be a subject of investigation and the field of private investigations is wide and diverse. The opportunities are as broad as you are creative. Being a creative thinker will be a bonus in the world of investigations along with being organized, persistent, and assertive.

DISCUSSION QUESTIONS

1. What do you think some of the benefits would be for private investigators to specialize?
2. What were the median annual earnings of salaried private detectives and investigators in 2002?
3. Where you surprised by the numbers, why or why not?
4. What are some of the business that private investigators can work (name at least four)? Which sounds most appealing to you and why?
5. Do many private investigators have college degrees? Do you think those that do have an advantage and why or why not?

PRACTICAL EXERCISE

Do some local research about private investigators in your yellow pages book. For optimal results, check under Detectives, Investigators, and Private Investigators. Are there more or less than you expected?

How many appear to be sole proprietorships, large agencies, and international? Are there any that specialize? What in; divorce, polygraphs, background checks? Do any handle homeland security or security services? How many employ retired law enforcement officers, any active officers? Write a short summary of your findings and give an estimate of how many agencies are listed.

Bibliography

Bureau of Labor Statistics. Office of Occupational Statistics and Employment Projections. http://www.bls.gov.OCO

Chapter 3

Methods of
Investigation

OVERVIEW

This chapter will allow the reader to delve into some
of the thoughts and strategies used by actual private
investigators. Various types of clients and cases will
be discussed allowing authentic strategies to replace
misconceptions.

OBJECTIVES

1. Bring the student into the authentic world of private
   investigations.

2. Establish an understanding of investigative process

3. Present insight into the why and how investigators
   conduct their tasks.

4. Differentiate between covert and overt investigations.

5. Identify methods of investigation and provide examples
   of their uses.

INTRODUCTION

Crime scene shows became very popular in the early 2000s. "CSI" (Crime Scene Investigation) takes place in three different cities, and there is "Crossing Jordan" and, oh yes, and the military version, "NCIS." Interesting and fun to watch, yet do the same individuals really recover bodies, sift through crime scenes, analyze evidence, evaluate crime evidence, fire test rounds of weapons, identify fibers under a microscope, interview witnesses, and arrest the bad guys? No, they do not.

As humans, it seems many of us want to trust what we see, even our vicarious television experience. We know television is primarily entertainment, yet when shows appear authentic, having no contradictory information, we tend to believe what we see.

In actual criminal investigations, there are many teams of specialists that are involved in prosecution of criminal cases. Each stage of the investigation and prosecution has its own experts to process crime scenes, take photographs, interview witnesses, analyze evidence, etc. through jury selection, and presentation of evidence in trial. There are likely 30 or more experts who handle a portion of an investigation through prosecution, not merely the five or six characters as shown in television shows… and that is just the prosecution side.

It is police and district attorney investigators and detectives who identify and interview witnesses, not the crime scene investigators. The crime scene investigators do their jobs in the field while the scientists do their jobs in the laboratory.

No one can count on television or novels to give them an accurate view of police tactics, medical procedures… or anything, else. No one can learn the correct circumstances and procedures until she is sufficiently deprogrammed from misconceptions including entertainment influences.

A documentary was broadcast recently about an alleged murder; the expert revealed that falls from stairs are "not like what you see on television". Ah yes, another "truth" invalidated.

Reality Checks

Private investigators gather information for their clients by 3 primary methods:

- Research
- Observation
- Interviewing

These techniques will be addressed in the chapter and detailed in the 3 chapters that follow.

The field of private investigation is no more dangerous than most office jobs where workers are in constant peril for paper cuts, carpal tunnel syndrome, and a sedentary lifestyle.

A field agent's greatest menace is driving in traffic while his attention is split between watching traffic and maintaining visual contact with a surveillance subject. Of course, there are some people who can manage to get in trouble performing the most mundane of tasks.

- Professionals don't go snooping around in other people's yards or peeping into their windows. Why? Because most investigators want to avoid being bitten by a dog or other household pet, shot at by an alarmed resident and/or landing in jail with criminal charges pending. (Those reasons aside, actually getting over a fence might present a serious deterrent to many of the older "experienced" types.)

- Physical prowess, a razor sharp mind, lethal hands, and x-ray vision are not prerequisites to a successful career as a private detective. Investigators of many different physical and mental abilities and skill levels can find good use for their talents in this field.

- Bad backs or bad feet will slow down anyone who has to sit or walk for long periods. Otherwise, accommodations can be made for most physical problems, as long as brains still work well. One does not have to hear, talk or walk in order to do analysis or research on a case.

- The rights set forth in the Bill of Rights are in place to protect the citizenry, from the government, not from private investigators or other private persons. Unless working in cooperation with police, private investigators have none of the protections or obligations conveyed by U.S and State constitutions, except as any other citizen.

- Those close calls with police detectives who will "yank your license" because you got underfoot in a criminal investigation are a function of the "TV Codes,". not any legal codes. The State ordinarily issues a professional license and will not rovoke or suspend it except for serious and/or repeated misconduct.

It is unusual for a private investigator to be on scene since someone would have to hire him for the assignment. A client might as well plead "guilty," instead of arousing suspicion by hiring an attorney and investigator before the crime scene processors are finished work.

Private investigators' evaluations of crime scenes are well past the processing stage, and it is almost unheard of for a defense investigator to find relevant physical evidence that crime scene processors missed. Private investigators don't attempt to solve crimes as a defense, and there is little opportunity for most to come in contact with police investigators.

Wire Tapping

Last, but not least is wiretapping. Tapping phones or recording phone calls even in a client's own home is not legal. A father can easily eavesdrop on his teenagers all he wants, rummage through the kids' rooms, install covert video cameras, and "bug" conversations with his friends.

> Qwik-Tip
> Not only are some of the aforementioned activities illegal; the cost to the client could be insurmountable in consideration of the potential loss of respect and trust between a parent and child. To assist the client by offering encouragement, advice or sources for equipment, just might earn one a conspiracy to wiretap charge, a felony.

There is not much his own children can do, yet their friend's parents are likely to be very upset when they discover their children are being monitored. Other parents could prosecute or at the least, file a civil case for invasion of their child's privacy. Citizen's seem to have a dim view of their privacy being compromised, in case you haven't noticed.

Some states require permission of all parties to tape record a private conversation, otherwise anyone can secretly tape record a conversation in which they are engaged. There is not an instance in which a "citizen" has the right to secretly tape record someone at anytime without that person's permission.. Keep in mind, it may be illegal to even eavesdrop on an intended confidential conversation although, held in a public place.

In the 1940s and 1950s, individuals in the private and public sectors listened in on phone calls of others, and set up listening devices in offices and homes to gather "intelligence." Gangsters "bugged" other gangsters and law enforcement listened in on whomever they chose.

At the height of the "Cold War" governments were wire tapping other governments, suspected spies, and law enforcement; it was difficult to distinguish the good guys from the bad guys which was likely a matter-of-opinion, anyway. American officials discovered crude listening devices in the walls of their new Russian Embassy, built by Russian workers.

Before Homeland Security that loosened restrictions, only law enforcement could legally tap a suspect's phone line, under a court order signed by a judge. There are both state and federal laws that prohibit wiretapping or eavesdropping on other persons. Some states allow exceptions to these laws. When a person is being threatened over the phone, or evidence of other serious crimes are being revealed the "victim" can legally record the conversation without permission.

PROFESSIONAL INVESTIGATIONS

Now that the student has is better able to distinguish between reality and fiction…

As mention previously, private investigators gather information, to help establish facts or discover an unknown for a client. It is the case circumstances and client objectives that constitute the major differences between private and other investigators, and money. The client's objective and purposes will determine how the case is approached and worked.

As a private firm, efforts on behalf of a client depend upon fee-for-service. The client can and will limit a firm's investigative endeavors on his behalf, by controlling the amount of money he is willing to pay. If the client needs $1,200 worth of investigation, yet agrees to pay only $500, then he gets his $500 dollars worth and can elect to allocate more funds, in the future.

Fictional investigators always seem to go way beyond what their real world counterparts would do. Private Investigators are business men and women hopefully engaged in money making enterprises, and seldom on charity projects.

Can you imagine going into a market prepared to pay only $50, for a full cart of groceries and expecting the store to give it to you for that amount, because you need it to fix dinner for your ten kids? Very few professionals will allow the client's problems to become their own.

This is not to say that every case is about money; some investigators are on panels for pro bono (free) cases for worthy causes and every once-in-a-while, someone's sob story gets to an investigator who cave's in. Most freebies though, go to family and friends, or group projects, not complete strangers.

What Investigators Do

Since an investigation is primarily an information gathering endeavor, the investigator's job is to discover facts and evidence that will benefit her client or employer's position in a given matter. Professionals gather facts, statistics, and evidence, (within an authorized budget) then commonly prepare a client report.

The client wants to know what new information was found, what it means to his situation, plus any insight investigators may have gained during the course of the investigation. Investigators are often the eyes and ears of a client; when it comes down to the reliability and appearances of the witnesses, and/or impressions or evaluations of the case.

Unlike law enforcement, private investigators are not legally obligated to search out the truth. In a criminal defense matter, investigators are searching for evidence that shifts the blame away from the defendant. Inquiries must be complete within the scope of the authorized budget. In other words, licensees are not responsible to bring forth all available evidence, merely to do a complete job in the hours allotted.

Professionals don't hold back anything from the attorney-client who is paying them. It is essential to report derogatory information to legal counsel, so she can be prepared to explain or discredit that information should it arise in trial. When a budget is exhausted, the investigator is under no obligation to continue even though viable leads remain unexplored.

PURPOSE OF INVESTIGATIONS

Insurance Companies

Insurance companies are legally bound to pay on legitimate claims. While a company can deny a baseless claim, the burden of proof is on the company to prove that a claim is unfounded or fraudulent. The initial investigation does not begin as an adversarial situation, and the investigator is seeking the whole truth.

Workers' Compensation Claims worthy of investigation are those involving:

- Injuries reported after days off
- Un-witnessed falls and/or injuries
- Injuries unassociated with work duties
- Stress related claims
- Worker is facing discipline
- Anticipated layoff
- Unknown pre-existing conditions
- Claims in which the accident account changes over time

The presumption of law is that an injured worker is an employee subject to workers' compensation benefits. Private investigators contract with insurance adjusters to conduct the company's aoe/coe investigations. This investigation answers whether or not, the claimant's illness or injury did *arise of employment*, or if it occurred in the *course of employment (aoe/coe)*.

In an aoe/coe case, the investigator will review the employment and medical records looking for discrepancies and inconsistencies. She will talk to other employees about what they know or have been told about the worker's alleged injury. She may extend her inquiry to friends and families of the worker seeking other possible reasons for the worker's complaints. A diligent investigation may bring forth a witness who reveals that the applicant complained about back pain a few days ago, after moving to a new apartment.

It is essential to evaluate the reports and check to determine if the resulting injury and complaints are consistent with the employees "first report of injury". If everything checks out, the employer has no reason to deny the claim and must accept responsibility to cover all medical expenses. If not, the employer can deny the claim and the worker will have to appeal the matter further through the Workers' Compensation Appeals Board.

Workers, who are/were legitimately injured, may continue to complain of pain long after they returned to coaching a little league team. Doctors often make an evaluation based upon the patient's subjective symptoms. Is it possible that treating physicians may realize that the longer they keep an injured worker off work, the more visits for which they can bill? When a case drags on, an independent medical examiner (IME) may be called upon to examine the patient and make a determination.

Workers' Compensation fraud can be one of several types involving claimants, medical providers and lawyers:

- False claims, no significant injury
- Exaggerated claims of injury
- Delayed recovery, malingering
- Purporting false or exaggerated discomfort
- Injury or illness, not work related
- Employed while collecting disability
- Non-disclosure of prior medical condition
- Medical providers over-billing
- Providers billing for services not received

Once a claim is accepted and paid by the insurance company, the employer has a reasonable expectation of when the worker can return to his usual job. When the worker remains off work and/or fails to return to work as expected, the insurance company and/or employer will want to verify the claim to assess whether the claimant is simply slow to recover, or whether the claim has reached the point of being fraudulent.

To satisfy the needs of insurance company clients, private investigators often engage in surveillance (secret observation) of claimants. For several days, field agents will begin early in the morning to determine in which kinds of activities the claimant engages, if any. Employers want to know if their employee is working another job while off work on a disability claim, or if he or she routinely conducts physical activities that the alleged injury should prevent.

When field agents videotape or record a claimant's physical activities, this is referred to as a "sub rosa" investigation. The phrase evolved from old English law and means that investigators work secretly and try not to be detected by the persons they are observing.

A medical professional may review the tape to help make a determination of whether the claimant is still disabled, or may well be able to return to work. Agents observe and tape over several days to counter any claims of "good day, bad day."

The insurance company can have five hours of tape showing the claimant who purports a neck injury, as he uses a pick ax to break up concrete and lay a new brick patio in his yard. When there is a single day of activity, the claimant can argue, "Yes, I thought I could handle that, but I had to take pain medicine all day and could hardly even get out of bed for almost a week." That single day of tape is not going to help the employer determine if the claim is still legitimate.

When a worker is on disability for work-related stress or depression, the insured expects her to spend most of their time at home in quiet activity. When the claimant has frequent social activities with friends, engages in biking or other sports, this is good evidence that she is able to return to all her usual activities, including her job.

Investigators may have the option of expanding their efforts in order to interview friends, co-workers and neighbors in an effort to get sufficient information to allow an insurance company to verify, or a deny claim. The larger the claim or value of the insurance policy will dictate how much work the insurance company is willing to spend to detect and eliminate fraud, thereby cutting substantial losses.

Fortunately, for those who specialize in workers' comp investigations, few insurers will follow through and prosecute fraudulent claimants to the full extent of the law. More public knowledge that one could be caught, prosecuted, jailed, and still lose his ill-gotten gains is a great deterrent to insurance fraud. Of course, detecting these crimes is good business for private investigators.

From the Files of Diane Evans

I recall a case assigned by a Chicago insurance company who wanted me to interview their claimant. Their insured lived in the exclusive Hollywood Hills area and claimed to suffer a burn on her face while cooking at home. With no intervening medical care, the woman traveled to New York some two weeks later to have plastic surgery then returned home. She billed her insurance company for $5,000. Because it was a low dollar amount, I was surprised the company didn't just pay it. I imagine that is what the "patient" thought, as well.

It is inconceivable that a woman with so serious an injury requiring plastic surgery, would have no medical care for two weeks, and then get on a plane with open burns on her face. Now maybe if she was transported by air ambulance, it would have been more believable.

Skeptical as I was, I checked out her story to see if I could verify any part of it. I called the Los Angeles Fire Department and sweet-talked the guy on the phone to check call records for "runs" to her address. He reported only a fire rescue call two years prior.

I was ready and set up an interview. I arrived at her home in the canyon only to find the electricity off, and her electric gate not working. I surprised both of us, when I agreed to climb over a low place in the fence and met her outside her bedroom.

She appeared to be in her mid to late fifties and her face looked perfectly normal for a woman her age. Swelling, reddening, scaring or any other signs of reconstructive plastic surgery was absent.

Behind the vines and cracking stucco walls was a spectacular home. I've seen old money rich in old Pasadena, California mansions which were rather like walking into a Ritz-Carlton Hotel. I was aware of the opulence surrounding me, but found it quite different from other homes I'd seen.

The long glass topped table where the claimant and I sat for the interview was at least an inch thick and appeared to have elephant tusks for a base. The table seated probably ten and each seat was covered with what looked and felt like actual tiger fur.

We began talking and the claimant tells me her husband was in the movie business and died a couple years ago. I think, that must have been the fire rescue call. She drops some Hollywood names like her good friend director, Oliver Stone and some lesser-knowns. Unimpressed, I smiled and nodded, then brought the conversation back to the fire and her plastic surgery.

"You look really great," I say. "Just what procedure did the surgeon do?" She points to her eyes and says she got some injections beneath her eyes. In my mind, she just conveniently admitted to insurance fraud. Because of my medical background and knowledge, I knew there was no way she could have recovered so quickly from extensive plastic surgery, and show no signs of bruising, swelling or healing incisions.

We chatter a little longer; then I wrapped it up and prepared to leave. To my amazement she began again, discussing her important friends and how

From the Files of Diane Evans, cont

many would need a good investigator, and could she have some of my business cards to refer friends, etc.

I said that I had forgotten my business cards, yet would be happy to send her a few after I returned to my office. I had no intention of doing so, realizing she was intending to bribe me with (probably false) promises of future work. I could only smile and thank her for her time. Fortunately, the power was back on and I walked down the driveway to my car. Now that put a real smile on my face. I sent my report off to the insurance company.

The dishonesty of people never ceases to amaze me. I can understand someone who steals in order to feed their family, yet this woman had no need. Selling just one of those tiger seat covers would have covered her trip to New York, with or without surgery. I'm guessing she might have a friend or relative who was a surgeon. Maybe she did or didn't have anything done, it makes no difference. I imagine the insurance company found it fairly easy to deny her claim and simply close the file. The claim was too small to litigate. The rich and famous avoid justice again.

Qwik-Tip: Ethics Check
Be extra careful dealing with people who appear deceitful and dishonest. Avoid the slightest appearance of possible unethical behavior. Should the case go south and you are drawn into it by someone who wants to redirect the heat, doing the client a "favor" may appear unethical. In the instance reported above if the investigator had provided the claimant a handful of business cards the argument could be made to discredit the investigator.

BIG BUSINESS

Pre-employment

Corporations and other large businesses are a rich and mostly untapped source of clients who can afford to pay well. Outside investigators, working on employment or work related situations are regulated by state and federal legislation. Savvy business clients may ask us to perform background investigations for new employees, knowing it is critical to his success in business. He needs to know his employees are honest, responsible and have the stated experience.

Outside investigators must comply with the Fair Credit Reporting Act. FCRA among other protections restricts pre-employment criminal searches going back more than 10 years. The State may have more stringent regulations that shorten that time frame. California for instance, has a 7 year limit for employees earning under $75,000; those earning more can be subject to a lengthier search. Employee consent is required to conduct a pre-employment background and FCRA spells out just how this is to be accomplished.

Investigators will check the employment application for accuracy by verifying previous employers and dates of hire, present and former address, and stated education. They also contact and interview provided references, and then may ask those references if they know others who could provide insight into that person's character. This allows them to develop a more accurate profile for the employer.

A criminal record will not necessarily keep a person from getting all investigation or other jobs, as long as it has been several years since the violation, the conviction was disclosed, and not of a serious or violent nature. Employers understand that good people, make some bad decisions, and as long as the candidate is forthright about the circumstances this negative information may cease to be an obstacle to employment.

In the Workplace

Alleged misconduct or illegal activity frequently arises in the workplace. Accusations of sexual harassment from both male and female employees are prevalent. With more transgender persons revealing their true selves, snide remarks from uninformed and un-approving co-workers are common, yet inappropriate comments and gestures create a hostile work environment for the worker who is different.

Something as simple as an off-color joke told in the presence of a worker who is offended by it, can create a hostile situation for that person. The majority does not "rule" in the work place. Lifestyle, religion, ethnicity, and other "differences" threaten some individuals who react by offending those who are unlike themselves. Bullies are bullies regardless of their ages. Employers have the responsibility to see that all workers are treated justly and fairly.

Our Constitutional rights to "life, liberty and the pursuit of happiness," extend to the workplace, as well. Under the law, no worker should have to endure a work situation in which other employee's actions are offensive, unpleasant and stress-producing. Each worker is worthy of the same respect and no employee should have to endure ridicule, teasing or abuse from co-workers or employers.

For example, a co-worker is always smiling at Betty, waiting and hoping to have lunch with her, and finally suggests they get together after work. Betty refuses politely and firmly, stating she is not interested in doing that. Next week cards and flowers appear on her desk and on Friday, he is still all smiles and waits so they can have lunch together.

Obviously Betty's admirer is out-of-touch with the 21st Century. There was a time when what he was doing was called "courting" and considered flattering. "No" sometimes did mean, "well maybe."Times have changed and "no thank you" does not mean, "Please, ask me again."

Since the employer has a legal obligation to provide a safe and comfortable environment and correcting offensive situations of which he is aware. This kind of workplace investigation will include reviewing employee complaints, employers' prior efforts to stop the offensive conduct, interviewing witnesses, or other workers, conducting background checks of suspects, and/or occasionally putting offenders under surveillance to determine their activities. An objective report will be prepared for the employer's who than has a course of action to take or who knows prior actions have corrected the situations.

Stopping Losses

Shrinking inventories and decreased profits are signs that a private investigator should be brought in to look for are employees who appear to be living beyond their means. That warehouse worker, who drives a Lexus SUV and recently bought a new house, just might make the top of their list of suspects until, and unless another source of income is found for him.

Once a suspect or suspects are identified, each one will be interviewed separately with the hopes of getting an admission, or better yet, a full confession implicating others. Professionals will refer to the process as an interview, yet it can quickly progress to an adversarial interrogation. "Interview" sounds much less threatening than "interrogation."

Employee theft is one of the few instances in which private investigators have the opportunity to interrogate, and get the bad guys to fess up. Professional investigators will use finesse and strategy rather than use force, intimidation, withholding of water, food or bathroom privileges, nor will one make false promises about the disposition of the case. Confessions made under duress or coercion will likely be ruled inadmissible in court, also creating liability for the investigative firm.

What investigators do best is to out maneuver suspects. Interrogators can be misleading, wave a file folder in front of a suspect saying, "Better tell us now, because we have all we need in this file" or "Make it easy on yourself and tell what you took, and who else is involved. I understand, if you meant to bring it back, etc." We might be able to help you out, if you help us." Not at all true, these are ruses to gain the suspect's trust and cooperation.

"Loaded" words like steal, thief, stole, crime, co-conspirators are not used... It usually helps to minimize the person's actions; a thief can think of himself taking something that didn't belong to him, but he didn't "steal" anything.

This use of tactful manipulation is much more effective that the old movie version where the "good cop" leaves the room and the "bad cop" throws the suspect against the wall and gets him to fess up. Very few confessions are coerced by threatening bodily harm and a long prison sentence. Experienced criminals know that if the prosecution had all they needed to charge a crime, which it would be done already.

Qwik-Tip: Ethics Check
Each licensee has a civil obligation to present the "truth" to her client, regardless of whether or not; the information obtained is sympathetic to the client. A client expecting professionals to "slant" an inquiry in his favor is going to be disappointed, because actual investigators don't work like the fictional ones.
Should the client not like what a professional does, he will need to find another who is less ethical than most. The client can usually get it done his way; however, the situation may well blow up in his face. What is your first guess as to who is blamed for a foul up? Only a foolish person will believe that the instigator of a sleazy operation is going to protect anyone besides himself.

Executive Protection

There are numerous opportunities for specialists in executive protection, security, threat assessment, corporate intelligence, theft of intellectual property, counter-measures for electronic surveillance, and a wealth of other specialties. Homeland Security has become big business across private industry.

SMALL & RETAIL BUSINESS

Small businesses have many of the same needs for investigations as their larger counterparts, only with smaller budgets. Even service businesses may need loss prevention strategies; employees have been known to cart off business machines and office supplies. A store's greatest losses are at the hands of employees, not shoplifters.

Shoplift Detail

To catch and arrest shoplifters, a detective will pretend to shop while actually observing a suspicious person. In order to make a citizen's arrest of a perpetrator, the store detective must observe the suspect conceal merchandise on her person, then maintain visual contact to make sure the merchandise isn't dumped before she leaves the store.

Once the suspect is past cashiers, the detective can be fairly sure she does not intend to pay for the item/s. Only the person, who witnessed the actual theft, can make a citizen's (private person's) arrest of the suspect, and use whatever non-deadly force is reasonable and necessary to overcome resistance.

Make a mistake and the store detective may be looking at criminal charges of false arrest, false imprisonment, kidnapping, assault, battery, and robbery, if he searched for, and removed items from the suspect. If the suspect dumped the merchandise in the store, both the investigator and the store can be looking at civil and criminal actions being filed against them.

In some states, a merchant may hold a shoplift suspect to conduct an investigation, yet can not search for or remove any merchandise from him. At best, the retailer can hope the person will return or drop the merchandise. If the suspect holds out and refuses to reveal his crime, all the merchant can do is escort him to the exit door, and tell him not to return.

On occasion, store detectives are not very adept at what they do and it is difficult to believe that they actually detect and arrest shoplifters. It isn't hard to notice someone who is looking over racks of clothing, instead of the clothing on the racks. Of course, the observer can't be sure that it isn't a shoplifter since shoplifters and store detectives do some of the same things.

Although most people don't notice there are most likely cameras at every cash register, dressing room entrance, and across the sales floor. Somewhere at the location, there is a bank of monitors subject to the scrutiny of store security. When security personnel see someone acting suspiciously, they will send an agent to the floor to personally observe the activity.

From the Files of Diane Evans

> One day in a Department Store, I recognized a guy on the elevator, who I took an Administration of Justice class with the semester before. He was not one of the brightest stars in the sky and the thought of him with a badge and gun was terrifying to me.
>
> My suspicions were confirmed, and I could only laugh when I saw him talking to the paper bag he held next to his ear. I might have just thought he was a little funny talking to the bag, but the radio antenna was a dead giveaway. Administration of justice classes teach a lot of valuable information, but they cannot teach the common sense, which my friend was apparently lacking.

Employee Theft

Paperwork that does not correlate as it should is the first indication that a business has an employee theft problem. The owner paid for and received 2,500 video games last month and the sales tapes show that 2,105 are sold. The inventory reveals 234 left in stock; revealing that 161 are missing in action. Not only will the retailer have to pay for the units stolen, he will lose the profit from those units. Those loses are than absorbed by other sales.

By verifying what stock came in, when and who unloaded it, and where it went from there will often lead you towards the right suspect. The ability to discover and deter internal theft is the main reason to maintain effective inventory control measures.

Delivery persons may work together with employees. Bar and restaurant owners usually learn this method the hard way. The dishonest employee will sign an invoice for six cases of beer as ordered, when only five are actually delivered on the hand truck and put in stock. Later in the day the driver will tell another customer (or a friend) he has a couple extra cases and sells them, splitting the profit with the bartender who accepted the short delivery.

Then there will always be "till taps" where money is taken from the register. With bartenders, the money may not get close to the cash register. Bartenders in busy neighborhood bars may pour several drinks before they collect from customers. A couple things can happen from here, and each benefits the bartender.

When regular customers depart, they will leave money on the bar for the drinks they consumed, assuming the bartender just forgot to collect, and will do so later. The bartender takes the money left for payment of drinks, and puts it in his tip jar. Bartenders may give drinks away to customers to get larger tips, or to impress a special honey or good buddy. All are forms of embezzlement.

From the Files of Diane Evans

I was in the bar business several years ago and had part-time night bartender, Ray, who was a waiter during the day. I could tell when I trained him that he was a whiz with numbers; I should have kept a closer watch on him. His night's sales were about 50% of what my other worst guy would do, but I could see by the mess on the floor how much money should be in the register.

He never stocked the beer cooler, so that gave me another indication of how much money I should have had in the register for his shift. I had previously changed the check-out procedure and the bartenders were no longer allowed to Z out (total) the register with a total of the night's sales.

This strategy would make it more difficult to keep track of what they pocketed, as opposed to what they rang up and put in the register. Most thieves use some kind of counting device, such as paperclips, pennies, or peanuts to keep track and to reconcile the drawer at the end of their shift, but not Ray.

I knew Ray was making himself my partner, but was at a loss as to how he was doing it. I decided to go in one night just before closing to find out. There were four customers sitting at the bar watching Ray's television instead of playing pool, feeding my jukebox or playing pinball like they are supposed to behave in a bar. They were probably drinking on me by that time of night, anyway.

I called Ray from behind the bar, said good evening to the so-called customers, and locked the door behind them. I went to the register Z'd it out and began to count the drawer. Meanwhile, I had Ray stock the cooler with beer and I calculated what should be in the drawer for just beer sales.

The cash drawer contained about twice the night's sales. I looked for some indication that he had used a counter or something to keep track, but I saw nothing. He didn't arouse any suspicion from customers because he put money in the cash register. He may have left the drawer open so he didn't have to enter "no sale" to open it, or he simply could have rung up only one drink from a round and returned with the correct change.

According to the stock replaced the numbers indicate there should have been more sales rung up than what was on the tape. In this instance I was 100% sure he was stealing and could only guess that because he was so quick with numbers, he kept it all in his head until he was ready to leave for the night.

A business owner can suffer significant losses from dishonest employees. She can be sure a thief is not going to very picky from whom he steals and will shortchange and overcharge customers, as well.

Shopping Services

Having no lack of imagination, retail clerks find numerous methods to steal from their employer. Strangely enough, all think that theirs is such a unique technique that no one will ever know or catch them. Shopping Services evaluate employee honesty and it is pretty exciting to catch one in the act. A shop owner may be at a loss because, regardless of the stock she purchased, she didn't have much of a profit to show for it. What she did have was a silent partner, helping himself to her earnings.

From the Files of Diane Evans

I went into her vitamin store, made a small purchase, and engaged this nice buff young man into a vitamin conversation, which was rather a stretch for me. My partner went in first and selected some tea, then counted out the correct change and approached the register waiting only for a moment.

In a huff, she said something to the effect of, "I buy this all the time and it costs $7.26 with tax and here is correct change, I have to go." She left with her merchandise and the clerk brushed the cash to the side of the register and continued talking. I ended the conversation then looked around for a few more minutes listening for the cash register. I selected another small item for a "lock in" purchase then headed for the front door.

I was halfway to the exit and still did not hear him ring up the tea. I thought maybe I didn't give him enough time, and walked back towards the register where this nice young man had a wad of $10 and 20 dollar bills in his hand apparently counting it. I asked another dumb question, then left. I estimated he had $80+ dollars in his grip and apparently was counting his take for the day.

This particular franchise had very liberal policies and gave employees the benefit of any doubt. An employee could have simply forgotten on what key to ring up the merchandise. Possibly it was a onetime occurrence and the employee had a special need. It could have been a crime of opportunity since investigators made it so easy for them, which was the idea in the first place.

The plan was to shop him several times a week for 2-3 weeksto make a fair evaluation. There was no question of this man's dishonesty, since he stole every single time someone made it easy for him. He lost his job after the first week.

Bars, fine restaurants, and even fast food franchises hire observers to come in and pose as customers. You get free food and drink, AND are being paid to consume it. Those are dream jobs for some, yet the pay isn't very much and you do have to write an evaluation after your meal.

Undercover Operations

To combat prostitution, female police officers dress up as street-walkers and males as johns (customers) then merely wait for someone to approach them. The interchanges last only a few moments and most investigators would be able to successfully pull off this ruse. It is fairly easy to deceive for a few minutes, as opposed to maintaining a deception of "who you are" for five or six months, a usual time frame for an industrial undercover assignment.

Once hired, the operative must create an identity and history for himself that is supported by his application. Co-worker's would be doubtful about this "mystery" employee who couldn't remember where he last worked, whether he had a wife or girlfriend, and where he went to high school.

The easy part is for the operative must create a verifiable history for himself that will be believable, and the more difficult task, is to be able to remember who he is. He must make himself "fit in" the situation for others to trust him and let him in on any illegal activity in the workplace.

From the Files of Diane Evans

My first undercover operation was supervising an investigator in the field. There was a $3,000,000 inventory on-site and the company printed and mailed multi-page advertisements to customers. Usually operatives are placed in an unskilled position, but the UC in this case was experienced with this kind of work making him less likely to arouse the suspicion of other workers.

This client used undercover operatives regularly. A few months prior, a UC operative uncovered a counterfeiting scheme being operated by the night supervisor who was using company equipment to print money.

Once assigned, the operative is responsible to make daily reports to his investigative supervisor concerning any situation or condition that has potential to negatively affect, or threaten the client's business.

As case director, I compiled the UC op's daily reports and prepared a monthly client report, which for security reasons, is sent to the client's home. All parties, including the client, operative and investigative firm are responsible to protect the operative and the integrity of the investigation. No one wants a clerk or housekeeper to happen to spot the report on the client's desk.

Rob, the operative, was a great observer and reported numerous safety concerns that the client did not correct, as long as we had an op in place.

Numerous safety conditions were reported. The stuffing line has little metal fingers to pick up each piece of paper to a stack, and then place the stack in an envelope. Because the paper used is light weight, the machine frequently jams; It must be turned off before manually removing the paper jam. On one occasion, Rob reported a female worker was clearing a jam and another worker started the machine while her hand was there. Fortunately, she was uninjured and didn't lose any fingers.

From the Files of Diane Evans

Numerous reports of management misconduct and missing safety equipment continued, otherwise the assignment was unremarkable. The operative is taken out in two to three months if he sees no evidence of suspicious criminal activity. When multiple persons and groups are involved in illegal activities, an agent remains in place for several months to build a stronger case.

Qwik-Tip
To easily create a history operatives borrow from friends or relatives who's "stories" they know well. This method makes it less likely he will forget any part of his cover story.

From the Files of Diane Evans

As a rookie I was on a short term (one day) UC assignment. My objective was to see if a new remodeling company was offering franchises for sale to prospects, before they was legally allowed. It seems the client's former employee, Dave, took an original idea and went into business for himself, angering his former employer. I doubt the client's motive was to uphold the law; it was more likely he wanted revenge.

I contacted Dave to talk with him about his store, and then met with him personally. I explained that I was a former bar owner and single mother, who wanted to reinvest in a business in which my son could work, and eventually take over, leaving Mom to bask in early retirement. Everything was the truth at one time or another in my life, or I never could have remembered my story.

It could be I oversold myself, because Dave offered me a working partnership in his "star" store. It was a "no go" for me who wanted the independence of my own franchise. He wasn't going for it either, and we parted ways with a handshake.

Counterfeit Products

At one time in Baja, Mexico, t-shirt shops were loaded with Disney characters. There were several variations picturing Mickey Mouse and Donald Duck. Donald is holding his arm out with one finger extended, and one could assume this was not a Disney product. Detection of counterfeit products is the main source of income for many investigative firms across the country.

When a company owns a trademark, like the *red target* of a Target store or Mc Donald's *golden arches*, the owners must actively protect it, or risk losing it to the public domain. These investigators may travel to flea markets, large shopping malls, strip malls, discount or liquidation store and even big box retailers in search of bogus products for their client.

High-end women's fashions are commonly duplicated for low prices. If you see a Louis Vitton handbag offered for sale at $60 that is the first clue it is not authentic. Various sports teams, Harley-Davidson and Disney are some of the top brands on the market, and shoppers often refuse pay $45 for a Tinkerbell sweatshirt, preferring a "knock off" or counterfeit product, at a swap meet for $10? Business is booming for cheap products.

There are millions of inexpensive CDs and, DVDs sold by counterfeiters on the street, and at fairs and even in storefronts. Easy duplicating and printing techniques are making it simple to reproduce music and movies for illegal resale. The music and movie industries are suffering accordingly from loss of sales. This society values its athletes and entertainers earning then six and seven figure incomes per year, yet, who wants to pay $18.00 for a CD when he can pay $7-8?

Qwik-Tip: Ethics Check
Entertainers are in business to earn a living; not to donate their time and talents for the public's enjoyment. The public can listen to music on the radio for free, since the station pays the artists for the privilege of playing their music. The price a disk only allows the purchaser to listen alone or with others as he desires. The owner of a disk can sell it or give it away, yet he has no rights to reproduce and distribute the material.
By purchasing illegally produced goods, the public is creating losses for the authentic creators, and those who make legal purchases pay higher costs to compensate for illegal buys.

Counterfeit shoppers search for imitations of their client's products. Shoppers are informed of manufacturers who can legally use the client's trademark and the brands they can sell under. Disney and other large designers sell limited trademark rights to manufacturers who then sell legitimately to retail stores.

The first things to notice about knock-off garments are inferior fabrics and stitching, then check the label and country of origin to be sure. When the shopper finds a suspect inauthentic article they will purchase it and get a receipt. When the merchant doesn't calculate sales tax and a "retail sales permit" is not displayed anywhere, those are other clues that his business may not be legitimate.

The shopper will get a good description of the seller, sales site and any signs that may be evident. They always ask for a business card, since they may want to make a wholesale purchase in the future, or at least this is what they tell the merchant. With a camera phone it is simple to take several photos of the site and merchant. These photos are used for future negotiations.

The investigation firm follows up on the counterfeit "buys" and contacts the offending merchants who will usually agree to destroy their inventory and pay a "fine" to the firm, rather than be criminally prosecuted. The client is satisfied to have the counterfeit products off the market.

Legal Investigations

Working with law firms is an excellent opportunity for anyone learning and expanding her skills. The firm could specializes in civil cases, criminal defense, threat analysis, corporate espionage, theft of intellectual property and many more cases where a good investigator is indispensable

Working for attorney-clients, investigators do some simple things like research prior court cases, prepare demonstrative evidence for trial, conduct asset searches in addition to conducting interviews, and taking witness statements. The most challenging cases are when an attorney places a case file in front of you and asks to, "Give me a defense on this." Now that is a challenge a professional is up to.

In one criminal defense case, the defendant was charged for manufacturing methamphetamine. He was a young man who was charged with his father and others. The attorneys wanted an aerial view of the location, which at the time, was prohibitively expensive. The legal team "made do" with a plot map and blueprints of streets and roads in the area, from which investigators constructed a diagram to be used as demonstrative evidence in court. The defendant was acquitted.

Hate Crime

From the Files of Diane Evans

The defendant is charged with a hate crime after assaulting a man while calling him a "wetback" and "dirty Mexican," among other things. One story is that the defendant was angry because the alleged victim yelled at one of the defendant's sons, and almost knocked the boy off his bicycle.

When the son went home and told his father what happened at the park, he neglected to mention that he and his brother were "buzzing" people while riding their bikes. The one boy came close enough for the victim to reach out, and try to grab the kid's bike to stop him.

Dad is angry when he comes to the park to confront the man; their argument becomes a fight and Dad allegedly began throwing punches and racially charged comments. Much to the defense team's surprise, a criminal case is filed in Federal Criminal Court as a hate crime against our client.

When I arrived to interview the defendant and his family, I saw a huge Confederate flag suspended from the ceiling of his garage. I thought, "Great, no prejudice here." The client and his family all denied hostility towards Mexicans or any other group and listed several friends and former neighbors who were of Hispanic descent. We interviewed them all and each spoke highly of their friend, and even after hearing the allegations, agreed to testify on his behalf.

Approximately 30 former neighbors and friends of the defendant and his children appeared to testify, many without benefit of a Subpoena compelling them to do so. To me this was a very strong stand for the defendant, that this many people were ready and willing to take the day off work without pay, and show up in downtown Los Angeles, to testify on behalf of their friend's character. The judge would not listen to all the witnesses and several were sent home without testifying.

The defense team doesn't win them all. As investigators, our job is to dig up the information, the attorney's is to present it and raise reasonable doubt, then the judge or jury makes a decision based upon the law and what they believe happened. This is how the system works

Criminal defense work is some of the most important work private investigators are responsible for. The defendant may be facing a death penalty, life without the possibility if parole or an extensive prison sentence. It is the defense investigator's responsibility to support the defense strategy, finding the errors and omissions made by law enforcement and seeking out authentic witnesses who can help create reasonable doubt.. Then present it in a way that the attorney can make use of it to discredit the prosecution's case.

In the Field

There are times that the only way the client is going to get the information they desire is by following and watching the subject of the investigation. The surveillant (one who is watching) attempts to conceal herself usually in a vehicle, and avoids attracting attention by blending into her surroundings. There should be nothing about her appearance, dress, vehicle or movements that should cause anyone to look twice in her direction.

The conditions will vary greatly from assignment to assignment, as will the client's objectives. Understanding the variables is what allows field agents to consistently conduct successful assignments without being "burned" (noticed by the subject.)

From the Files of Diane Evans

> You cannot imagine the life activities of which you are unaware, unless sitting quietly in your car at night on surveillance. One particular evening I was in a commercial area trying to spot the subject as he drove into the driveway of his apartment building. I had his address, a description of his vehicle, and no shortage of vantage points since the pickup was on a main thoroughfare.
>
> In a commercial area the need for secrecy is lessened, and most people don't give you a second thought. When parked in front of an adjacent apartment, one nice lady came out and asked my partner and me if investigators needed help. I explained investigators were waiting for our friend to arrive since investigators had nowhere else to stay, and only an address of where she lived. She brought us cookies and lemonade.
>
> The next evening investigators changed our vantage point and watched while a catering van let out a dozen young women who walked towards the boulevard. A man in a car stopped to talk with one, and she got into the car with him and drove away. About a half an hour later, she was back. When the van returned a couple hours later the driver let out another group, and took the first group away. I am fairly sure what I was seeing, was a well organized prostitution ring.
>
> Another evening I was keeping an eye on a parent who the client feared might take a young child away and try to conceal her. I'm sitting behind a restaurant looking across the street into a Burger King where I can see the client and child, along with the subject.
>
> Meanwhile, I happened to glance over to the rear of a carwash where a man was carefully cleaning "lint" from the vacuum machine. I could only guess this is how the ingenious employees stole from customer's cars without being caught. They just sucked it up and went back later to get their booty.
>
> As I look back at Burger King, I see the subject carrying the child toward the rear of the store near the exit where her vehicle is parked. I think

From the Files of Diane Evans, cont

> I held my breath until she returned with the child who apparently had to go to the restroom.
>
> In my early years, there was a client who was apparently delusional, yet my employer took the case and put me on it. There was not much leeway as to where I set up my vantage point, in order to see the well-lighted front gate I was across the street parked in the middle of nothing. I was watching when four boys showed up on bicycles and parked in the entrance. I heard rustling in the leaves and a few minutes later, heard the unmistakable sounds of pop tops being removed from aluminum beverage cans. The sounds made by the kids let me know it was beer, not soda they were drinking. I watched while two of them answered nature's call against the bushes. It is fun to be a little mouse watching everything that happens.

A later chapter provides an in-depth account of surveillance, how it is accomplished and more about the purposes of clients.

INDIVIDUAL CLIENTS

Not all investigation firms will work for an individual client which is fine for many others since they enjoy the variety in cases presented by individuals. A large number of professionals are sole proprietors who provide a variety of services, and prefer to do the work themselves, or occasionally contract with another licensee for help when needed.

Individual clients often don't understand the realities of investigative work or the costs involved. There are plenty of times one will say, "All you need to do is…" To which the investigator has to take the time to do some education and get the prospective client up to speed.

Individual clients tend to be time-consuming anyway, and investigators feel a moral obligation to learn why the client wants what she wants. Even when she convinces the investigator her request is warranted, the investigator is likely to require her permission to notify her long lost nephew, Willy, before giving his contact information to her.

Qwik-Tip:
You will learn with experience as others before you, that it is not a wise decision or practice to allow your client to direct the case. There is an adage, "never try to teach a pig to sing, because it is a waste of your time and it annoys the pig." You have the expertise and need to take charge, the client may watch too much television, and then, when his strategy is non-productive, he is upset with you. You don't want a surgeon who will allow you to tell him how to take your appendix out.

The client has a goal or desire, yet it is your prerogative to determine how you accomplish the tasks you undertake. You have an obligation and a fiduciary relationship with your client; you must operate within the law without threatening the integrity of the investigation.

Know your responsibility to keep your endeavor legal and confidential, and you are likely to have skills, knowledge, contacts, and techniques to get the job done. You do not have to tell the client how you are going to accomplish his objective, since do so could compromise special sources or trade secrets.

It could be that good old "Aunt Tillie" is just out of the slammer again, and wants to hit Willy up for a few thousand dollars. Aunt Tillie could be unrelated to Willy, and simply a stalker who does not know how to accept "do not bother me."

Qwik-Tip - Ethics Check:
When a client refuses to give permission to notify the subject notice of her interest, then the case is turned down. Without revealing the subject or potential client name, it is a good idea to pass on the circumstances of the inquiry to other professionals.

For example: "We had an inquiry today for an aunt that was looking for her nephew, but refused to allow us to notify the nephew before we released his contact information. Use caution."

This gives other investigators a head's up, and hopefully this person, who may be up is to no good, won't find anyone to take her case under her stipulations. Private investigators are not legally obligated to do this, yet as professionals we must be aware of the impact of problematic reunions.

So how do private investigators accomplish all these miracles? Investigation in the private sector is primarily an information business. Our clients want to know something about a particular person or situation, and don't know how to get. That is the reason they are willing to pay a professional to find out for them.

Very simply, private investigators meet goals by:

- Conducting research
- Talking with people
- Watching what goes on

They do research in public offices, libraries, publications, online and through the un-secret invisible net. There are much better search engines than Google or Yahoo that will be presented. Fee based proprietary databases of consumer records, court files; tax and property records are readily available in the industry.

The techniques are uncomplicated… investigators gain information by listening. They may ask direct questions then listen for what the person says, as well as for what is not said. An innocent individual involved in a fraudulent traffic accident scam will tend to relive the experience as the story is told. Conversely, the scamsters are well-rehearsed and display little emotion.. The "bad guys" will refer to their injuries much more often..

Other cases will require the investigator to be cagier, in order to protect the integrity of the investigation. Some assignments may involve a field operative sitting down next to a subject in a bar and starting a conversation by saying, "that guy is such a jerk, I need a beer."

Private investigators learn to pay attention to the subject's posture, use of words, halting speech and dozens of other meaningful traits. Later they may compare statements from different people at different times, and those of different individuals, attempting to find inconsistencies in order evaluate the information.

Qwik-Tip: Ethics Check
You might think in a public setting, that we get yourself close to those we want to know about then eavesdrop on their conversation. It is okay to be sneaky or shrewd, but in California, it is illegal to eavesdrop or record an intended confidential conversation, so that one may be out for you in your state, also.

Field agents watch people and what they do, whom they speak with and where they go. They may follow on foot or public transportation, but ordinarily are secured in their own vehicle. Of course, this activity has to be accomplished without being "burned" (spotted) by the subject of the surveillance.

Physical inspections of locations assist when trying to locate stolen property or safety factors in child custody matters. An operative may be in a stationery position outside a factory watching to see who drives in after the gate is secure for the night. This effort could provide a short list of theft suspects. Investigators will strategize with the information obtained.

An assignment may be handled entirely by one individual, or a team. They have to pull together what they learned, then to make some sense of it to provide the product our client is paying us to produce, the report.

When the team is unsuccessful, they report steps taken and make recommendations, if warranted, for future efforts. Investigators cannot advise a client whether he has the necessary information to pursue his endeavor, yet they can advise him of what other information may be available.

All cases mentioned in this chapter can and were resolved by using investigator's senses of sight and hearing with a lot of ingenuity, analytical skills, and some rudimentary knowledge.

SUMMARY

This chapter helps to answer why so many misconceptions exist about private investigators, and have provided concrete examples to reinforce the realities of the profession. An overview of the techniques used in several types of private investigations is presented. Readers have gained understanding about the clients and cases investigators tackle placing emphasis on accuracy and real life situations. Further details of techniques with more case examples, will follow in subsequent chapters.

DISCUSSION QUESTIONS

1. How has your opinion of private investigators changed?
2. Can you see how easy it is to take what we see in movies and television and believe it is true?
3. How can an investigator morally defend murders and rapists?
4. If you are opposed to criminal defense investigators, how would you want to proceed if you or one of your family members were accused of a crime?
5. Should we defend all defendants or merely the ones we believe are innocent?
6. Which of the methods used in investigation do you consider most reliable?

7. What would be a problem if you allowed your client to tell you how to conduct an investigation?

Chapter 4

Sources and Resources

OVERVIEW

There are voluminous sources of public government information, both written and published materials that researchers and others can make use of on a daily basis. There is seldom a case in which investigators don't do some kind of record checking or verification. It may be merely an address or phone verification, or the case could require a complete dossier on an executive who is about to be promoted to national prominence.

Building on prior chapters, we'll expand upon the written and published materials available to those of us, who know where to find those jewels. We'll touch on a number of Federal issues, and sources for United States and state level public records. Search tips are presented and the "hidden web" will be revealed. Numerous online sources are introduced, as well as techniques for evaluation of websites.

OBJECTIVE

1. Discuss their knowledge of government function, applicable laws, and available records.

2. Research of public records is discussed including methods of retrieving those records for public use.

3. Explain the Internet sources and learn to use search engines more productively and gain access to the so-called "invisible web."

INTRODUCTION

Definition of Public Records

For simplicities sake, in this text the phrase "public records" is used generically and includes:

- Indexed government documents
- Public telephone and city directories
- Compilations and Internet based directories
- Private compilations offered for sale
- Commercial sources of public information
- Other unrestricted published material for general distribution

What's Out There?

Just about anything anyone would ever want to know about a person is just a few keystrokes or mouse clicks away on the WWW, right? Well, it may be closer to "wrong" once you learn how to search the "deep web."

A professional's most reliable sources of information are from public government records. When the subject of an investigation owns real property, holds a professional license, has a traffic accident, or merely gets a traffic ticket, that information is readily available to everyone who knows where to find it. Occupation and business licenses, federal registrations, delinquent student loans, criminal and civil litigation histories create additional avenues to pursue.

Every government agency generates voluminous records on a daily basis. The various departments compile data, register professions, regulate business and commerce, and enforce laws, offer protection or services, in addition to numerous other functions such as taxing sales, individuals, and businesses. Each agency creates and holds records of its audits, expenses, memos, activities, applications and case record files. Personnel time sheets, job descriptions, and performance evaluations are maintained, plus the countless records of telephone and email messages. There are a multitude of historical maps and diagrams, photographs, plot maps, building permits maintained by the governments of every city, county, state and federal government. So where does it end?

Qwik-Tip
For the sake of privacy, personnel, income tax, medical and similar records are NOT available to anyone who inquires.

Most commonly, investigators need to verify a subject's license, registration, property ownership, etc. and those tasks can be accomplished over the Internet from the government agency or a public record reseller, also referred to a record vendor. Some record vendors incorrectly identify themselves as "information brokers".

An information broker is a professional researcher, ordinarily with a graduate degree in library science or business retained by large corporations. No license is required since they research public records and published material from special libraries both on and offline. Pepsi wants to know what is going on with, Coke, just like Microsoft keeps tabs on Apple, and one of they ways to accomplish that is to hire a professional researcher.

Open records are the foundation of our democracy, yet a citizen's right-to-know requires appropriate balance to protect another individual's rights to privacy. Juvenile records of all kinds are off limits, except to the minor's parents or the subject after reaching majority. Also protected are adoption, court, and school records involving those less than 18 years, although some states do have open adoption records once the minor reaches majority.

The federal Freedom of Information Act requires the government to open up documents for public viewing, while the Privacy Act restricts personnel records and other private matters to the person named in the record. These topics will be discussed further in a later chapter.

Financial records, amounts of earnings or taxes paid are confidential unless and until these matters are adjudicated in some manner. Once a taxpayer goes to court to contest an IRS ruling, his tax returns are made public as part of the court proceeding. Delinquent tax amounts become public when the government records tax liens against an individual. All otherwise private business and personal records brought into evidence in a civil trial become public record.

Names of public assistance recipients will not be published, nor are the names searchable by the general public. Medical treatment in public and private institutions is confidential, and covered by the legally sanctioned "privileged" relationship of physicians and patients. The recently amended 1996 Health Insurance Portability and Accountability Act (HIPAA), has been instituted to protect patient's hospital and medical records on the local level.

> Qwik-Tip
> The Freedom of Information and the Privacy Acts apply only to federal documents and records.

A government employee's personnel file is confidential although public records often reflect the pay scale for the position. His or her performance reviews or disciplinary actions would remain private, yet available to the employee under the Privacy Act.

Evidence presented in civil, criminal, bankruptcy, admiralty, international and tax law cases are public, as long as juveniles are not parties. Various environmental functions, mapping of land, historical preservation, building of highways, and public structures likewise generate voluminous public documents. While seldom of interest to the casual record searcher or investigator, these are generally readily available for the asking.

State Records

The states are charged with protecting personal information and making public information available on the state level. Each state government has its own Constitution, public record laws, and privacy laws.

For instance, the California Records Management Act defines records as "all pages, maps, exhibits, magnetic or paper tapes, microfilm, photographic films and prints, digitized images, punch cards and other documents produced, received, owned, or used by an agency regardless of physical form or characteristics."

Analogous to the federal Privacy Act, the California Information Practices Act allows a government employee, or other subject of otherwise private records, a right to view records that concern them personally. Personnel records and police files fall into this category.

In it is the California Public Records Act that allows or denies access to our government records and state documents. Litigation history, real property ownership, professional licensing, franchise registration, retail sales permits, and criminal charges are the types of public records investigators and researchers seek out most often. We will refer to these as indexed public documents.

Keep in mind the published source material in the public domain, such as telephone books and city directories. Local libraries are full of books, newspapers, magazines, and journals containing names of prominent individuals, businesses, and participants of newsworthy events.

Since most fictional investigators are engaged by individuals, it is likely you believe that to be correct, Individuals are a source of clients for some firms, while other firms only take cases from law firms or "big business". Since most individual clients don't offer much repeat business, it would be necessary to constantly market the business.

A firm may be engaged to investigate a business the client wants to purchase, or a target could be a large (potentially) fraudulent real estate development. I Investigating toxic spills and environmental contamination is not just for legal assistant Erin Brockovich, who took on the job of investigating. Since she was working on her own and not being paid, she did not violate any laws. There are no limits to the various matters private clients bring into an office; investigators can be hired to look into a police department, university, Fortune 500 Company, or the local ice cream vendor.

Businesses

A business may take one of four basic structures in California. The simplest form is a sole proprietorship held by an individual owner. City business licenses are required and the owner must file a County Fictitious Business Name filing, to open a bank account if not operating under his surname. Also know as a "DBA" (doing business as) the filing is required when the business name does not make clear the ownership, such as "Rick's Electric" or Martinez & Sons.

A general partnership has two or more owners each with full financial responsibility for the entire operation, making that obligation financially more stringent than marriage. Each partner is responsible for a full 100% of any legal obligation. They will have a city business and requirements for a FBN are the same as for a sole proprietorship. Limited partnerships have two or more general partners and an unlimited number of limited partners who only invest in the enterprise, with no management or operational role. This is a risky investment for limited partners, who have no recourse should the general partners run the business into the ground.

Corporations are legal entities requiring at least one officer who usually operates the business. Ownership is by stock issuance. Closed corporations are usually held by families or other close knit groups who buy and sell stock only within the group. The officers are frequently the only stockholders. Huge corporations such as IBM, Texaco, and AMEX trade stock publicly.

Limited Partnerships and Corporations must register with the Secretary of State who maintains records on the business owners, identification number, and provides the name of the person designated as agent-of-service. Should a business be sued the summons and complaint can be served to an owner, officer or designated agent-of-service.

Individual business owners are required be identified, at least, by surname in the business name. When the business name does not include each surname (legal partnership or corporate name) or if the name suggests the involvement of others, individual owners or partners file a statement with the county, listing the all owners' and officers names and addresses. These statements are known as fictitious business name statements (FBN) or referred to as doing business as (DBA)

Corporations doing business as a name other than the legal corporate name must also file. A corporation is a legal entity and, as such, is entitled to operate under different business names, as long as the proper fictitious name statement is filed. Should William Anderson Enterprises open a chain of "Big Billy's Burgers", they would be required to file FBN statements for individual store names at each address in each county.

Public Business Records

FBN/DBA statement expires in five years and must be renewed, or sooner upon the filing of a change of address or change of owners. Most business owners comply with this requirement initially since the statement is required to open a business bank account. There is no penalty for failing to file or renew. A company may, or may not be active regardless of the status of their DBA statement.

Researchers can view and obtain a copy of the filing through the County Clerk's Office. The record can be accessed usually by business or owner name. Business licenses are public information and cities collect fees and license business annually. In some cities, the annual fee is in proportion to the business income. The amount of the fee is not public, unless delinquent.

Common sense would indicate that since Limited Partnerships and Corporations are registered by the Secretary of State they would also be able to provide the names of the major stockholders of open corporations. That may be true is some states, however, the California Department of Corporations performs that service in the state. As mentioned before, the state's department names will vary. Corporations and Ltd Partnerships register with the Secretary of State. The Secretary of State provides names and addresses of the business, the corporate officers and the designated agent-of-service for legal process. When researching business entities you will likely check on the city, county and state levels.

Libraries are full of member directories of professional, business, who's who, award winners, famous people, and even directories of directories, and directories of associations. Since many investigation subjects are companies remember there are tons of data on businesses in the public library. Expand your thinking further since "library" includes academic, special libraries, and law libraries.

Colleges and public libraries provide database searches for library patrons and may extend searches to students and those with public library cards. Students and library card holders are often able to access library catalogs and databases from home computers. Paralegal and law students can receive reduce rates to access otherwise very expensive legal databases.

Record Vendors

If all the above isn't enough to put the average person in information overload, there is much more to think about. Private companies purchase 1,000s of public records electronically then transfer the data into their own systems. The record vendors often reformat and generally improve usability and accessibility of the data, for a charge, of course.

Why pay, when you can get it free? As a licensee earning $50-75 per hour, time is better spent soliciting new clients, actively working on cases or writing reports. Researching can be time consuming and may be better left to those with an aptitude for following logical trails with a strict attention to details.

There are a slew of web sites that compile sources and URLs of interest to investigators. Many are free links to public record indices that may be accessed by record vendors who charge a fee. It is a good idea when searching for public records, to search from more than one source, especially if the only cost is time.

Online sources allow a searcher to index files (search) for a subject name and document number, but the actual record in not available by electronic means. If you are going to do it right though, the only way is to have an experienced human retrieve and review the actual file.

There are government entities, businesses, private groups and professional organizations, and colleges and universities that compile valuable information on their websites for easy access. Keep in mind that sites are created by entrepreneurs who may also be compiling or creating their own databases with consumer information. It is always a good idea to check a sites privacy policy. Some entities and governments charge a fee for accessing public record indices, yet many do not. Payment online is by credit card.

Creation of Documents

The first government document produced on ones behalf is a birth certificate. The record contains the child's name, the date and time of the wondrous event, mother and father's names, birth dates, birthplaces, addresses & occupations, plus the names of the hospital and attending physician.

It indicates whether the birth was single or multiple, and the number of previous births for the mother. The doctor in attendance signs the certificate and it is recorded in the county of birth, with a copy forwarded to a statewide index.

When the baby is born at home without a doctor or midwife in attendance and the birth registration is delayed, there is another document completed and recorded. Birth records may or may not be public, depending on the state.

Before the next tax deadline parents will rush to the Social Security office to apply for a Social Security card for their precious little tyke, so the government can track them… oops we mean, so the child can become a legitimate tax deduction for her parents.

> QwikTip:
> Student school records are not public info. Should the parents divorce, , or if one is a victim of crime or a traffic accident these circumstances may create additional records that can be obtained. Each is restricted, one way or another.

"The Early Learning Program" in the local school district is essential for preschoolers. Numerous sports and activity classes are available for little ones through city community centers. A child is barely out of diapers, yet their personal paper trail will have a solid beginning with records generated in all levels of government.

A child's preschool assessments and aptitudes are documented and retained. Participation, eligibility, or ineligibility for special programs is also noted. Grades, achievements and extracurricular activities likewise, will be memorialized supplementing the existing myriad of government records.

A young man may have a city work permit or state learner's permit to drive a car. College admission applications become part of community or state college records. There is a court record generated for the minors' the first traffic ticket and males register for Selective Service; all this happens before the teen can register to vote at age 18.

The document records increase more rapidly as we mature and begin working and pay income taxes, into Medicare and other payroll deductions. Should we become entrepreneurs ourselves, we'll require a city business license, a county fictitious business name statement, a professional license and/or state registration for our corporation, generating another batch of records.

Our dream comes true when we obtain a national pilot's license, or graduate from a public college or military academy. We can't forget all those student loan documents! There are even published lists of those delinquent on student loans and persons who cannot do business with the government?

Marry your sweetheart, have a child, purchase property, build a house, sell your business, and carry on the other activities of life in our society generating records and entries throughout public and government agencies. The continuous generation of these records is what investigators refer to as a "paper trail."

Adult life is a larger series of government registrations, applications, filings, permits, vital records, affidavits, deeds, business filings, professional licensing, certificates, property ownership, building permits, animal licensing, oh yes, and taxes. Through the ordinary course of living, we have countless interactions with all levels of government each dutifully being noted and memorialized in government record. Even upon death, the government has to know about it!

Many such documents are frequently requested and readily available. Some are available only upon formal request while many others are not available at all, for public viewing under any circumstances. Availability and access to particular records will vary from county to county and from state to state.

Indexing Records: Logic or Illogic

When searching for an individual's name make note of entries for exact matches and for those listed with no middle initial. If you do not know the middle initial, you will be wise to note all entries with the same first and last name, regardless of the initial.

Note the:

- Type of record
- Dates included
- Subject name
- Other parties
- Numerical or other codes
- Record number
- Date of filing

Qwik-Tip
Document copies and case files are held by "number" and if there was an error in recording the number the clerk will be unable to locate the file, and the search will have to be repeated. When there are many entries, it is best to purchase a photocopy of the index rather than risk transposition errors.

For a subject named "David Joseph Patterson" note exact matches, should there be any, and all David Js and any David listed without a middle name or initial. When learning it is better to get too much information, rather than not enough. When the surname is uncommon and the budget allows you may search for partial names or possible family members.

Companies

You might get lucky and discover previously unknown related companies. If doing an in-person search with an adequate budget I would also look just to cover possible misspelling or data entry errors. When you can find something someone else missed, it makes you look good and impresses the client.

While searching a telephone book, or other printed directories you may realize that there is no standardization for alphabetical order. Number names are generally listed before letters names. 1-2-3 Delivery could be listed before A-1 Rentals, yet there is no guarantee. If you cannot find 1-2-3 Delivery listed this way, you might want to check One-Two-Three Delivery, to be thorough.

Business names with initials such as, A.A. Management will generally come at the beginning of the listings with A & A Builders follows. Others systems do not regard spaces and punctuation and would list A & A Builders first. I check for variations and possibilities on an index, as long as I am not paying for each name. "Seaview Bakery" could be listed before or after "Sea View Furniture."

Be meticulous with names like "Mac Intyre, Mc Intire and Macintire" or "De La Rosa, Dela Rosa and Delarosa." Some records will be strictly alphabetical with no consideration for spaces or punctuation, while others will consider any word or letter before a space, as a separate and distinct word. Electronic directories are becoming more alike, yet you still need to know about inherent differences.

Some systems make allowances for spaces and capitals while others do not. "Mac Donald, Ralph" could be before or after "Macdonald, Helen." "La Rosa, Barbara and Larosa, Phillip" could likewise be found in either order. It is not unheard of for a computerized system to separate off a name prefix and you could end up with "Rosa, Barbara La." Really!

Hyphenated last names can be confusing to identify and search. The client may provide you with the name "Phyllis Taylor Bristol." Once you are into the investigation you discover that she is commonly listed as

"Phyllis Taylor-Bristol". Go back and do it over again! That one you should have verified before you began searching.

Be careful that you don't miss anything. At the very least, it is embarrassing when someone else finds something that you swear was not there. At worst, you could face legal action if your client suffers damages, because you omitted available information.

If you don't find what you are looking for, or even if you do, it is wise to check other possibilities on the index. Remember that while most data is scanned some is keypunched by humans who are known to make mistakes. Depending on case budget and circumstances, you might want to check for spelling mistakes and/or spelling variations. Take the time and thought necessary to avoid omissions and mistakes.

In person and/or free index searches will allow you to search for name variations. You may not have the correct spelling for a particular name and may want to search for both Peterson and Petersen, if the time and budget allows.

Sneaky and otherwise evasive people will change or misspell a name intentionally. "Carrol Stevens" could easily be changed to "Carl Stephens... or Karl Stephans." You will have to dig deeper to find those people.

Figure 4.1 Sample from the Nevada Marriage Index
Alpha list...
Williams Teresa
Williams William
Williams Winston
Williams, Ann
Williams, Bernard
Williams, Charles

It may have been corrected in recent issues, yet the Nevada Marriage Index from the late 1980s is just a little quirky as shown above. Some names were entered with a comma and others weren't.

For instance, it will list "Williams Winston" then "Williams, Ann" (with a comma.) Various clerks apparently entered the names differently. That computer system reads rather than ignores the comma and other punctuation. Be on the lookout for these kinds of inconsistencies.

Keep Thinking

If the subject's surname is unusual and not found after checking one or two indices, it could be the provided subject name is misspelled or you wrote it down wrong. Check a large metropolitan phone book or conduct an online search to see if you can find the surname there.

If you check a telephone directory in a metropolitan area and still do not find others with the same last name, the surname is probably non-existent or spelled incorrectly. Do not embarrass yourself; waste your time and the client's money by preparing a report in the wrong subject name.

Verify the spelling with the client to see if it is correct before you issue a report of "no record found." Not (anybody can find something.) You can charge for necessary repeat searches when the client provides incorrect subject information.

Notes from Index

When you take information from an index, you will begin by noting the name and dates covered by that index. This applies whether online, by commercial vendor, or microfiche; e.g. "L.A. Municipal Civil Court-Plaintiff 1980-1989"

You will find this process a whole lot easier and more accurate if you use a set form or format for your notes. If in doubt, write it down. It is better to get too much and throw it out than to have to go back and get what you missed.

Note everything on the line where you find the subject name:

- Subject name (exactly)
- Date of the record
- Other party or entity
- File or case number

Be contentious when writing down names and file numbers. A misspelling or transposition error could be costly. At the very least, you could personally incur the cost of a repeat search, and at the worst, you could lose your client.

Certified Copies

When the document copies you require are for a court case or other legal purpose, obtain certified copies. You would need a certified copy of a death certificate to present to an insurance company to collect on life insurance. A certified birth certificate is a must to accompany a passport application or initial driver's license.

Certified copies are acknowledged by the issuing agency to be true, accurate, and authentic copies of the original government record. There is a usual charge of $10-15 per page to certify documents; copies are printed on special paper or contain a red or purple seal to indicate the certification.

Perusing Public Records

An in person visit allows you to examine as the authentic court files and other original documents. You will usually be offered the original DBA (doing business as) or FBN (fictitious business name) statements. You will likely view photocopies of documents such as property deeds, tax liens or UCC financing statements.

The request forms used, records maintained, various methods of record storage and access will vary from department to department. Your county could be analogous to a borough, parish, or island in another state. The names will change, yet the functions are duplicated from state to state. In most states there will be as many ways of creating local governments as there are counties or parishes in the state.

Fortunately for researchers, government records are likely complied and stored numerically and chronologically rather than by a personal name. A civil case file is assigned a sequential number as the complaint is entered and filed by the court clerk. Each recorded document bears a number in order of recording, usually with the first two numbers relating to the year.

Unless you already have a document number, it will be necessary to search the alphabetical index by subject name to obtain the case file number to retrieve the file. You may access to a computer, or microfilm or microfiche for older records.

Once you have a file number you can request the record brought to you to read and take notes, and/or buy copies from the clerk. Public offices do not allow you to bring your own copy machine or remove any document from the case file.

Most recent records and files will be readily available except in very large departments. In some venues, it will be necessary to call a day or two in advance to have the files pulled from "archives" before your arrival. Save yourself some time and aggravation by calling before you make the trip there to determine if the file or record you want is available, or whether you must first order it.

At the records room you will fill out a brief request form. Hopefully, the files you request are brought to you in a few minutes by the clerk. For security purposes, you may be required to provide or submit a government identification card before the clerk will give you the records. This is to help insure you return the record when you are finished.

These are public and there should be no record kept if who had access to what file.

If the file isn't located by the clerk, consult the docket to identify which courtroom or party last checked it out, so the file can be tracked down for your review. You may not have access to active cases, but there is no reason not to try, if you want it. It never hurts to ask and the worst thing you can hear is, "Sorry, it is not available."

There will be tables or counters nearby where you can work. You can read the file at your leisure and make notes as you wish. Do not open the clips of a case file or otherwise mark or remove any paper. Do not remove it from the area.

Qwik-Tip
It is a felony to remove anything from a case file or to remove the file from the viewing area.

These same indices may be available through an agency website for free, or via a fee- based commercial record vendor. There are commercial firms that do the manual searches for a fee per name searched.

On-Site Record Review

The best tips I can offer are:

- Dress neatly
- Use your charm
- Be patient

Yes, these are public records and yes, you have a right to see them... and computers go down, you could be in the wrong office and files are checked out or "lost." Irritating the clerk on duty is the best way for not getting files when you want them.

It isn't clear which will get you less, looking like you took a break from your yard work to drop by the clerk's office or having the wrong attitude. Appearing irritated or impatient, being demanding or presenting oneself as "important" is the best way I have seen to get someone a nice long wait.

If you are courteous, dressed in business attire you just might be misidentified as "counsel" and race right through the process. I speak from experience.

Be well mannered and polite, yet don't go overboard and risk appearing condescending. A genuine smile works wonders coupled with "Hi, I was wondering if you could help me when you have a chance?" Remember to use the clerks name and say "thank you."

Often you can blurt out a quick question and get an answer to send you where you need to go. Try "Excuse me, but am I in the right place for...?" (This is not the time to get chatty.)

If you have the clerk's full attention and are being directed to another room or building, ask for the name of someone there. When thanking the clerk, if you do not know already, ask her and introduce yourself, especially if you're are going to be a "regular" customer. When you get to room 239 in Building B, ask for a person by name. "Is Bill here? Tammy in the clerk's office said I needed to talk with him."

Case Dockets

These readily available records provide fundamental court case information. The docket is a synopsis of the case listing the parties, cause of action, motions, and decisions arranged chronologically by case number. If you only need to know if there was a conviction, or the amount of a judgment then you can refer to the docket.

Use the dockets to save time. It is smarter to check the docket to determine the outcome of a case before you waste your time waiting for a file or coming back the next day. I would hate to wait around for a file only to find a nearly empty file because the case was dismissed.

> **Qwik-Tip**
> With most files I will get a docket then allow the client to select which, if any documents are necessary.

For older cases, do these by indexing the case name for a case number then go to the proper docket book and review that page. The newer dockets are computerized, and are searched by name or case number. The clerk will ordinarily conduct the search and provide you a printout for you for a small fee. He will also appreciate you paying in correct change or a small bill.

Court Record Briefs

Start reading at the beginning... in the back of the file. New material is always placed on top. You will note the parties names, attorney names, the cause of action, allegations, dates, special circumstances, charges if a criminal case, and the disposition of the case.

Always note the status of the case. Is it still pending? Was it dismissed? Is there a conviction or judgment? If you only need the status, you can save time by checking the docket. Electronic dockets are available at the clerk's office for newer cases

A court case brief is just that, "brief." Do not hand-copy each page in its entirety. Read the complaint then various documents and summarize what you read. "Plaintiff claims defendant was negligent by allowing his 12 year old son to drive his truck. Pl. claims great bodily harm and severe emotion distress, etc..."

Certified Copies

When the document copies you require are for a court case or other legal purpose, obtain certified copies. You would need a certified copy of a death certificate to present to an insurance company to collect on life insurance. A certified birth certificate is necessary to accompany a passport application or initial driver's license.

Ordering Copies

Very seldom will you be required to copy an entire file. A client often wants only a copy of the complaint or a few other documents.

There is no sequential numbering of pages in court files, so you cannot indicate pages for copying in that manner. You may fold over pages or mark with paperclips or Post-a-Notes. Ask the clerk how he wants the pages marked for copying.

You pay for copies when you request them; costs are in the range of $.50 to $2 per page. If the department is very large or very busy, you may have to come back in a few hours or the next day to pick up your copies. Cash is the preferred method of payment although some offices accept checks or credit cards. It is best to come prepared with smaller bills.

> Qwik-Tip
> Sometimes it is more convenient to have the court mail your copies. This process can be simplified when you provide the clerk with a self-addressed postage paid USPS 2 Day-Priority Envelope for up to 2 pounds. I have even left a blank check marked "not to exceed $25" and had change fall out when I received the copies and opened the envelope.
> Another tip: if you are working for a client get your copy fees advanced. Otherwise, you could have money going out of your pocket that the client could be slow to pay or refuse to reimburse.

Grantor-Grantee Index

The County Recorders' office has copies of real estate documents, tax & mechanic liens, notices of default, foreclosures, abstracts of judgment and some 200+ other "recorded" public documents all filed by name, year and document number.

If not computerized there are two sets of microfiche or tapes to consider. One set are the indices that lists the individual or business names and document numbers for various periods, usually 10-year blocks labeled as follows:

- 1990 - 1999   Dar - Edw
- 1990 - 1999   Edw - Fra
- 1990 – 1999   Fre - Gra

The other set has copies of the actual public documents arranged by document number indicating the year labeled as follows:

Doc # 99 - 171234 to 99 - 182456

Doc # 99 - 195624 to 00 - 000352

Doc # 00 - 007524 to 00 - 013256

Numbers start over each year.

First, index the subject name to get the other party name, document type, document number, and number of pages. Be sure to note whether the search name is designated as a grantor or a grantee on the index.

If you can't figure out the system, you can always ask a clerk. Just remember, the clerks are there to provide access to records for the public, not to personally educate you. When court runners and document researchers are hard at work, some are unhappy when interrupted with questions, so do not be surprised if you receive a curt answer. These people are working hard to get their work done and leave…. or go to another court.

Go to the next set of tapes that includes the document number you need then find the document you want to view. If you are going to brief the document you will note the document type, parties names & addresses, dates, document number and specific details such as parcel numbers, prices, terms, loans or tax amounts.

Be sure to record the legal description if the document relates to real property. These are several lines long. It is usually acceptable to write just the first 15 (or so) words...then the last five.

Be meticulous when recording numbers. Experience will help you balance the need to be efficient and cost effective while being absolutely accurate. At the very least, your transposition error will cost you in time and parking for a repeat search.

If I am not clear about what documents the client needs or want to avoid the expense of ordering many unnecessary documents, I provide a copy of the index to the client. Then the client can select only the documents relevant to the case and not incur needless expense. Obviously, online searching is the most cost effective method of locating and obtaining document numbers.

DOING BUSINESS AS (DBA)

Investigators frequently access fictitious business name statements. They either need to know the owner of a particular business or which businesses an individual owns. The indices are usually two parts to search either, by owner or business name. The clerk will make copies for a fee.

ACCESSING PUBLIC RECORDS

The "custodian of records" for a particular government agency maintains government public records. With the exception of some federal court files, there is usually no cost associated with simply viewing court files, fictitious business name statements, or copies of tax liens and property deeds.

The indexed government records are stored by a case or document number. The custodian of records will maintain a name index that you can peruse to find the cases or documents that relate to your inquiry.

Certain public records such as real estate records are in great demand. Title, real estate and escrow companies are willing to pay for the convenience of having access to their own copies or direct access to the index. Government Agencies sold copies on microfiche (4"x 6" film), microfilm, magnetic tape, or CD disk that could be loaded into that company's own database. Well, at least they did in the olden days when DOS was first introduced. Most current indices are stored electronically.

There are hundreds of "public record vendors" that purchase, and then resell government index information. Often they will reformat the government information making it much more useful to the public. Their customers are willing to pay for the convenience of off-site searching and improved results.

When you must be absolutely sure of your results, then you are going to have to personally search the government records... or pay someone else to do it. Electronics are great, but not perfect.

Local Records

Counties and cities, have the power to enact local ordinances that restrict records access even further. Accessibility to most county records is similar, yet, there is no guarantee that all the same records will be accessible in each county.

Record Content

The function of the government agency producing the record will determine the documents content. The Secretary of State registers and regulates corporation, franchises, limited partnerships, and notary publics. The Department of Consumer Affairs licenses many business and/or occupations and provides verification for many licenses online.

Business applications will include the complete business name, tax identification numbers, names and addresses of owners or officers, the agent-of-service, background of principles and assets held by the company, as well as many other small bits of information that could be of interest to an inquisitive researcher.

Without knowing for sure, you could guess that a marriage application would contain the names of the bride and groom, their respective ages, birth dates and birthplaces, family names and possible business or occupations, and you would be correct. A death record would obviously include identifying information, last address, next of kin, birth date and place and cause of death.

Personal applications for registration or services will contain personal and business names, birth dates, family members' names, marital status, Social Security numbers, personal identifying information, addresses, former addresses, employment, former employment, licenses held, education, assets held, business interests, company names, and possibly admission of criminal convictions.

A divorce case file includes names and ages of children, statements of earnings and expenses, lists of assets and liabilities and sometimes some good ol'dirt. Many states are no-fault divorce state; yet requests for restraining orders, allegations of infidelity and abuse are not, unheard-of.

Don't overly concern yourself about what you expect to find in each record. The nature of the record and your good common sense will indicate the type of information you can expect to find there… and there are frequently some nice surprises

Obtaining Federal Records

Some federal government records are requested in advance or under the Freedom of Information Act, however most indexed government records are readily accessible. All one must do is walk in the appropriate office and make a request for the record.

Older document those will be stored in the National Archives. You will need to contact the federal court in your jurisdiction and request information. With the growth of the WWW, it is simple to research local court requirements. You can index and locate federal court files by telephone or via the courts' Pacer System online. Pacer is a fee-based service, yet there is no charge for the first $10.

Government records are frequently utilized by investigators, collectors, realtors, law firms, and individuals, members of the press and other businesses, generating a substantial demand. Private companies purchase the indices of these records them make those accessible online for a fee. Busy professionals gladly pay for the convenience of online searches. Due to low demand (and decreased profitability) many of the lesser populated counties' records are unavailable through commercial vendors.

Qwik-Tip
I found out the hard way that Henderson, Nevada was closed on Fridays, except for the jail. Energy shortages and local cost cutting measures can restrict counter access at some venues. Keep in mind that smaller county or city offices may have abbreviated access hours. Call ahead before making the drive to government offices in sparsely populated areas.

WWW Sources

Various government, business, and individuals publish and deliver content from the WWW via the Internet. There is no shortage of either fee or free sites. Many provide valuable content for no charge, to attract visitors and make money by charging advertisers who hope to catch the eyes of visitors who will "click" on their link.

Counties are putting their court file indices online in compliance with state laws. This allows the researcher the convenience of locating records and case numbers before they have to leave the comfort of their computer chairs. Busy professionals would rather find there is "no record found" before they trek down to the courthouse and park, etc.

Doctors, lawyers and many other professional licenses are verified online, usually at no charge. You can phone for verification; however, that often requires long waits and contributes to neck strain. There are instances in which you could have traveled to the court, in the time you spent waiting on the phone for information. Speaker phones allow working while waiting.

Do not overlook your local public or school library for free on-line access to proprietary databases. Libraries and colleges pay for access that allows the public to connect online free. You may have your choice of county public or law library and municipal or city libraries. It is truly amazing what you can find when you start looking around.

American Business Information, Hoover's, and others publish business directories that you can access free at the library or online for a small fee. Anyone who pays can get the information, but those are not accessed "freely," unless you keep paying.

Qwik-Tip
Only trademarks, layout and design of factual statistics and directories may be copyrighted. Copyright concerns creative works, but not factual directories. Government publications belong to the people and can be acquired and used at will.

The various banks, credit card companies, and credit bureaus sell their database information to banks, investigators and others for specific purposes. Although once considered private, consumer information is now "up for sale." Mostly used by marketers, consumer info is not otherwise widely available or accessible to the general public. The information remains semi-private, or semi-public, depending on how you view it.

Public record vendors such as MerlinData and Confi-Chek use the web as storefronts and conduct business exclusively online. Companies like these purchase and sell indices of government records, and charge for some otherwise free government records available on the web. The convenience of one-stop shopping Entrepreneurs also creates and sells priority database information maintained by private concerns.

Another category of available information concerns information or data freely accessible by the general public. Published works, such as phone and industrial directories, magazines, professional journals, newspapers are in the public domain. You can make copies for your own use, but cannot recopy for others or reprint the work under your own name. Observe copyright laws and get permission before you appropriate someone else's "intellectual property."

Reunion registries, email directories, and business databases maintained on the World Wide Web (WWW) can be used widely by anyone with payment of a small fee. You can begin with Classmates.com and Reunion.com for starters.

Buyer Beware

The WWW has radically increasing society's access to data; yet it will likely never hold all answers for reliable investigative queries. Information is abundant; unfortunately, there is no guarantee of timeliness or accuracy.

Question big promises for moderate fees, and expect results that are more modest. Paying $39.99, is not going to get much more than a search of online telephone books that you can do yourself. Some companies may use the low fee to get customers interest then raise the cost far beyond a legitimate comparable search should cost.

The buyer needs to be savvy before giving her money away. Talk to a real person and don't be afraid to ask questions. Is the company licensed? Find out exactly what you are buying, the source of information, and the cost. Legitimate companies will not mind your questions and will take time to explain. Is the initial low cost simply a come-on to get you to spend more money? Most of us don't mind paying $100 for information we cannot get elsewhere, yet we want to know in advance that is what will be required.

Do not forget to ask about your recourse if the information provided fails to fulfill your objectives. Use the Better Business Bureau's online website to check out companies before putting out your hard-earned money. http://www.bbb.org.

Investigators and Information

If your subject owns real property, holds a professional license, has a traffic accident, or gets a traffic ticket that information is readily available to everyone who knows where to find it. Business licenses, animal licenses, and civil litigation history create additional avenues to pursue.

Inexperienced investigators may sign-up with several public record vendors who provide index searches (lists) of public records. Because they never learned how to properly interpret the information they found, they can go no further. Many researchers pass themselves as investigators, yet they know how to *find* information, not how to *use* it. The uneducated leave it to the client to figure out what to do with that stack of database reports they pass off as a report.

This is unfortunate since the information gained from government records are reliable, easily verified, and stands up in court. It takes just a little more time and effort to interpret and access the provided information once you have some understanding of how the search results are utilized.

Getting Hooked Up

What you know as the "World Wide Web" is the system of governmental, educational, and business servers connected via telephone lines, and now satellites. Until the late 1980's the Internet was the domain of scholars, librarians and scientists until one day we heard of CompuServe and Prodigy. It was with the advent of AOL that really got the Internet ball rolling.

The information industry is solidly in the electronic age, and is not ever going backwards. It is all around us. Public libraries, community centers, community college libraries, adult schools, and senior centers are equipping workstations with computers and free Internet connections. Cafes and bookstores offer Internet stations for an hourly fee. There are inexpensive ways of finding out how to use computers to access and utilize the Internet. Here is an online Internet tutorial co-sponsored by Verizon. http://www.superpages.com/verizon_ilt/.

Internet Use and Content

From a record searching point of view you can access the Internet and reach various websites that contain needed information or you might link directly to a university library and conduct your research on the university's computer database.

Websites frequently come and go or can become very busy, preventing your access. Pages are renamed frequently and/or moved making the URL appear useless. Don't give up! Take off letters to slashes "/" of the end of the URL until you get it to connect where you can look for the new link. Try different days at different times before you abandon your efforts.

If do not have the website you want, you can conduct a topic search using one of many "search engines" created specifically for that purpose. You can find some very popular ones are listed below:

- http://www.google.com
- http://www.excite.com
- http://www.lycos.com
- http://www.altavista.com
- http://www.northernlight.com

If your first search doesn't give you what you want, resubmit it another way. Change or add words or try a single or plural form of a word. Find the "search hints" button for search tips. Check out the advanced search, hints or tips before you compose your query. Different search engines will get different results, so experiment until you get what you need.

Government Searches

- http://firstgov.gov/Topics/Reference_Shelf.shtml
- http://www.pueblo.gsa.gov/cic_shop/cicshop.htm
- http://www.archives.gov/national_archives_experience/charters/charters_downloads.html
- http://pacer.psc.uscourts.gov/
- http://www.fjc.gov/federal/courts.nsf

Website Evaluation

Do not make the mistake of blindly accepting whatever you find on the Internet as accurate and reliable. Children, university students, criminals, and hate groups have equal access to the mostly unregulated web. Teens can produce some sophisticated sites.

Do some simple analysis. What domain is the site under? Gov, .mil or .edu should be reliable. Org, .net, .tv, .info or .com can be purchased by anyone and usually for a commercial purpose. What is the purpose of the site, to sell, educate, or convince? Pop-up ads are a good sign the intention is to sell and the content will be secondary to generating income.

Who sponsors the site? There should be an "about" page with actual persons named. Real contact information must be provided, not merely an email address. Look for a copyright or revision date to indicate timely information. Inclusion of addresses and phone numbers tend to reflect reliability.

ONLINE RESOURCES

Invisible Web

We access the web with search engines; the current most popular of which is Google. It seems like the sillier the name, the more popular the product. A search engine finds web pages by sending out "spiders" that crawl over web pages and follow links to other sites then follows those links, creating an index as it goes which allows us to search. Spiders don't even have teeny brains to interpret and validate what they see.

There is much web content that is not readily available on common search engines; "dynamic" (created on the fly) pages can not be crawled by spiders. There are some specialized search engines though, that know what other things to look for in web content that can get you going on an entirely different direction.

"The Invisible Web Search Engine." is at www.incywincy.com. You can enter "searchable database" in the search field; and in 110,055 choices in 0.02 categorized hits, Plus numerous advertisements.

#####...the following section is unchanged from the previous edition is you can use it...#####

Change your search terms to "searchable database crime" to find 5,324 references categorized by Reference, Regional, Society, Science, Computers, etc., because the more specific your search, the more relevant your results.

A tutorial on how to use the invisible web

- http://www.lib.berkeley.edu/TeachingLib/Guides/Internet/InvisibleWeb.html

Those Dark Hiding Places

- http://library.rider.edu/scholarly/rlackie/Invisible/Inv_Web.html

Your relevant result is a click away!

- http://www.upspiral.com/

Find searchable databases

- http://www.redzip.com/

Directory generated by humans, XLNT quality

- http://dmoz.org/

Internet Public Library

- http://www.ipl.org/

Invisible Web Directory

- http://www.invisible-web.net/

Librarians Index to the Internet

- http://lii.org/

Wikipedia Free Ebctckopedia

- http://en.wikipedia.org/wiki/Main_Page

Newspapers or Magazines Online

- http://www.ecola.com/

Directory

- http://web.info.com

Public Records by location, free search, low fee for some records

- http://www.searchsystems.net/

Free people search free with address; background $20

- http://www.ZabaSearch.com/

Free Searches, $ reports

- http://www.Intelius.com/

Online Searchable Death Indexes & Records

- http://www.deathindexes.com/

Figure 4.2 Directory of Resources

Alcoholic Beverage Control

Licenses bars & liquor stores. Records are held in regional offices and duplicated on the state level. Applications and any accusations are public record. Verify license by business name or street address.

Archives, National (US)

Preserves and holds U.S. government records. There are land records, military records, passenger lists, passport applications, personnel records and many others. There are branches located in San Bruno and Laguna Niguel, CA.

Armed Service Locators (US)

See Military Locator below

Assessor, Tax

County. The tax assessor determines the value of all taxable property, prepares property tax rolls, administers property tax exempt-ions and reassesses property upon transfer. Separate records are held on real property (secured property) and on mobile homes, boats and planes (unsecured property).

Both the secured and unsecured rolls are set up to search by owner's name or owner's address.

These records can be useful in locating an individual or his assets. Private companies have taken the secured rolls from all 58 California counties and compiled them into one database that will allow simultaneous searching statewide for one fee. Otherwise to conduct a statewide search, you would have to go to each county seat.

Animal Regulation

City/County. Licenses pets and maintains animal bite reports. Could be a long shot, but you may want to index your subject's name as a pet owner. Some departments are quite aggressive about licensing pets.

Auditor-Controller

"Bookkeeper" for the city/county. Maintains expense records for officials and employees, in addition to records of general expenses and payments.

Bar Association

In most states licenses and regulates lawyers through the Bar Association. As with all professional licensing, you can verify current license by phone and issue written complaints.

Birth Records

County/CA. The birth certificate will provide full name, date and time of birth plus parent's names &, ages, birthplaces, occupations, addresses and possibly information about the doctor and hospital.

Records are available at the county or state level. California indices are available online at http://www.rootsweb.com.

Boating and Waterways

Regulates yacht brokers and vessels for hire.

Figure 4.2 Directory of Resources (Cont.)

Building & Safety (Public Works)

City/County Issue building permits and perform inspections on private construction. Look for contractor's names, amounts paid and names of persons authorizing work. Copies are available to the public.

Business Licenses

Cities obtain revenue from business taxes. Application and past due taxes are public record. Lists name and addresses of owner.

Campaign Contributions

Under the County Registrar-Recorder. The law requires that candidates and political action committees file statements regarding the source of funds and how the funds were spent.

Child Support Enforcement, Federal Office (US)

See Social Security below

Civil Services Commission

City/CountyState. Provides employment verification for government employees.

Clerk, City

Maintains records of city council activities, property transactions and city elections including campaign disclosure statements.

Clerk, County

Records Board of Supervisors minutes and maintains campaign disclosure statements, corporation files, election returns, naturalization records, notarial records, process service registration, statements of economic interests and voter's registration.

Commodity Futures Trading Commission (US)

Regulates Commodity Brokers

Consumer Affairs, Department of

Some 200+ occupations require some kind of licensing, certification or registration by the state or local government. Each requires testing and/or fees to be paid by the licensee.

Records held by the state will include current license status and may also include residence or business address, dates of school attendance, school attended and complaints or disciplinary action taken.

The amount of information you can obtain from these sources may only be limited by your own ingenuity. You can call the licensing bureau directly or access the information through a record vendor or online for free. The current DCA URL is http://www.dca.ca.gov for online license status.

If you need information regarding the ethical practices of professionals you can refer to the appropriate Business and Professional Code which is available in both public and law libraries.

Licenses numerous occupations and professions as follows:

Accountancity, Board of

Acupuncture, Examining Committee

Animal Health Technical committee

Figure 4.2 Directory of Resources (Cont.)

Architectural Examiners, Board of

Athletic Commission, State

Automotive Repair, Bureau of*

Barbering and Cosmetology, Board of

Behavioral Science Examiners, Bd of

Cemetery Board*

Chiropractic Examiners, Board of

Contractors State License Board

Court Reporters, board of

Dental Examiners, Board of

Dental Auxiliary, Board of

Dispensing Opticians, Registered

Electronic & Appliance Repair Bureau

Engineers and Land Surveyors, Board

Funeral Directors & Embalmers, Board

Geologists & Geophysics, Board of Registration

Guide Dogs for The Blind, Board of

Hearing Aid Dispensers Committee

Home Furnishings & Thermal Insulation Program

Landscape Architects, Board of

Medical, Board of

Midwifery Licensing Program

Nursing Home Administrators, Bd

Optometry, Board of

Osteopathic Examiners, Board of

Pharmacy, Board of

Physical Therapy Examining Committee

Physician's Assistant Examining Committee

Private Investigators*, Bureau of Security &

Professional Engineers and Land Surveyors

Psychology Examining Committee

Registered Nurses, Board of

Respiratory Care

Speech Language Pathology & Audiology Examining Committee

Tax Preparers Program

Veterinary Medicine, Board of Examiners

Vocational Nurses & Psychiatric Technicians

Figure 4.2 Directory of Resources (Cont.)

Controller-Unclaimed Property (CA)

Holds assets such as abandoned bank accounts, undeliverable government and tax refund checks and those from persons who died without wills. Inquiries can be made in writing or online at http://www.

Corporations Department

Charged with protecting the public from fraudulent business practices and sales of financial services and products. Records stock issuance of open corporations. Regional offices can provide indices of permits, licenses, and certificate files.

Corrections, Department of

Maintains state prisons. For inmate verification by phone you must provide complete name and birth date.

Court Records

The counties administrate both the municipal and superior courts in their jurisdiction. In order to be more efficient many of the counties now have consolidated courts that mute the former distinctions

All other dollar amounts, adoptions, injury cases, divorces, probates, name changes, and conservatorships are under the jurisdiction of the Superior Court.

Criminal records are available for both misdemeanors and felonies. You can index the records and examine case files at he county court clerk's office.

Courts, Civil

Starting with Small Claims and going through Superior, court records are an information gold mine. Small claims cases deal with low dollar amounts, but an individual is more likely to have been sued in Small Claims than Superior. (You will have to index SC on a local level. Higher courts can be either locally or by private companies). Divorce records include extensive asset information and are sure to include property settlements. In Superior Court you will also find cases regarding custody of minors, adoptions, and those regarding estates of minors, incompetent persons and deceased.

Courts, U.S. District

Records for civil, criminal and bankruptcy are public record. Bankruptcy records will reveal the subject's Social Security number, date of birth, address, bank accounts, stock ownership along with their debts. See Courts above for civil and criminal information.

Coroner-Medical Examiner

County Investigates deaths those are unnatural and/or unattended by a physician within 20 days of the death. Death certificates are obtained from the County Recorder.

Death Index, Master (Fed)

Social Security maintains a list of individuals who died after having paid into or collected Social Security. Non-working children, tourists or unidentified deceased will obviously not be listed.

Figure 4.2 Directory of Resources (Cont.)

Inquiries can be made using the name only or combined with the date of birth or death or by using the Social Security number alone. The search will provide full name, SS#, date/place of death and zip code where lump sum check death benefit was sent.

Records are sold to and can be indexed in the private sector. Most larger genealogical libraries have free access. A CD ROM containing records until 1995 is sold very inexpensively with a genealogy program, Family Tree Maker. Free access is accessible online through http://www.ancestry.com.

Divorce Records (CA)

In California you can obtain a "divorce certificate" from the state. To obtain the case particulars you will need to review a copy of the divorce case file at the appropriate county court and can also get one there.

The court file will contain data about the minor children and extensive personal and asset and financial information of the couple. This is an excellent source for background investigations of all kinds.

Equalization, Board of (CA)

Collects sales taxes and distributes shares to the various levels of government. Applications for retail sales permits and past due taxes are public record.

Fair Political Practices Commission (CA)

Regulate candidates and political action committees. Can provide origin of funds and expenditures.

Federal Aviation Administration (US)

Under National Transportation Safety Board. Licenses & regulates pilots and aircraft. You can index pilots or aircraft owners. Social security number is license number. All aircraft accident reports are held by NTSB in Washington, DC.

Federal Parent Locator Service (US)

See Social Security

Fire Departments

City/Co Maintain public records of fire and paramedic runs by date, time and location. Fire investigation reports also maintained, but are not generally public information.

Grantor-Grantee Index

The County Recorders maintain copies of real property transfer documents, tax liens, notices of default, judgments, UCC filings and some 200+ others for public viewing.

Besides real property records you will find, assignments, change of name, disclaimers, divorces, fictitious names, guardianships, incompetency, judgments, liens, name restorations, notice of tax liens, power of attorney, release of liens, satisfaction of judgment, warranty deed, and many, many others.

Health Dept., State

Compiles records of births, deaths, marriages, and divorces from the counties.

Figure 4.2 Directory of Resources (Cont.)

Highway Patrol

Responsible for patrolling state roadways. Maintains records as do other law enforcement agencies. Regulates school buses, emergencity vehicles, and their drivers. Compiles statistics on vehicle theft and serious traffic accidents for the state.

Horse Racing Board

Licenses and regulates all horse racing and track personnel.

Insurance, Department

Licenses and regulates insurance agents and brokers with telephone or online verification.

Interstate Commerce Commission (US)

Regulates trucking firms, moving companies, and other business that travel across state lines on the nation's highways.

Investigation, Federal Bureau of

Chief law enforcement body of the U.S. Maintains files on stolen vehicles and missing persons. Non-public records can be obtained by utilizing the Freedom of Information and Privacy Acts.

Libraries

U. S. Government Depositories

Regional centers around the nation have copies of most government publications.

Marriage Applications

County clerks retain applications for those who get a marriage license. The applications require that the bride and groom provide addresses, occupations, birth dates, birth places, parent's names, and include prior marriages and dissolutions.

Many who obtain a license don't marry, yet the license application is completed with the same identifying information as the marriage certificate. These records are accessible on the county level.

Marriage Certificates

The license application information will be provided, in addition to the wedding date and location and names of persons attending and officiating.

In California, and some other states, there are confidential marriages that do not require a license and are not public record. The purpose is to protect children born out of wedlock. In order to get a copy of these you must have the county, names of both parties, and the date of marriage.

Regulations in other states vary greatly. It will be necessary to contact the states directly and/or access records through commercial databases.

Medical Board

Licenses and investigates complaints against physicians, acupuncturists, audiologists, hearing aid dispensers, physician's assistants, and other allied health professionals.

Figure 4.2 Directory of Resources (Cont.)

Military Locator (US)

Members of the United States military can be traced through the military locator for each branch of service. You must provide subject's full name in addition to his/her social security which is now the service ID number.

Under the Freedom of Information Act you are permitted access to name, rank, salary, duty assignments, telephone number, awards, and decorations. If an individual is retired a letter may be forwarded.

If Child support or Paternity is an issue then you will want to direct your inquiry to: Armed Services Community and Family Support; Attention: TAPC-PDO-IP; 200 Stovall Street; Alexandria, VA 22331.

In cases of family emergency, serious illness or death of immediate family, the American Red Cross can also be of assistance. You will need the same information as above.

Motor Vehicle Records (CA)

Available Records:

Driving history

Plate reports

Vehicles owned

These DMV records are not available to the general public, but to businesses (inc. investigators) for permissible uses with commercial accounts.

The investigator may need to have an idea what a subject looks like before conducting a physical surveillance. The driving history reveals the driver's physical description, restrictions, any tickets they received, and the vehicles they were driving when the citations were issued.

Although address information if someone has moved out of state there may be a notation such as, "CA license surrendered by Michigan". This tells you where to take your search.

We may need to know who owns a particular vehicle. If you know the license plate or vehicle identification number, you can order a plate report. DMV will provide the registered owner, legal owner, tickets, and other details. Knowing where parking tickets were issued may give you an idea of where the subject lives, works or hangs out.

When the owner financed the car he had to fill out an application. By using a pretext on the legal owner, you might be able to find out where the registered owner works or banks, or you could get a birth date, social security number or other valuable identifying information.

In most states you can obtain the history of the vehicle since it was first licensed in that state and possibly a copy of the license application. These are expensive (in the range or $25-$45), but allow you to check signatures and obtain former addresses.

Figure 4.2 Directory of Resources (Cont.)

If you are conducting asset searches you will want to run the subject name to determine if there are any vehicles Registered at a particular address. You will have to check for vehicles at each address where they might register vehicles.

Your vehicle search could turn up cars, boats, trailers, motorhomes, motorcitycles or trucks. If your surveillance subject lives in an apartment or condo the search will help you identify the vehicle he or she may be driving.

If there are tickets issued you can view them through the court then check out the address on the citation. You can run the plates of the vehicles he was driving and find out who owns the vehicle. Often this will give you a spouse's name. If he or she was cited in an employer's vehicle, you now have a lead to an employment trace.

Private investigators and other businesses in California can set up commercial accounts to obtain DMV records. They are issued a "requestor code" to conduct inquiries by telephone, mail or through a commercial vendor. Drivers and owners are not notified when an inquiry is made by a commercial requestor. The fee for maintaining an account is $50 every two years.

Due to a 1989 state law, address information is not available to private investigators for any reason. Further information and applications can be obtained from Motor Vehicles Department in Sacramento.

National Weather Service (US)
Provides forecasts and historical weather data for the entire U.S.

Passport Records (US)
The Department of State maintains passport records and you can readily obtain passport records of deceased. Freedom of Information requests are required for other third party requests.

Personnel Records Center, National
Provided personnel records on government employees. Contact Office of Personnel Management, 1900 East E Street, Washington, D.C. 20415. Some information is available under Freedom of Information Act. If you know the agencity the subject worked for you might contact directly or ask them to forward a letter.

Police Departments
City. These agencies maintain reports on arrests & booking, auto theft files, crime reports, gun registration, parking tickets, police permits, tear gas registration, traffic citations, uniform accident reports, and warrant files.

Accident Reports are generally released only to "interested parties" (people who have an interest, not those who are just curious). In most venues only serious accidents are reported. If a report was taken it will include name, address of drivers, passengers, and witnesses plus locations and vehicles involved.

Police, State (CA)
Now merged with CHP.

Figure 4.2 Directory of Resources (Cont.)

Printing Office, U. S. Government

Prints and distributes many pamphlets that are of use to investigators and other researchers.

Process Servers

Registration and bond information maintained by county clerk.

Real Estate, Department of (CA)

Licenses, regulates, and if necessary, disciplines agents, and brokers.

Secretary of State (CA)

Oversees many aspects of big business. Regulates corporations, foreign (out of state), and domestic. Obtain officers and status of corporations. Get the names of the general partners of limited partnerships. The limited partners (the investors) are no longer required to be listed. Uniform Commercial Code (UCC) filings are records of certain business debts. May provide SS#, additional business names, and address of individuals. There is a charge for these services and also commercial database access. Notaries are also required to register.

Securities & Exchange Commission (US)

Corporations that trade stock must file reports with SEC. Various corporate information is available. Regulates stockbrokers.

Selective Service (US)

Maintains records of young men eligible for military service. Non public information.

Sheriff's Department

County Maintains similar records as the police departments and also inmate information for county jails. In custody inquiries must be made with full name and birth date. Sheriff's office will report if the person is in custody.

Social Security Offices (US)

Federal Parent Locator. Division of Social Security. May be used to locate an absent parent to enforce a child support agreement or to locate a parent who has absconded with a child in violation of a visitation or custody agreement. Contact your local office for further information.

Social Security has also established a letter forwarding service to meet compelling humanitarian needs. Where there is mental anguish, serious illness or a death in the immediate family they will attempt to forward a letter to a missing person through their last known employer. In instances where the person may be due an inheritance, they will also forward the letter for a $3 fee.

If you want them to forward a letter, you must write a brief letter of explanation to Social Security. The letter intended for the missing person should be placed in an unsealed, plain envelope with the person's name, and social security number if known. Nothing of value should be enclosed. If the person's social security number is not known, you must include date, and place of birth and parent's names. No acknowledgment will be sent from Social Security that the letter was ever forwarded or received.

Figure 4.2 Directory of Resources (Cont.)

Enclose your letter, the unsealed envelope with the letter to the person and $3 if the person is due any money. When you write your letters, keep in mind the conditions required by the Social Security office and how your letter will be forwarded.

Office of Public Inquiries
4100 Annex Building
Social Security Administration
6401 Security Blvd.
Baltimore, MD21235

Tax Appeals Files
All tax returns that are appealed through the courts become public record.

Tax Board, Franchise (CA)
Responsible for collecting personal income and business income tax.

Transportation, Department of (CA)
Maintains local, state, and federal roadways

Transportation Departments
City/County Maintain public streets, and roads. Detailed maps of streets and intersections are available to be copied.

Transportation & Safety Board, National
See FAA above

Unclaimed Property (Controller) (CA)
In most states abandoned bank accounts, income tax refunds, dividend checks, and utility refunds revert to the state. If there is no activity or the individual can't be found in seven years the assets are turned over. In California these lists of unclaimed property are published annually in newspapers. Individuals can write or phone to determine if any assets are being held for them.

Veterans Affairs (US)
This agency will forward letters to veterans when they have a current address. Contact Veterans Benefits Administration; Administrative Support Staff (20A52); 810 Vermont Avenue, NE; Washington, DC 20420. Requirements are similar to Social Security above.

Vital Statistics (State Health Dept.)
Birth, Death & Marriage records are considered vital statistics. These events are recorded in the county where the event occurred then compiled by the State Department of Health.

You can obtain copies of these records from either the county or the state. If you don't know the county you will have to index and order records from the state. Costs of copies are in the range of $10-$12 dollars for certified (attested to be true) copies.

These records all provide a wealth of information for skip tracers and invest-gators gathering background information.

Figure 4.2 Directory of Resources (Cont.)

You can write or usually order by phone with a credit card and providing the name of the individuals, date of the event and the reasons for requesting the records.

The US Department of Health has prepared a booklet, "Where to Write for Vital Records", which gives the requirements for all the states. Available through the US Government Printing Office.

Voter's Registrar, County

The records are maintained for political purposes. Recent regulations have made this information unavailable to the public, but the "media" is one class that can still access the records.

A voter's affidavit contains the document number, the name, address, birth date, birth place, signature, and possibly a phone number and occupation. Old indices are available on microfiche and database. The document number is required to view the affidavit.

Worker's Compensation Records (CA)

Individuals who have been injured on the job will have cases filed with the local Worker's Compensation Office. In California cases can be viewed at local boards, but if you don't have a case number, you must be indexed by phone or mail in San Francisco. Accessibility will vary by state. Records will produce addresses, employers and medical histories at the very least.

Additional agencies and links can be found online at the ISS Network Resource Links http://issnetwork.org.

Figure 4.3 General Directory of Resources

Better Business Bureau

http://www.bbb.org

Broadcast Media Sources

Many expose and reality theme programs offer program transcripts for purchase at the end of each program. If you know the name of the program and broadcast date you can generally obtain the information you need directly from the producer or from large

Figure 4.3 General Directory of Resources (Cont.)

libraries that have the published indices. Instead of that option, you can search program listings through such services as Compuserve. Other companies such as, Nexis, provide full text on-line.

Business/Financial Sources

Most of these require extensive training before becoming proficient.

Dow Jones News/Retrieval

Picks up credit reports and extensive financial information on big business. Retrieve articles from Wall Street Journal, Barron's and other financial publications. International.

Global Scan

International, multi-lingual on-line gateway service to business and finance reports. Includes public and private corporations.

NewsNet, Inc

On-line business news.

Federal Trade Commission

http://www.ftc.gov

General Information Databases

Require special training.

Dialog Information Services, Inc
Infomaster-EZ Link
Mead Data Central

The biggies. Used extensively by the business world and professional information brokers.

Government Printing Office

http://www.gpo.gov

Information Brokers

These companies provide rapid access to published material of all types. Their sources include newspapers, trade journals, scientific data, legal decisions, and business reports. Most of their information is available on line through large databases like Mead Data and Dialog. Brokers charge an hourly fee then pass on the database charges to the client.

Seek Information Service, Inc

818 242-2793

Figure 4.3 General Directory of Resources (Cont.)

Internet Tutorial

http://www.superpages.com/verizon_ilt/

Medical Information Bureau

Maintains records from insurance companies much like credit reports. Non-public information.

Professional Organizations

Association of Certified Fraud Examiners

Holds training seminars.

California Attorneys for Criminal Justice

Associate memberships for investigators involved in criminal defense investigations. Newsletter & seminars.

California Association of Licensed Investigators

Quarterly newsletter, monthly dinner meetings, and conferences. http://www.cali-pi.org

ISS Network

Offers assistance and support for CA licensing. http://issnetwork.org

Investigator's On-line Network

Network of investigators nationwide. Primary purpose is marketing.

So. Cal. Fraud Investigators Association

Membership limited to those involved in fraud investigation and prosecution

Nat'l Association of Certified Fraud Examiners

Continuing education/seminars

National Association of Certified Investigators

Offers certification/training/publications

Southern California Online Users Group

Aimed at professional researchers, yet open to anyone. Conferences.

Products

Shop and compare before purchasing. The following offer an assortment of surveillance and counter surveillance equipment and electronic devices.

Figure 4.3 General Directory of Resources (Cont.)

Guardian Personal Security Products

   The Privacity Connection

Intelligence Incorporated

   Publications

PI Magazine

   Published monthly. Mostly for fiction writers.

Paper Trails

   Stephen Levine and Barbara Newcomb

   Butterworth Heinemann

   Law Journal Seminars-Press

   Gould Publications, Inc

Professional journals and reference materials

   Eden Press

   Thomas Publications

A combination of professional journals and fun reading. Worth checking out.

- Public Record Vendors
- http://www.IQData.com
- http://www.irbsearch.com
- http://www/loc8fast.com
- http://www.locateplus.com
- http://www.knowx.com
- http://www.merlindata.com

Record Research Sources

   California Newspaper Service Bureau, Inc

Especially valuable for state searches in Sacramento. By pre-pay.

Choice Point

   Major player in California market. On line source for courts, driving records, address changes, UCC, docket scan, federal records, and many special searches by subscription. User friendly.

Courthouse Data, Inc. (KnowX)

   Established firm moving into California Corporate record research. Good pricing for high volume.

On-line Searches

   Primarily private name and address searches. Easy, quick & inexpensive. Deposit required.

Figure 4.3 General Directory of Resources (Cont.)

Red Cross

Helps locate missing persons for family members.

Salvation Army

Maintains a missing persons bureau. Contact your local office if you think that your subject might have fallen on hard times.

Search Engines

http://www.google.com

http://www.excite.com

http://www.lycos.com

http://www.altavista.com

http://www.northernlight.com

SUMMARY

We presented a review of various public and government documents available to researchers and methods to personally access those files. You now have a much better idea of just how vast the World Wide Web has become; and learned additional methods to access otherwise hidden web content. This is not an exhaustive list; however, it is an adequate beginning point to construct one that will meet your needs.

DISCUSSION QUESTIONS

1. The Freedom of Information Act requires government agencies to release some types of information when requested. Why do you think this law was passed?

2. Under what circumstance would a government agency not want to release information?

Chapter 5

Interview and Interrogation

CHAPTER OVERVIEW

Private investigators obtain information from research, from people and from observation of people and things. We will now center on people as information sources.

CHAPTER OBJECTIVES

1. Differentiate meaning between interview and interrogation

2. Explain the purpose for either the interview or interrogation

3. Describe the stages and techniques involved in both the interview and interrogation.

4. Explain the nuances and legal differences between private investigation interview and interrogations from those of public law enforcement.

Interview and interrogation are the processes of obtaining information from the persons. At first glance, this may seem to be a relatively straightforward effort. However, the human being is a complex and changing source of information and thus, must be handled properly. As such, the investigator must consider the different factors and conditions present to utilize use a wide variety of techniques that we will discuss in this chapter.

THE INTERVIEW

Purpose

The purpose of an interview is to gather information from a person. Interviews are simply fact gathering discussions. It should be stated that the interview will be conducted with someone with whom you do not anticipate having an adversarial interaction with. On the other hand, an interrogation is intended to obtain information from an individual who does not want to provide any incriminating information or turn on a friend. The interrogator must overcome the resistance of the person in order to get a true story. We expand on this in our discussion about interrogations.

Although we are looking for the truth, it cannot be ignored that the private investigator is working for a client who has a specific purpose or need in mind. In a large majority of the cases, that purpose will have a basis in the law. Most commonly, investigations revolve around legal issues involving criminal, civil or administrative law. Criminal investigations include simple crimes such as petty theft all the way up to first degree murder. Civil investigations may involve tort law such as negligence, personal injury, defamation or divorce. Administrative law may involve workers' compensation, bankruptcy, and labor disputes.

However, legal cases do not always involve proving that someone was wrong or liable for one reason or another. Often, investigations are done for the purpose of assessing some proposed action. For example, in what is commonly referred to as due diligence, one company or corporation may seek to purchase or acquire another company. This is a very complex process. In order to make an informed decision the buyer may need to know:

- What is the ratio of debts and liabilities compared to gross earnings?

- What assets and values does the company have to offer?

- Who is running the company and who are its employees?

- How many employees are on payroll and what are the costs of benefit packages?

- Has there been a history of worker injuries that is above average?

- Do they pay their bills on time?

All of these questions and more require extensive investigation and interpretation before any decision will be made to purchase. Hence, the interview will be designed accordingly.

The person being interviewed can be called the interviewee, witness, target, claimant subject or applicant. Typically the person being interviewed has personal knowledge of a situation or some event. Ultimately, the purpose of the interview is to obtain information that is correct, complete, and thorough. For this, there is no one book, technique or approach that will work in all cases. While there are useful techniques there will never be a substitute for common sense, practice, and feedback from other professionals.

Related Considerations

Before discussing interview techniques used by private investigators we should take into account a few other related considerations. It is helpful to start by pointing out how the disciplines of communications and psychology interrelate with the interview process. Having a basic understanding of these areas can aid the private investigator in their quest for knowledge through interviewing. As mentioned earlier the human being is a complex creature, we will touch on a few of the reasons why in our look at communications theories and psychology.

In communication and psychology theories, one must consider how information can be lost between the investigator and the subject being interviewed and vice versa. Some of the issues that should be considered are:

- Personality disorders

- Emotional stress

- Level of maturity

- Influence of alcohol or drugs

- Internal/physical stress

- Attention span
- Vocabulary
- Language differences
- Presumptions
- Verbal and nonverbal messages
- Cultural differences

We will elaborate on just of few of these items. Certain professions and occupations rely heavily on their own unique jargon. The investigator should clarify the meaning behind these terms and not be bashful about asking for further explanation. Civil and criminal private investigators often interview police officers. Law enforcement professionals are known for their prevalent use of acronyms and codes. However, the difference in codes between departments can be significant. The code '211' in one department may mean 'robbery in progress' but in another agency it could mean 'dead animal in road'. Not only will it help the interviewer uncover the information they need, but clarifying jargon and codes will help those who need to read the interview report or transcription later on.

Vocabulary and language variations can result in different messages and meanings being exchanged. Say the interviewee speaks English, but Spanish is their first language; find out how fluent and comfortable they are conducting the interview in English. Sometimes people might be embarrassed to let on they don't know something as well as they think, or think others feel they should. Occasionally an interpreter is needed, which opens other concerns that must be handled

Citizens from Great Britain and America speak the same language, yet have many different colloquial expressions. If someone said to you "I'll knock you up" what would come to mind? Well, if they are from England, they are telling you they are coming to visit and knock on your door.

Lack of knowledge of certain cultural differences can lead to misinterpretations or flat out embarrassment on both sides. Americans are 'low context' culture; meaning we focus our communications in words. Americans prefer to write or speak their message and tend to be direct. Whereas Asian cultures are 'high context' cultures; communicating through body language, tone of voice and physical gestures. If you are interviewing someone from an Asian background they may appear to be evading to your questioning. But what might really be happening is they are not familiar with direct questions and are unsure of how to respond.

The Japanese are a 'collectivist' culture, whereas Americans place focus on individualism. In a collectivist culture saying "no" is considered negative. Therefore negative answers are replaced with positives, but collectivist listeners interpret the high context signs and understand when a 'yes' is really a 'yes', and when it is really a polite 'no'. This might be worth keeping in mind if your interviewee is Japanese. A hesitant "yes" might really mean a definite "no".

If your Japanese interviewee points their middle finger at you, should you take it as a derogatory insult? No, the Japanese use their middle finger to point with rather than with the index finger. Hopefully your Brazilian, Greek or Turkish interviewee will be just as understanding of you when you wrap your index finger and thumb into the 'ok' sign. In those cultures that symbol has similar obscene meaning as the American gesture of flipping the middle finger.

Be mindful of your own body language when interviewing someone. Are you one to show your relaxed attitude by putting your feet on your desk? This is a common practice among Americans. However, to English, Saudi, Indian, and other foreign nationals this is an unforgivable insult. To a Buddhist is it considered rude.

Verbal and non-verbal communication is a special field of behavioral analysis. Author and researcher, Stan Walters is one of the more recognized experts in the field interviews and interrogations. His in-depth study of what is called kinesic behavior has led him to write such books as "Principles of Kinesic Interview and Interrogation" and "The Truth About Lying". Anyone interested in advancing their comprehension of human behavior in the interview or interrogation setting would benefit from reading these texts and others regarding human behavior.

In psychology, one must consider personality types. Though it is beyond the scope of our purpose here, we can make some general classifications. For example, personality types can be broken down in to three different interpersonal orientation types. Or they can be lumped into three different problem solving personalities.

The Interpersonal Orientation Personality Types

- Control- these people like to take charge
- Inclusion- these people like to join groups and be around others
- Affection- these people like to have close and personal relationships

The Problem Solving Personality Types

- Task orientated- these people are good with details but fail to see the big picture
- Goal orientated- these people are not good with details yet excel at getting the big picture
- People orientated- these people are accepting, compassionate and helpful

Although it is essential to try to understand the person being interviewed, it is equally important for the P.I. to understand their own personality. Knowing how we are perceived by others is fundamental to understanding how people respond to us. The skilled investigator will carefully consider each of these personality types in planning and conducting any interview.

Other emotional and psychological issues include matters of maturity level. Exceptionally young witnesses must be dealt with very carefully since children are very susceptible to suggestion and tend to be people pleasers. The very young pre-schooler or kindergartener may not be sure of the difference between reality and fantasy or could be intentionally misleading because it is fun. While investigating incidents involving traumatic events it may be prudent to have the child interviewed by a specialist in the field of child psychology.

Pre-adolescents and teenagers present special circumstances as well. Often at this stage in life, young people will feel most comfortable confiding in their peers. They may not trust adults. The technique of building a rapport is helpful here. (Rapport will be discussed later in this chapter). Additionally one must consider the legal issues involved in interviewing a minor. Parental permission or presence during the interview maybe required.

From the Files of Diane Evans

In my professional list serve the topic in interviewing child witnesses comes up on a regular basis and the discussion is always the same. "You must have parent's permission and presence during the interview, because in my company that is the way we do it." Many of my colleagues assume, because an action is a department policy somewhere, that it must be a law. Actually, many insist it is a law, yet when I request a "cite" (the code section number) so I can check it out, I don't hear back from them.

There may be a law requiring a private investigator to obtain a parent's permission before speaking with their little witness, but that would be in opposition to our First Amendment Rights of free speech and expression. Police departments will have policies about talking to child witnesses, yet this is likely NOT a statewide law that compels a parent's permission or presence.

I am not an attorney, nor have I played one on tv. It is my opinion as a California licensed private investigator, which in my state there is no legal code that prevents me from talking to a minor child with no parental consent is required. However, common sense may be more important than legal codes in this situation. The youngest witness I recall interviewing was about

From the Files of Diane Evans

eight years old and his mother was present for the interview. I had to do it again with the child on his own. We don't want a parent to interfere and coach the child on what to say.

Secondly, as an adult I do not want to put myself in a position of being alone with a young child without a parent's knowledge. How are you going to get access to a child, at school? Not a good idea, now that I think about it. I have conducted interviews in homes, offices, my car, parks, restaurants and on the steps of an apartment building.

My cutoff for parental permission or participation is somewhere about 13-14 when most kids are on their own after school, hanging out with friends. The last thing I want is to have some 12 year old kid telling me he was somewhere he shouldn't have been, while Dad is sitting there with an un-approving expression on his face. The kid will likely hold back to keep from facing Dad's wrath, and therefore will not be credible as he tells the truth at another time because of conflicting stories.

Interviewing Elderly Persons

The very elderly present somewhat similar challenges as children do when it comes to interviewing. Like young children, seniors may have trouble accurately correlating their thoughts and recollections. Separate events and different time frames may be recalled as one single experience. Regardless of age, certain prescription drugs and mental disease can affect behavior and memory. While seniors are subject to short term memory loss experiences from twenty-years ago may be recalled with great detail.

Make sure the interview subject can hear you. The best way to do this is to ask them "any problems hearing me?" If they use a hearing aid do they have it in now? Don't make the mistake of assuming all elderly are hard of hearing and begin the interview by shouting.

In the field of psychology there is a division devoted entirely to the study of eyewitness evidence; formally called eyewitness testimony. Eyewitness evidence is one of the most hotly debated subjects in the law. Due to the fallibility of human memory and recall, many innocent people have been misidentified by victims and witnesses resulting in wrongful convictions for crimes. Fortunately, as a result of advances in forensic science many of these inmates are being released from prisons and even death row. As such, a tremendous amount of psychological research has been done by psychologists and medical doctors into how the mind stores, retrieves, and recalls information about an event. A truly good investigator will have a firm grasp of this subject.

According to the National Institute of Justice (NIJ) Technical Working Group for Eyewitness Evidence; eyewitnesses frequently play a vital role in uncovering the truth about a crime. The evidence they provide can be critical in identifying, charging, and ultimately convicting suspected criminals. That is why it is absolutely essential that eyewitness evidence be accurate and reliable. One way of ensuring we, as investigators, obtain the most accurate and reliable evidence from eyewitnesses is to follow sound protocols in our investigations. [1]

Recent cases in which DNA evidence has been used to exonerate individuals convicted primarily on the basis of eyewitness testimony have shown us that eyewitness evidence is not infallible. Even the most honest and objective people can make mistakes in recalling and interpreting a witnessed event; it is the nature of human memory. This issue has been at the heart of a growing body of research in the field of eyewitness identification over the past decade. The National Institute of Justice convened a technical working group of law enforcement and legal practitioners, together with these researchers, to explore the development of improved procedures for the collection and preservation of eyewitness evidence within the criminal justice system. [2]

The investigator must take various factors into consideration before beginning the interview and remain mindful of those during the interview. If not properly addressed it can hinder the end objective, which is attainment of correct and relevant information from the witness.

PREPARING FOR THE INTERVIEW

Review Available Information

With the above information as a backdrop, the investigator is better able to begin a proper fact-gathering interview. Prior to interviewing any person, an investigator must have a very clear understanding of the purpose of the interview and any possible positive or negative information that is sought. Typically, the purpose will be to assert some legal theory or defense. The investigator should thoroughly discuss all legal theories, case strategies, and purposes with the client and/or legal counsel.

Time is of the Essence

It is important for an investigator to interview people as soon as possible. With time, people forget important facts and may lose interest in the case. And, in many cases, witnesses will move and can be difficult to find.

Determine the Location of the Interview

Generally, it should be in a location conducive to a relaxed environment where a free flow of information is optimized. On occasion, it might be helpful to return to the scene of a crime or other incident as a means of helping the person recall the event.

Ensure Resources are Available

Be prepared. You will hear this throughout the text, but a key to being a good private investigator is being prepared. You don't want to interrupt the witness in the middle of a critical moment because you have to search for pen and paper. When discussing the purpose for the interview with your client they may instruct you to audio or video record the interview. Have the tape recorder, camcorder or other devices ready along with spare tapes, batteries and extension cords. Even more distracting than searching for pen, paper or batteries would be to have your cell phone ring. Shut off your phone or at the least the ringer and request your subject do the same. If you are conducting the interview in your office, advise co-workers of the appointment time and to keep the room free from interruptions.

From the Files of Susan Ford-Baltazar

While it's ideal to have a comfortable air-conditioned office to conduct interviews, it's often a luxury in my field. And when I say field, it can literally mean a field. I do workers' comp cases for a large insurance carrier. Those working as manual laborers such as; movers, farm workers, roofers, machinist, are at greater risk for injury than say a receptionist. When a worker is injured on the job their co-workers are often the best source of information. In order to expedite the interview process and to prevent disrupting the work flow anymore than necessary, it makes the client happy if we can do the interviews at the work site.

This was true in the case of a farm worker's injury. The farm operator was already short staffed and the crop harvest had only a short window. So I found myself in a cilantro field on a hot afternoon interviewing the claimant's co-workers. The only place to sit was a tattered couch beside a trailer. When I finished my legs were covered in red welts from bug bites. Depending on the nature of the work, a private investigator can find themselves conducting interviews just about anywhere. I keep a little of everything in my car for those occasions; extra batteries, bottled water, spare tape recorder, hat, flashlight, and now, bug repellant!

Interview One at a Time

It is highly inadvisable for an investigator to interview witnesses while they are in the presence of any one else. Hearing what one witness is saying may influence other witnesses and cause them to doubt their own experience and recollection. In which case, a witness may adopt what he or she hears from the other witness thinking that their own perception may be incorrect. It may also be the witness will simply accept what another witness says in whole or in part for fear of appearing to be unobservant or un-intelligent.

Background Check

The investigator must be prepared with as much factual information as available prior to the interview. The investigator may speak to any other interviewer or investigator who talked to the person before. Obtain background information about the subject and review all case files and any other information that is pertinent and legally available. Armed with the background information, the investigator sets out to plan how the interview will be conducted.

It is always wise to conduct a background check prior to an interrogation, but it can be very beneficial in the case of interviews as well. Your client may be looking for witnesses to back up his or her case. Say it's a workplace sexual harassment law suit. An attorney has hired you to find evidence supporting his client, Ms. Smith, and her claims that she was subjected to intense on the job harassment. During an interview with one of Ms. Smith's former co-workers the interviewee tells you names, dates, and incidences of harassment she endured. Before you get too excited, and run to the attorney with what you think is 'pay dirt', think about this; what if this woman that you interviewed has filed over six lawsuits in the past five years? What if all of them were against former employers and made claims of discrimination and sexual harassment? While it's not always feasible to conduct a background check prior to interviewing every witness, it certainly would be prudent to do a follow up afterwards if you think you have found your 'star' witness.

CONDUCTING THE INTERVIEW

Establishing a Rapport

How you come across to the interviewee is important. It is very helpful to find common ground; this helps the interviewee to feel comfortable and open up to you. Part of establishing a rapport is how the interviewee perceives you. First impressions are influential and hard to change. Put some thought into who you are interviewing and where. Is this a first time meeting with the client? If this is the case, most likely they will be meeting you at your office. Convey professionalism, this person needs to know that you are competent and responsible. Men should consider wearing a tie, or sport coat; maybe even a suit if the client is a business banker. Woman, wear a skirt suit, pants suit, dress slacks with a blouse or sweater. Have you lunch or breakfast finished; don't be eating when they arrive, and don't leave lunch on your lapel.

What if you are not meeting your client at the office? As is in the case of Susan Ford- Baltazar, her interview took place in a cilantro field. A skirt suit probably wouldn't be the best choice. If you are a criminal defense investigator it might be quite common to conduct an interview in a jail or prison. In these cases dress extremely modest and professional. Jails and prisons have strict dress codes, even for legal visits, check with the facility beforehand. Just as important as where you meet your interviewee is 'who' your interviewee is. Are you meeting a high powered attorney or a single mom in government assisted housing? They need to relate to you and they will make a first impression based on your appearance. Do you think the young single mom is going to relate to you if you show up in a Gucci designer suit, expensive watch and jewelry? You want them to open up and feel comfortable with you.

From the Files of Carol Hawks

While working for a private investigator that specialized in criminal defense work I often encountered witnesses who were reluctant to speak with me. I recall one woman in particular told me "I ain't gonna help you get that murderer off" and then slammed her front door in my face. I understood where she was coming from; I was working for "the bad guy" in her mind. Knowing that it is easy to stereotype or label someone you have never seen, I didn't think she'd be interested in hearing about my client's woes, hard luck story (or even his possible innocence). But I thought if I made myself pathetic enough she might be willing to listen to my despair. I knocked on the door again and using the most obvious thing we had in common, being female, I told her how I was new at this job and the men in the field would like nothing more than to see me fail. If I could do a good job on this case it would really show them up. I may have even choked back a tear. She may have not been willing to help my client, but she was willing to help another woman struggling in "a man's world". She invited me in her home and let me conduct the interview.

Inquire as to Witness Knowledge of the Incident or Case

It's helpful to have the interviewee tell you what they know about the case or incident first. This way you can modify your questions. People are curious and if it's an especially interesting case they may want to know more details. They will be aware that you have the 'inside scoop' and may pry. They may do it out of curiosity so they can be the first to spread the news to their friends, or they could have some culpability in the incident and want to gage, if and how much, they have been exposed.

Be careful not to become the interviewee. You don't want to reveal confidential information, nor do you want to tip off a guilty party. The other thing you want to be careful of is tainting the interview. This will be discussed further in the chapter.

The next phase involves the questioning. A skilled interviewer will use techniques that help the witness remember events and details, and encourage them to offer up information. Having planned out the types of questions to be asked in the order in which they will be asked will improve the interview. The most common type of question is the open-ended question. This type of question simply asks the person to explain as much as possible without worry of limit or criticism. An example of this would be asking a witness to recount a traffic accident. In this case, is often best to ask the witness to recall the event from beginning to end; as a chronology. This type of question elicits the most amount of information the least amount of effort. You can use the open-ended questions to stimulate the interviewee if they get stuck. Keep them on track and talking by asking questions such as, "did she say anything or communicate anything to your after that?" or "how did you feel at that moment?"

The closed-ended question is just the opposite. It is designed to elicit a simple response such as "yes" or "no" or a choice between a series of options. This is typically done where the type of information desired is known such as which direction a car was traveling. The closed-ended question may be used to help sum up the facts obtained during the open-ended questioning. With these two question types as a base, the investigator can ask them in the proper order to obtain information that is thorough, complete, and accurate.

A properly trained investigator will avoid asking questions that appear to require a desired response, such as the leading question, and to avoid asking questions that are confusing or difficult to respond such as asking many questions in sequence before and answer is given. An example of a leading question is one that requires a yes or no answer; such as "the man you saw entering the Quickie-Mart was taller than Mr. Smith, isn't that true?" Also the investigator will be careful to steer the witness away from guessing. Let the interviewee talk on, try not to interrupt. This is what the pen and paper are for; write down items you wish to have clarified and save them for the end.

Typically throughout this process, the investigator will verify information that is given by summarizing it back to the person. Once it is determined that the interview has been successful, the investigator will conclude the interview and ask the person if they would be willing to answer future questions as needed. In most cases it is necessary to do what is called a follow-up interview. As new information is gathered, it might require re-interviewing the person to expand on or clarify known or new information.

This concludes what is a basic summary of the techniques that the investigator uses in the interviewing process. While it would be impossible to include all potential issues related to interviewing, the following point will likely come up in interview situations that investigators will do.

Protected Information

It is very important to for the investigator to consider whether he/she is entitled to receive information that is sought. The information may be private, confidential, privileged, or maybe protected by some other "need to know only" basis. For example, there are dozens of new federal laws that increase privacy rights in the areas of health care, financial information and similar private records. If the person the investigator wishes to speak to is a party to the lawsuit and is represented by legal counsel, the investigator is generally not allowed to discuss anything with that person without getting the permission of that party's attorney. In criminal cases an investigator for the defense may not be able to contact the alleged victim at all.

Figure 5.1 Arizona Constitution Article II

The Arizona Constitution, Article II; §2.1 (5) provides:

[A] The victim of a crime has a right to refuse an interview deposition or other discovery request by the defendant, the defendant's attorney or other person acting on behalf of the defendant.

Summary of Interview Process

To summarize what was stated, we have inserted the following check list from the U.S. Department of Justice's National Institute of Justice *Eye Witness Evidence* report. The full text of the report can be found at: http://www.ncjrs.org/pdffiles1/nij/178240.pdf

PRE-INTERVIEW PREPARATIONS AND DECISIONS

Principle: Preparing for an interview maximizes the effectiveness of witness participation and interviewer efficiency.

Policy: The investigator shall review all available witness and case information and arrange an efficient and effective interview.

Procedure: Prior to conducting the interview, the investigator should:

1. Review available information.

2. Plan to conduct the interview as soon as the witness is physically and emotionally capable.

3. Select an environment that minimizes distractions while maintaining the comfort level of the witness.

4. Ensure resources are available (e.g., notepad, tape recorder, camcorder, interview room).

5. Separate the witnesses.

6. Determine the nature of the witness' prior law enforcement contact.

Summary: Performing the above pre-interview preparations will enable the investigator to elicit a greater amount of accurate information during the interview, which may be critical to the investigation.

INITIAL (PRE-INTERVIEW) CONTACT WITH THE WITNESS

Principle: A comfortable witness provides more information.

Policy: Investigators shall conduct themselves in a manner conducive to eliciting the most information from the witness.

Procedure: On meeting with the witness but prior to beginning the interview, the investigator should:

1. Develop rapport with the witness.

2. Inquire about the nature of the witness' prior law enforcement contact related to the incident.

3. Volunteer no specific information about the suspect or case.

Summary: Establishing a cooperative relationship with the witness likely will result in an interview that yields a greater amount of accurate information.

Figure 5.1 Arizona Constitution Article II (Cont.)

C. Conducting the Interview

Principle: Interview techniques can facilitate witness memory and encourage communication both during and following the interview.

Policy: The investigator shall conduct a complete, efficient, and effective interview of the witness and encourage Post-interview communication.

Procedure: During the interview, the investigator should:

1. Encourage the witness to volunteer information without prompting.

2. Encourage the witness to report all details, even if they seem trivial.

3. Ask open-ended questions (e.g., "What can you tell me about the car?"); augment with closed-ended, specific questions (e.g., "What color was the car?").

4. Avoid leading questions (e.g., "Was the car red?").

5. Caution the witness not to guess.

6. Ask the witness to mentally recreate the circumstances of the event (e.g., "Think about your feelings at the time").

7. Encourage nonverbal communication (e.g., drawings, gestures, objects).

8. Avoid interrupting the witness.

9. Encourage the witness to contact investigators when additional information is recalled.

10. Instruct the witness to avoid discussing details of the incident with other potential witnesses.

11. Encourage the witness to avoid contact with the media or exposure to media accounts concerning the incident.

12. Thank the witness for his/her cooperation.

Summary: Information elicited from the witness during the interview may provide investigative leads and other essential facts. The above interview procedures will enable the witness to provide the most accurate, complete description of the event and encourage the witness to report later recollections. Witnesses commonly recall additional information after the interview that may be critical to the investigation.

THE INTERROGATION

As with the interview, the purpose of the interrogation is to obtain the truth. The primary difference between an interview and interrogation is that with the interrogation is seeking information that could be used to the detriment of the person being interrogated. It should be pointed out that an interview can turn into an interrogation in a split second. An investigator's initial purpose may simply be a fact-gathering interview. With further discussion, the investigator may come to find that this person was involved in the crime or matter being investigated or may find that there is a new crime or matter. It is at this point that the interview becomes an interrogation. However, in the majority of cases, the investigator knows at the outset that his purpose is one of interrogation.

The information that is obtained in an interrogation is generally classified into one of two types. The first type is called an admission. An admission is simply a statement by the person being interrogated that a fact or other information is true or not true. The admission does not necessarily carry with it some sort of liability or detriment to the person being interrogated. It may well be though that an admission taken together with other facts will yield a conclusion that the person being interrogated is liable or culpable. For example, an admission might be that the person carried store merchandise out of a store. In this case, the person is not stating anything more than a simple fact. However, if it is shown that the merchandise was not paid for, this fact, coupled with the admission may ground liability for theft.

The confession, on the other hand, involves a statement by the person being interrogated that he or she directly admits to being culpable, liable or guilty of a crime or law. In our store merchandise example above, a confession would mean that the person admits that he or she took the merchandise without paying for it and knew that it was wrong.

As we will see, interrogation is a very tricky endeavor which, to be successful, requires an investigator with advanced training and skill.

PURPOSE OF THE INTERROGATION

At a fundamental level, the purpose of interrogation is to establish whether the person being interrogated is or is not liable or guilty of some law or crime. Long gone are the days of heat lamps, finger pointing and glaring detectives. Today's interrogations are far more sophisticated and are better characterized as a negotiation.

Establishing an Initial Belief in Guilt or Innocence

The purpose then is first to establish whether or not the investigator believes the person being interrogated is in fact liable or guilty. In a large majority of cases, the person being interrogated is not likely to admit or confess for fear of the consequences. The investigator uses techniques discussed below to facilitate the attainment of the admission or confession.

Nonetheless, the investigator must be constantly aware that the person being interrogated may not be liable or guilty. As such, the investigator will use techniques discussed below to help establish whether or not the person is telling the truth. If at any point during the interrogation the investigator believes that the person is not liable or is innocent, the interrogation may then turn into an interview or the discussion will simply end. However, if the investigator believes firmly that he or she is talking to somebody who is liable or guilty, the interrogation will take a new direction.

Establish the Law or Crime that is to be Proved

In a large majority of cases, an interrogation is done while investigating a crime or other civil wrong. As such, it is typical for the investigator to be looking for admissions or confessions that satisfy the legal elements of a crime or tort. For example, suppose an investigator is trying to establish that the person he is interrogating is liable for battery. Battery is defined as "the harmful or offensive touching of the person of another" (this definition is most commonly used in civil court cases such as personal injury as opposed to criminal battery). Here, the investigator wants to obtain admissions or confessions that the person being interrogated purposefully touched the person of another in a harmful or offensive way.

STAGES OF THE INTERROGATION PROCESS

An interrogation involves many different phases, approaches, and techniques. As such we will only touch on this area at a basic level. There are some techniques which we will not cover it all as they are trade secrets which will remain known only to law enforcement and fulltime private security officials.

The interrogation stages can be broken down into three general categories. They are the preparation phase, the interrogation itself, and the time frame that follows interrogation.

Preparation Phase

In the preparation phase the investigator is involved in an in depth and complete gathering of as much information as possible as follows:

General information

What information has led up to the belief that this person is liable or guilty? Are the sources reliable? What type of law has been violated or broken? Is it possible that other similar or different laws have been broken? Is there anything suggesting innocence or a defense to the lawsuit believed to be violated?

The investigator wants to have as much of the known evidence in one place if possible. He or she can then sift through it, organize it and make basic assumptions prior to the interrogation. Of paramount concern is the credibility of the evidence, and an open and objective attitude.

Information about the person being interrogated

It is equally important to know as much information about the person being interrogated as anything else, any background information that is legally available to you, such as employment applications, credit applications, prior civil suits (whether as plaintiff or defendant), prior criminal convictions, financial history and any other information that might appear to be relevant. It must be emphasized that this information must be legally available to the investigator.

There are many potential legal traps for the unwary investigator here. The investigator must speak to legal counsel or appropriate supervisors to be certain that any information is obtained properly.

It is not unusual for there to be another investigator who has interrogated this person before. The investigator should find out how this person has reacted in prior interrogations such as issues of honesty, cooperation, communication style and potential issues of belligerence or violence.

Location of Interrogation

Next is the preparation phase; the investigator has to find a location for the interrogation. The location should be neutral and conducive to the environment where the person interrogated will feel free to be honest. The person interrogated is generally placed in a spot where there will be few distractions. Noise, open windows, distracting pictures and any other interruption within view or earshot should be handled appropriately.

It is not uncommon for the investigator to remove items from the interrogation room that might pose a possible threat to the safety of the in the investigator. Pencils, books, and even office equipment have been used in the past to injure investigators.

The investigators also carefully consider whether or not evidence will be present in the room. There are reasons why one would not want the evidence in the room while another times it might be used to facilitate some purpose.

The investigator also has to consider whether not he or she is going to audio or video tape interrogation. If this is done, the investigator must knowledgeable about the laws surrounding the recording of private or inculpatory conversations. Investigators also consider such trivial things as whether not to take notes, what clothes to wear and whether or not to eat or drink prior to the interrogation. Again, the interrogation process can be very complex, sophisticated and full of little nuances.

Miscellaneous Issue

Some of the last issues in the preparation phase consider how long the interrogation should take and whether not support staff should be present. Most interrogations are emotionally draining for both the investigator and the person being interrogated. After certain point, there is a diminishing return with continuing an interrogation. When the person being interrogated needs to use the restroom, requires water, or if the investigator needs paper for statement or telephone for phone call, having another person around can be tremendously helpful.

It is not uncommon for an additional person to be present during interrogation as a witness. This is often done in cases where the investigator and the person being interrogated are of the opposite sex. With the witness present, allegations of sexual harassment and other inappropriate behavior can be thwarted. While caution should be taken, it is not uncommon for two investigators to be doing the questioning in an interrogation. Alternatively, one investigator might interrogate for a while and then swap out with another. We've all heard of the good cop bad cop technique which, for the most part is discarded of today. However, there are useful and legitimate techniques that are used. And, finally, it is very rare that another suspect or opposing party will be present during the interrogation.

THE INTERROGATION AND TECHNIQUES

The interrogation itself is a juggling act for the investigator. Though somewhat oversimplified, the investigator is concurrently considering or dealing with one of four issues. They are detecting deception, handling denials, rationalization and obtaining the admission or confession.

Detecting Deception

The first issue has to do with detecting deception. Investigators who perform interrogations properly are specially trained and skilled at reading body language, referred to as nonverbal communication, as well as things that are said by the person being interrogated. Each part of the body can reveal unconscious or purposeful behavior that can indicate truthfulness or deception. The head, the eyes, the arms, the legs and feet each have separate behaviors that are typically indicative of truthfulness or deception. One example refers to what is called as the freezing effect. Here, the person being interrogated sits rigidly in the hopes of preventing any body language that might otherwise indicate deception.

Lack of eye contact, covering of one's mouth when speaking, turning away from the investigator, scratching of the nose and ears, dry mouth, sweating, a pulsing carotid artery at the neck are but a few of the hundreds of examples of deceptive behavior.

Signs of truthful behavior include but are certainly not limited to a relaxed pose, regular and appropriate eye contact, sincere gestures, arms at the side, etc.

Truthful and deceptive behavior can also be determined verbally. The deceptive person tends to stall when asked a question, will appear to be insincere in their responses, may avoid important aspects of a question, or might try to avoid a question by changing topics such as accusing the investigator of harassment to name a few. The truthful person is likely to answer questions directly and without concern for the purpose of the question. They will be sincere in their responses and are much less likely to change the topic.

As with any science, detecting deception requires more than simply watching for truthful or deceptive behavior. The investigator usually starts out by establishing a baseline with this particular person. Some people regularly exhibit behavior which appears deceptive when in fact it is not. The investigator will start with test questions to elicit responses that are known to be true. Examples would be asking the person to recount their activity before interrogation or stating their name and address. It might be possible to discuss other innocuous or benign activity so that the investigator can see the person responding it truthful way.

Typically, interrogation starts out with a get-to-know session. The investigator wants to build a rapport and a relationship of trust with the person. This will often last for from ten to twenty minutes. Topics such as favorite music, the weather, favored vacation spots and hobbies might be discussed if appropriate. Usually avoided are topics such as religion, financial matters, political issues, and other areas of a personal nature.

Once the baseline is established and the rapport built; the investigator starts into the sensitive matters. Investigators often know what specific statements or assertions will make the person uncomfortable. It is at this point that the investigator begins to take note of what may be deceptive behavior. Here, again, the investigator is looking for the baseline or series of behaviors that may be deceptive and unique to this person.

It is also a typical for the investigator to look for more than one deceptive behavior at a time before concluding that a response is deceptive. These are called clusters. It is rare that a person will exhibit only one deceptive behavior when being untruthful. As an example, if the person is especially nervous, he or she will be sweating, will exhibit dry mouth, and will attempt to freeze their body to mask any other potential deceptive behavior. By looking for clusters, there is an increased accuracy in determining truthfulness.

It should be noted that some people are nervous simply by being in the presence of an investigator. We have all been driving down the street when a patrol car pulls and behind us. While we know we are doing nothing wrong, it still puts us into a nervous and paranoid state. This is the same thing that some people exhibit merely by being in what they perceive to be an interrogation. However, these people usually loosen up during the first ten or twenty-minute rapport-building discussion.

It is not uncommon for investigator to determine the likelihood that the person being interrogated is not liable or guilty of anything, based in large part on the truthful or deceptive behavior. It does not serve the investigator's purpose to continue an interrogation with somebody who is obviously not involved.

TECHNIQUES

Making Accusations and Handling Denials

Once the investigator is convinced that the person being interrogated has exhibited enough deceptive behavior, the investigator will begin a process of making mild/indirect to potentially strong/direct accusations.

Suffice it to say that at this stage the interrogation enters what is effectively a negotiation process. The investigator will be certain to confidently handle any denials made by the person being interrogated. While the investigator continues to test the truthfulness of the person, his or her confidence will grow that the person being interrogated is culpable in some way. Carefully asserted and considered accusations are used and denials are properly dealt with. The purpose here is to let the person being interrogated know that their culpability is known and that they are being talked to in hopes of getting their cooperation.

If appropriate, the investigator will offer the person being interrogated breaks to use the bathroom or similar offerings to make the person being interrogated feel more comfortable and to avoid the appearance of being too tough.

Rationalization

The next phase of the interrogation itself has to do with what is called rationalization. At this point the investigator has been successful in establishing his confidence in the person's culpability and now works to find out the "why" of the actions or offense. This is called rationalization process because it is the purpose to find out what reasoning was used to commit the act that resulted in a violation of law. Was it for money, to spite or take revenge, to help a friend, or similar purpose?

Typically the investigator is trying to minimize or downplay how horrible the violation might be. Rather than calling it "theft" one might call it "take"; rather than calling it "struck" one might call it "made contact." By appearing to understand where they are coming from it's possible to get the person to open up and discuss their reasons behind the act or event. For example, if there is strong proof that the person being interrogated has stolen something, the investigator might offer reasons why a person committed the act. Perhaps it was because they were desperate for money, or they have a drug problem that makes it difficult to resist such an act, or perhaps it was to try to help out a friend. The investigator might refer to it as an error in judgment rather than calling the person evil or bad. One must be careful not to suggest something that might not be true. The investigator is after the truth and it would not be wise or fair to minimize something to the point that a lesser offense is the only thing supportable.

Eventually, if the investigator is successful, he has accurately gauged that this person is not being truthful, has appropriately accused and handled denials, and has offered rationalizations which has brought the person being interrogated to a point where he or she is ready to admit or confess.

The Admission or Confession

Now in the last phase of the interrogation itself, the investigator is ready to conclude the interrogation. Using a variety of techniques, the investigator has established all possible violations of law or areas of culpability, to the proper extent, and the person being interrogated has made all admissions or confessions.

Next, the investigator typically will ask the person being interrogated to provide a written statement; most of the time this person will do so. The written statement may be just a free-form explanation written by the person being interrogated or it may be guided in one form or another. Obviously it cannot be coerced nor should the person feel compelled to write anything that is not true or is inaccurate.

Normally the person is asked to include; that their statement is being given of their own free will and without promise of anything in return. It is not uncommon for the investigator to handwrite questions to which the person will answer in their own words. This is common with people who are not particular cooperative; people, who are very tired or worn out, or people who have limited educational or language skills.

In the private sector, it is not uncommon for the investigator to seek a restitution agreement from that person in the amount of damage that was result of this person's action. This is most frequently done in cases involving theft. It is also typical that these cases are sufficient after an interrogation and are then referred to criminal prosecution, if this is a case involving criminal law.

FOLLOWING THE INTERROGATION

The final of the three aspects of interrogation is the activity that follows the interrogation itself. It is very rare for an investigation to end after interrogation. The information obtained from the interrogation is often corroborated and combined with other evidence for analysis. On occasion, a person may be re-interrogated as the case develops.

Special Considerations

Most of the special considerations of the interrogation concern legal issues. In the case of the government such as law enforcement, it may be necessary for the investigator to read the person their Miranda rights. If the questioning seeks to obtain incriminating statements and the person does not feel free to leave it is required that the person be read the Miranda warning. If this is not done, any statements made may be inadmissible in a criminal proceeding.

Another legal issue has to do with false imprisonment. If the person being interrogated does not feel free to leave this might support a false imprisonment theory both criminally and civilly against the investigator.

Yet another legal issue has to do with defamation. If, before or after the interrogation, the investigator makes derogatory or untrue comments about the person to be investigated this might support a cause of action for defamation against the investigator.

The possibility of one of these legal issues becoming a problem for investigator is not remote. And, many times the accusations against investigator are not true and done out of spite or to deflect attention away from the person interrogated.

LAW ENFORCEMENT AND THE PRIVATE SECTOR DIFFERENCES

The Interview

The primary difference between law enforcement interviews and those conducted in the private sector is their purpose. Communications theory, psychological issues, the type of questions asked in the interview and the interview environment are issues that really don't change much.

Government – Law Enforcement

For law enforcement, the purpose of conducting interviews usually concerns prosecution of a criminal case or a violation of some administrative area of law. As such, the end result is the determination of guilt where the person or entity being investigated will be liable for fines, penalties, restriction of some activity, cancellation or suspension of a license, or other monetary sanction. In more egregious cases, a person or persons may be incarcerated. As such, the interview is designed to net information that is very likely to lead to the determination of liability under some government code.

And, while government investigative units often have tight budgets, the amount of manpower associated with an investigation often turns on the severity of the crime or violation. The people who are served by these investigators are the general public as they are the ones who provide government funding through taxes.

Private Sector

In the private sector, the purpose of the interview may be broader. The purpose of the interview is generally limited to issues that concern the client directly. The inquiry might be to establish guilt or innocence, as in the case of law enforcement. In this scenario, the investigation might be to investigate someone else who has committed a crime against the client. Conversely, it might be to determine the guilt or innocence of the client himself.

Or, the investigation may turn on some sort of other civil area of law. Issues such as tort law, contract law, business or agency law, employment law, or the determination of the value of a proposed purchase are among many other areas of law. These are often the purpose of an interview.

The investigator is often either asked for, or will offer, proactive or preventive measures in the process of doing an interview. Law enforcement, for example, may offer to perform a crime prevention inspection of the home or facility. In the private sector, investigators may suggest internal controls, changes in the way business is done, or other measures that will reduce the risk of negligent or intentional conduct.

The Interrogation

It is in the area of interrogation where there are sharpest contrasts between the public and private sector.

Government – Law Enforcement

For law enforcement, the purpose is rather straightforward and limited in purpose. In the vast majority of cases, the purpose is criminal. The person being interrogated is being interrogated to establish his or her criminal culpability, and possibly to establish other possible suspects. The purpose of course is to determine the truth. The process of weeding out the innocent from the guilty is the highest-level purpose. However, once it is believed that a person is liable or guilty of some crime, the purpose is to prosecute that person to the limit of law.

It should also be noted that government and law enforcement investigators enjoy immunity from certain types of civil lawsuits. This is done because law enforcement officers would otherwise be very reluctant to pursue cases for fear of being sued. In the balance, it is believed that society is best served by limiting civil lawsuits against public investigators so that they may protect the public from criminals with greater freedom.

As we discussed before, the legal differences are also rather dramatic. The purpose of the United States Constitution primarily is to limit the authority of the federal government. As such, many of the constitutional amendments protect an individual from the acts of government - obviously to include law enforcement. Among these restrictions is the right not to be compelled to incriminate oneself, the right to an attorney during questioning, and being informed of other rights when an interrogation is performed in a certain way, for example the Miranda warning.

Private Sector

In the private sector, unless the investigator is acting at the direction of law enforcement, i.e. as their agent, none of the aforementioned constitutional safeguards apply.

As with interviewing, the purpose and results of an interrogation can be very different from that of law enforcement. There are generally many more facets and competing interests that have an impact on how a person is interrogated and what is done as a result of information obtained during the interrogation.

The best way to point out how complex interrogation issues can become is by providing an example. Imagine that your client is an investment business, and company officials suspect one of their employees is embezzling money from one of their trust funds. In addition this employee does not get along with her supervisor and has alluded to others in the company that she has been sexually harassed by the same supervisor.

You need to assess what the issues of the case are going to be. How strong is the case that you currently have against the employee? Is it overwhelming or is it scant? If there is not much evidence to start with, and after interrogating the employee you come out of the interrogation with little or no further evidence, where does that leave you?

The employee may decide to file a sexual harassment suit against her supervisor and the investment business. She may do it out of spite if she thinks interrogation was initiated by her supervisor in order to intimidate or harass her. However, if she is involved in embezzling, she may attempt to deflect attention by filing a suit. So, you still have an employee who your client believes is embezzling money, and now, there is a sexual harassment and assertion of general harassment suit filed. So, before conducting the interrogation, it might have been wise to reconsider the timing.

Perhaps other investigations into the sexual harassment case and the relationship with the supervisor should be done first. Or, you might wait until you can find more evidence to be certain that the embezzling employee can be successfully terminated and prosecuted. If the latter is the case, this employee will no longer be with the company (to continue to steal). An interrogation may not need to have been done, and if it was, the likelihood off any claims that the interrogation was done for harassment or some other ulterior purpose will be mitigated.

Taking this example one step further, let us assume that the interrogation yields plenty of evidence both to terminate the employee, to criminally prosecute and to seek restitution. The criminal prosecution may yield some unwanted publicity. Imagine what this investment company's customers are going to think when they hear that someone of trust in the company has been stealing their money. That kind of press is negative to a company's image. In fact, in many real world cases, this kind of bad press has caused far more damage in lost business than the embezzlement itself. It may be that the company would rather not seek criminal prosecution.

Additionally, unlike their public sector counterparts, the investigator in the private sector does not enjoy the same immunity from certain civil lawsuits. This is just one more consideration in the manner in which the interrogation is conducted and what is done afterwards. There are other differences between the public and private sector which are too numerous to list here. However, we've covered many of the more well known differences.

SUMMARY

We have covered a very broad area and perhaps one of the most important areas as part of the private investigator's job. A private investigator is charged with getting the truth and to do that he or she must obtain information from many sources; the most important and complex source. other people. Understanding the purpose of an interview or interrogation, and the techniques used, becomes one of the most valuable, useful and challenging disciplines for the private investigator.

ADDITIONAL RESOURCES

Tainting the Interview

Earlier in the chapter we discussed how you should elicit as much from the interviewee about their knowledge of the case or incident. We pointed out a few reasons why the investigator should be careful about what they say. The following article from the FBI Bulletin goes into much greater detail about how and what the investigator says and does at the beginning of the interview can taint the outcome.

Article 5.1 Strategies to Avoid Interview Contamination

[A] The victim of a crime has a right to refuse an interview deposition or other discovery request by the defendant, the defendant's attorney or other person acting on behalf of the defendant.

Summary of Interview Process

To summarize what was stated, we have inserted the following check list from the U.S. Department of Justice's National Institute of Justice *Eye Witness Evidence* report. The full text of the report can be found at: http://www.ncjrs.org/pdffiles1/nij/178240.pdf

PRE-INTERVIEW PREPARATIONS AND DECISIONS

Principle: Preparing for an interview maximizes the effectiveness of witness participation and interviewer efficiency.

Policy: The investigator shall review all available witness and case information and arrange an efficient and effective interview.

Procedure: Prior to conducting the interview, the investigator should:

1. Review available information.

2. Plan to conduct the interview as soon as the witness is physically and emotionally capable.

3. Select an environment that minimizes distractions while maintaining the comfort level of the witness.

4. Ensure resources are available (e.g., notepad, tape recorder, camcorder, interview room).

5. Separate the witnesses.

6. Determine the nature of the witness' prior law enforcement contact.

Summary: Performing the above pre-interview preparations will enable the investigator to elicit a greater amount of accurate information during the interview, which may be critical to the investigation.

INITIAL (PRE-INTERVIEW) CONTACT WITH THE WITNESS

Principle: A comfortable witness provides more information.

Policy: Investigators shall conduct themselves in a manner conducive to eliciting the most information from the witness.

Procedure: On meeting with the witness but prior to beginning the interview, the investigator should:

1. Develop rapport with the witness.

2. Inquire about the nature of the witness' prior law enforcement contact related to the incident.

3. Volunteer no specific information about the suspect or case.

Summary: Establishing a cooperative relationship with the witness likely will result in an interview that yields a greater amount of accurate information.

C. Conducting the Interview

Principle: Interview techniques can facilitate witness memory and encourage communication both during and following the interview.

Policy: The investigator shall conduct a complete, efficient, and effective interview of the witness and encourage Post-interview communication.

Procedure: During the interview, the investigator should:

1. Encourage the witness to volunteer information without prompting.

2. Encourage the witness to report all details, even if they seem trivial.

3. Ask open-ended questions (e.g., "What can you tell me about the car?"); augment with closed-ended, specific questions (e.g., "What color was the car?").

4. Avoid leading questions (e.g., "Was the car red?").

5. Caution the witness not to guess.

6. Ask the witness to mentally recreate the circumstances of the event (e.g., "Think about your feelings at the time").

7. Encourage nonverbal communication (e.g., drawings, gestures, objects).

8. Avoid interrupting the witness.

9. Encourage the witness to contact investigators when additional information is recalled.

10. Instruct the witness to avoid discussing details of the incident with other potential witnesses.

11. Encourage the witness to avoid contact with the media or exposure to media accounts concerning the incident.

12. Thank the witness for his/her cooperation.

Summary: Information elicited from the witness during the interview may provide investigative leads and other essential facts. The above interview procedures will enable the witness to provide the most accurate, complete description of the event and encourage the witness to report later recollections. Witnesses commonly recall additional information after the interview that may be critical to the investigation.

DISCUSSION QUESTIONS

1. Other than a civil or criminal case, why else would a private investigator conduct interviews?

2. Why are private investigators held to higher standards and subject to legal ramifications than are police on how they handle interviews?

3. Recall an incident when you were communicating with someone who was not being truthful to you. How did you know; what was it that gave you that impression? Was it their voice, what they said; didn't say, or their body language?

4. Name some factors that could contaminate or at least influence an interview?

5. You have been subjected to questioning many times, a few examples are; a job interview, college entrance interview, or when meeting your dates or friends parents. 6. Have you ever guided or shaped your answers based on what you thought they wanted to hear? What clues or factors in their behavior tainted your answers?

END NOTES

1   NIJ. U.S. Department of Justice, Office of Justice Programs, National Institute of Justice report. (1999). *Eyewitness Evidence: A Guide for Law Enforcement*

2   Ibid

Chapter 6

Written And Recorded Statements

OVERVIEW

We will review fundamentals of interviews while introducing the reader to the techniques of obtaining witness statements. Our discussion will include the responsibility of the interviewer to his client, while accommodating the need to be complete and objective to the witness. Pretrial information exchange is included along with some strategies used by well-informed investigators. Details are provided on purpose, preparation, techniques, and reporting of investigative witness statements.

OBJECTIVES

1. To prepare students to conduct interviews and produce statements from witnesses.

2. Readers will be able to determine whether or not, to memorialize a witness interview and the techniques used. Strategy, as well as law is discussed as it applies to statements.

INTRODUCTION

Most people have a favorite dish or meal that they are proud to prepare. Spaghetti and chili are favorites, especially chili. You never heard of a Tuna Casserole Cook Off, did you?

Some cooks begin by choosing ingredients like meat, spices, and beans, while the more exotic are including armadillo or alligator and beer. (Non-meat eaters, please stay with me on this.) All the dishes the contestants create are called chili, and each chef claims his method is the best.

However, not everyone else agrees to the particular taste, ingredients, and preparations that make the best chili. It is like that with some interviewers who have been doing what they have been doing; because that is the way, they do it. There is a lot of ego involved in both pursuits and each interviewer has his or her opinion about the right way to conduct an interview and take a statement. Most are not open to other ideas of presentation.

MINDSET

Since it is impossible to take a witness statement without first interviewing the witness, we will review the basics. The process begins with the attorney and the type of case presented. It continues with case strategy and the client's objective.

As you can imagine, the depth of interview will be in relationship to the importance of the issues involve. A lesser skilled interviewer can obtain the statement of a traffic accident or personal injury witness and over time, prepare and gain the skills required when a defendant's life or liberty are on the line.

This course will focus on less critical interviews of subjects or witnesses of traffic accidents and personal injury accidents. In reality, these are the first interviews you are likely to conduct, unless you already have some training in this field.

The information a person has, or does not have about a particular incident is brought forth by means of a witness interview. The purposes of a written statement are:

- Make a record of the witness' words for reference
- Refresh a witness's memory before testifying

- Provide the attorney with testimony he can expect at trial
- Lock-in a witness who may try to change testimony later
- Have a means of selecting the most valuable witnesses
- To know what obstacles the attorney may have to overcome with this witness
- May be used in absence of the witness under some circumstances

I will use the example of a civil defense witness rather than get into confusing descriptions of plaintiff and defense and the roles they play. In a civil case, the decision is made for or against the defendant, usually by a jury. The jury will hear both sides and then have to decide which side presented the most convincing case. The verdict is decided by a preponderance of the evidence; the winning team scores more points.

It is the defense team's job to find and present evidence, that supports the defendant's side of the story. The defense is not required to present evidence against the client and must act in the client's best interest. The investigator picks up and points out discrepancies among various statements from the same witness, and may even see if a witness will follow a line of questions he knows is untrue.

The attorney-client uses what the investigator finds to bolster her client's case. It is to the defendant's advantage to present the attorney with the truth, to allow her to enhance the positive while deflecting the plaintiff's witnesses. This is our adversarial system and the principles apply to both the civil plaintiff and civil defense teams.

If you are reading this and thinking, that alone gives you advantage. However, if you are thinking the defense team should not trick people or get them to go on about untruthful statements, I tend to disagree. In a court case you are obligated to prepare evidence that works on behalf of your client. These are common tactics used by both sides, so try not to worry.

You are under no obligation to neither protect any witness, nor refrain from "tricking" him if it will further the defendant's case. If an investigator should tell you, it is wrong to trick an opposition witness then I assert that he does not have a good grasp of his job requirements, regardless of the number years he has been doing interviews.

Many investigators have crossed over from law enforcement and it is possible some have unconsciously brought along their preference for the "plaintiff." In this work, you must constantly put aside what you think you know, in order to be objective. To take in this course, you have to be willing to let go of what entertainment teaches us about the field.

You must be familiar of the laws in your state that govern the actions of private investigators. There is no reason, including ignorance, which will excuse you if you conduct an illegal act in the process of working on behalf a client.

PREPARATIONS

Before you attempt to interview a witness, you need answers to the following questions. At the risk of being trite, the more information you have going in, the more information you can bring out.

- What is the purpose of the interview?
- Is this a friendly or hostile witness?
- Is this the first interview?
- Is there background on the witness?
- Does the attorney-client have a theory on strategy?
- Could this witness to be reluctant or defiant?
- Does the witness claim to have no knowledge of the matter?

In other words, know what you may be walking into with this witness. We may have no idea of the witness' attitude until we "hit the front door," yet we need to prepare for any eventuality. This may be the one and only contact with this witness and we need to make the best of it.

You may, or may not make an appointment with a particular witness. This element of surprise does not allow him an opportunity to be swayed by well-meaning, yet uninformed friends. My colleagues may ignore strategy by consistently insisting upon appointments under all circumstances.

You arrive for an interview and the witness is half asleep, appears ill or possibly intoxicated, what do you do? You can allow him to have a cup of coffee to wake up and may be offered a cup yourself. You may graciously accept or decline as you wish; of course when you accept, drink most of it. When declining, also do so graciously; "Thanks much, but I have already had my morning (afternoon or evening) allotment."

Some investigators prefer not to interview under adverse conditions and that is their call. The interviewer will return at another time risking their opportunity with this witness. The subject might decide he does not want to get involved and may start screening his calls and not answering the door. Now what is he going to do?

Under adverse circumstances, ask the witness if he feels like he is able to talk with you today; if no, jot that information down, attempt to make an appointment and ask the witness to write his name on a statement as follows:

> I, Ralph Waldo Emerson, do not wish to be interviewed at this time, as I am not feeling well today. I made an appointment for next Tuesday (insert date) to speak with (interviewer name) about an accident I witnesses last month.

Signed: Ralph W. Emerson (date)

The non-statement only takes a moment or two, yet accomplishes two things:

- Prove to the client that you did contact the witness
- Use the statement to your advantage when the witness has a change of heart, "You said you would agree to meet with me."

Our job is to talk with a particular witness, whether she wants to or not. It is not about only interviewing the people who are easy and willing to talk with us. If a witness refuses to tell me his side of the story, I will ask if the plaintiff told him not to talk to anyone else. If yes, I will speak to her sense of duty and her contribution to society, by taking advantage of her opportunity to make the system work.

If you threaten or use your parent tone of voice, expect to have a phone hung up in your ear or a door slammed in your face. As mentioned earlier, initially the witness refused so talk with the investigator so Carol used the common ground of women in the workplace to gain the witness' cooperation. Whether we as professionals can appeal to someone's sense of justice, their own personal interest, or our own "supposed" personal need, we use what magic we can create to gain cooperation and do our jobs. It is so much better than begging, crying or stomping our feet.

When we succeed in convincing someone to talk to us, we have already established a relationship with that individual and are on common ground, establishing a great foundation for an ever-greater interview. The reluctant witness may be so, because she has relevant information, yet does not want to expose herself by revealing all she knows. She may simply be someone who is closed and un-used to sharing her experiences with others.

Once you get permission from a "shaky" witness, proceed with your interview. When it is your side's advantage, leave the statement as it is. If the statement is critical and you must know how accurate it is, you can phone the witness in a day or two when he should be feeling better. At that time you can re-read the statement over the phone and get his agreement to his story or make changes. If time allows, you can drop by with a revised copy for signature.

The reason you want to grab the opportunity to speak with a witness as soon as you can, is to obtain the freshest most accurate story. Once a witness talks to friends and those friends tell him not to get involved or what to hold back, you have lost any advantage you may have held. Too often, the accident witness statements are taken several months or even years, after the event. You won't be hired until the attorney is hired and the case is scheduled for mediation or trial.

Pre-Interview

- Read statements from this witness
- Review statements and reports of all others concerned with the case
- Review photos, view vehicles or other evidence and/or visit the scene
- Prepare to get a truthful account, keeping the client's strategy in mind
- Dress in a manner that is consistent with the intended witness and location
- Choose a location that is quiet and agreeable to the witness
- Arrange to take a witness for your protection if the witness is a minor or may be unstable

There is no excuse for not being fully familiar with the circumstances that affect this witness or his accounting of the story. The witness may state she just does not know what help she can be, since it happened so long ago.

From the Files of Diane Evans

> A few months into my career as an investigator I witnessed a traffic accident. I knew at the scene which driver was at fault and probably based my decision on the appearance of an elderly gentleman who appeared shaken. I couldn't wait for police arrival and left my card with the injured man as a witness.
>
> Several months later when an insurance investigator phoned me at work, I apologized and said I probably couldn't help much, since I had forgotten the details. I gave him the names of the other passengers in my vehicle.
>
> He asked if I would consent to the interview and I did with a caveat that I did not remember much. What was crystallized in my mind was the image and perception of the elderly man seated on a bus bench.
>
> That interviewer was great. He asked the right questions and once he took me back, I was able to answer his questions and tell him why I held the impressions I did. "I recall the light was red for me as I was stopped waiting to make a turn." The trained interviewer made the difference between getting a "statement of no statement" or a detailed account from a witness, who watched as the accident unfolds in front of her.

Appearance

An investigator is not going on to a construction site to talk with a carpenter in a Jones of New York suit. We humans tend to trust those we perceive to be like ourselves. Conversely, you should not go to interview an executive wearing jeans and a sweatshirt. "In Rome, you do as the Romans." For most statements, it is appropriate to dress "casual Friday," This may be an unbuttoned collared shirt and casual slacks or a skirt

Skip the business suit or jacket unless the interview is with someone who will be dressed as you are. When going to speak with a college professor you should use your best grammar, yet if the witness is a teenager your grammar will be only slightly better than the witness. About the only time you should think of wearing jeans would be to talk to a teenager or a ranch hand.

Decorum

- Use all the good manners your mother taught you
- Use all the good manners you learned in school, church, or temple
- Be genuinely interested in what the witness is about
- Be open, friendly, and low key then work up a genuine smile

- Be yourself, yet refrain from conveying any air of your superiority

- No gum chewing or candy sucking

- No smoking, whether or not, the witness does or offers you a cigarette

- Avoid slang or profanity and speak without incrimination

- Leave your personal problems, feelings, and opinions at the door

- Do not reveal personal information about yourself, except to provide a business ID minus your home address.

- Make no threats or promises, yet be persistent, when necessary

- Project your sincerity, objectivity, and desire to establish the truth

- Use your compassion and composure to help put the witness at ease

Not everyone knows how to conduct him or herself in a business atmosphere, which is why these reminders are presented. Most are self-explanatory.

Arrival at Location

- Be on time, no more than 5 minutes early, and never late

- Never, park in the witness' driveway; walk a block or two if you have to

- When someone answers the door, introduce yourself and inquire if he or she is Mister or Miss [witness name].

- Enter the house on invitation or ask if you may enter

- Engage in light conversation with witness and thank him or her for meeting with you

- Suggest she finds a quiet place in his home for you to talk

- Tactfully eliminate others from the room

- Sit when invited, or ask if you may seat yourself

- Get out your notepad and pen then keep it closed while you explain why you are there and present the witness with a business card

- Ask if he has any questions; and answer to the best of your ability

- State you would like to make some notes if that is all right with him, and then open your notebook

- Ask the witness about himself, where he works or ask about something in his home without taking notes
- Thank him, and then get down to business

When you are getting approval or permission from a witness to take notes it is only a formality, yet people feel good that someone asks them if they mind. By getting permission, it could be simply "if you don't mind." By not objecting, the witness is allowing you to proceed, which is consent.

It is not in the client's best interest for you to advise the witness, that he is not required to talk to you or anything else that might be "fair" yet work against the client. You are working for the client, not the witness. If things are different in your part of the country or an investigator tells you they are, then ask him to show you the "cite." That means the Code Section. There are investigators who make up "laws" to justify how they do their work. They seem to think because they do something a certain way that there must be because there is a law about it. That is not necessarily so.

INTERVIEW

- Begin with a request, "can you tell me about that day, what were you doing before you arrived at the shopping center"
- Leave your parent voice at home, and speak more like a teacher who is asking questions of her class
- Listen without interruption, then restate witness's story and make a note or two
- Listen for inconsistent use of pronouns, names, nouns, and adjectives
- Get an account of the incident without interruption, then clarify and make more notes
- It takes practice, yet when you are really listening to what is said, you do not need notes and will catch inconsistencies.
- Use your notes to show a witness' inconsistency "See, I wrote…"
- Return to the day of the accident and begin to obtain details in chronological order
- As the witness begins to detail the events, begin the formal statement

Keep your questions open ended to allow for a narrative response with explanation. The witness may have practiced a misleading statement, yet will be unable to provide details or be able to reverse the story. For example, when one goes to a shopping center, he/she can tell you what they was doing before, who they were with and why they went to the center in the first place. The made up story will be difficult to recall and can usually only be told in sequence. You can ask a question out-of-sequence to "test" the witness.

As you proceed get the who, what, when, where, why, and how of the activity in question. Who else was there? Who else would know? What was each person doing? What verbal statements were made and heard by this witness? When and where was the incident? How did it happen? How long did it take? How did the person feel?

Here is an example:

> I am sitting at my computer working, with my cats for company. It was about 2 in the afternoon on (date) when I heard a rumbling and the building shook for a few moments. It began at a low force then increased and it was over in a few seconds. Living in Southern California I made a quick diagnosis of "earthquake" our most frequent natural disaster. I was glad the cats were inside and safe and that the power is still on. One of the things I heard was my patio cover outside my office door. I was hoping it would not fall apart. After refreshing my soft drink, I returned to work, no worse for the wear.

A good interviewer can pull out inconsistencies and make witnesses stammer as they try to repeat and recall information. Depending on client strategy you may, or may not want the witness to know that you know, he is untruthful. When you step out of your personal place (leaving your insecurities and what does she think of me, behind) and become confident and competent "Investigator Charley," or whoever you are; you are much more efficient and perceptive as an interviewer.

WRITTEN STATEMENT

Guidelines for a written statement are:

- You can use printed forms, as we have done at the end of this chapter or, a lined legal pad, or any napkin that is handy (There is no legal requirement to use a particular paper)
- Note witness name, address, phone, occupation or other identifying if that person moves before court
- Note interview location, date, time, people present
- Write the witness statement in your hand in first person, as the witness speaks
- Determine is witness is personally acquainted with subjects of investigation
- Paraphrase the witnesses' words to sound like is something he might say
- Resist temptation to correct grammar or soften profanity or crude words
- Do not skip lines or attempt to make paragraphs
- Correct mistakes by crossing out letters with a single line
- Sincerely listen and occasionally check back with the witness to acknowledge you attentiveness
- Guide witnesses and keep them on track, expanding the depth of the interview
- Refrain from asking stupid questions; those that are unrelated to you purpose

We can loose our advantage and compromise our client when we allow a witness to write his own statement. Generally do not allow this. Examples follow:

Statement of Sammy Wilson

On December 8th last year I remember seeing a car accident when I was going home from school. I left the parking lot and turned onto Campus Drive then stopped at the red light to make a left turn onto University Boulevard. While I was waiting to turn I heard tires screech then saw this old dark red Chevrolet Cavalier, I think, crash into another car that was coming from the other side of University from Campus Drive. The car that got hit was a newer model silver foreign car. It was like a Toyota, Mazda, or something. I know my light was still red, but I am not sure what the other lights were red or green. The Cavalier must have been going fast because the screech lasted a long time before the crash. The crash was in front of me and it looked like the Cavalier must have been going east on University and the silver car was just pulling out of Campus into University. The Cavalier hit the silver car right on the driver's side door and made a big dent. I was sure someone must have got hurt. Some other people stopped to see if the people in the cars are okay. I didn't know what to do and was just sitting the until one of the helpers, an older man with grey hair and glasses, asked for some help. He asked me to help him and I went over to the Cavalier where the older man was talking to the driver of the Cavalier who looked really screwed up. The driver of the Cavalier was a guy about 20, with kind of dark complexion and dressed real nice in a suit. He smelled like puke and beer and was talking, but didn't make no sense. I think he wanted me to take him home, but I don't know nodody there and I sure wasn't going to do that. The silver car is screwed up on the side and that driver was a middle-aged woman. She had long dark hair and wore glasses that were broke. She didn't smell like anything, except maybe a perfume factory. Between the two of them and another guy smoking I thought I was gonna puke. The lady was nice though and didn't seem like she was hurt or nothing. I think it must have been the guy who caused the accident, cause he was going so fast. The cops showed up and they talked to me for 1-15 minutes then finally let me go home. I went home when they said I could. I don't know none of these There is nothing else I wish to add at this time. I have read this statement and had the opportunity to make corrections. None was needed.

END of Statement.

I declare under penalty of perjury that the aforementioned facts are within my personal knowledge and if called as a witness I can testify competently thereto.

Signed. Sammy Wilson   Date: _____(date)

Statement of Sammy Wilson

I was going home from school and getting ready to pull onto University Street. That damn red light is so long, it was still red and I thought it was never going to change. I was about ready to take my chances and run the damn thing. I had to get home because it was Monday and I had to see the NFL game. It was during the playoffs for the Super Bowl and I just had to see it. Then this old red sedan smashed into a new Mitsubishi Galant. I got out and checked on the guy driving the red car who was looking bad. The lady in the Galant looked okay. I got out of there before the cops came, and got home right after the kickoff, but damn it I missed the first touchdown.

END of statement.

Any question as to who wrote which statement? The witness does not have a concept of the purpose of a statement. His priority is the football game. I doubt that your client will want to pay you for the second statement.

COMPLETION

- Ask if there is anything else the witness wishes to add to the statement
- Allow witness to hold statement in his hands to number pages, make, and initial corrections
- Ask witness to write in his hand, "I am giving this statement of my own free will and without promise of compensation"
- Take the statement in your had and read it aloud to the witness and get his agreement verbal
- When witness agrees, write "End of Statement" then draw single line to signature line
- Return the statement to the witness for date and signature.
- When signed, put the completed statement in your folder, thank the witness then leave

POST STATEMENT

- Memorialize any post statement comments
- Prepare a client report including a witness evaluation
- Include a copy of the statement and/or tape

- Keep originals secure in your custody until requested by counsel

TAPE OR NOT TO TAPE

- This is really the client's option; ask what she wants
- Taping is usually allowed for opposition witnesses
- Ill-advised for cooperating or unknown witnesses
- Video should be above and/or behind interviewer as to not distract witness
- You must NOT audio or video tape without the witness' consent

Whether or not we tape, has to do with laws of discovery, which require a pre-trial information exchange between sides in regards to statements obtained, interviews and opinions of experts expected to testify in trial. It is only "our" witness the client intends to call that we need to identify to the opposition. If we get important information from "their" witness that they didn't get, that is their problem. We just did a better job than they did.

By consent, this means with the witnesses' knowledge. In order to show your recording is voluntary and consensual you make an announcement. What I generally do is to chat while getting my notebook and two pens nearby. I will take out my tape recorder when necessary, and if possible, place it outside the witness' direct view. The microphone will be closer to the witness than that the interviewer, since the interviewer will probably be speaking more clearly and confidently. Introduce yourself again and give him a business card.

Occasionally, someone will ask me whose side you are on. You might say, "Hhmm, I don't know nobody ever asked me that before.(sincerely) If it is really important to you I might be able to find out." What you did was to push the witness back a bit, then bring him closer again. You would only use this technique when the witness appeared hostile or overbearing.

Answer something to the effect of, "You know, my boss never tells me that." (You always have a boss) Your job is to talk to people then your reports go back and somebody gets to figure out what happened. I guess the want us to be neutral.

Start the tape and begin by making a statement giving date and time, and then ask the witness to state and spell his name for identification, and then I proceed with the interview as described above. This taped introduction accomplishes voice identification, and serves to indicate the witness knew of the recording; her tone of voice may be analyzed by an expert to determine any points she shows stress and may be not reporting things truthfully.

Whether or not, your state has a "one party" or a "two party" requirement for taping phone calls. You would not proceed in those states to tape a witness unless it was with his/her knowledge. The reason is case-related rather than legal or personal. If ever have to appear in court to backup the interview, the plaintiff's attorney will rip you apart for violating the witness' right to privacy; not that you did anything against the law, but he will make it sound the a reprehensible act. It his job to make you look bad and I want to eliminate that advantage for the other side.

SUMMARY

We reviewed techniques for interviewing and introduced the purpose; methods and techniques for accomplish the tasks necessary. You have information on when it is, or is not advisable to audio or videotape a witness statement. Students have learned the importance of dress, demeanor, and confidence in regards to obtaining witness statements.

DISCUSSION QUESTIONS

1. There are two more sample statements at the end of this section that you are to include in your discussion and assignments.

2. Have you taken statements before, if so does this material add some depth to your endeavor?

3. Discuss the two primary techniques for obtaining a witness interview and statement?

4. Regardless of the technique you choose, what type of questions do you ask?

5. Your purpose is to obtain a statement from an alleged victim of a personal injury accident that occurred in a retail store. Think outside the box and reveal what you will tell her when she asks, "Who sent you?"

ASSIGNMENT

Read and analyze the statements presented in this chapter. See if you can find anything that is missing and should be included.

1. Earthquake experience of author
2. Statement of Sammy Wilson
3. Statement of Barbara Currie
4. Statement of Caesar Martinez, Jr

Chapter 7

Surveillance

CHAPTER OVERVIEW

In the Methods of Investigations chapter, the text discussed the different approaches used by private investigators with surveillance being one of them. This chapter will expand the topic to include basic equipment, fundamental principles, standard procedures, and various types of cases stressing the importance of an operative's appearance and choice of vehicles. Presenting readers with true accounts of actual cases provides a strong foundation for learning, seldom available elsewhere. The contributions of seasoned professionals allow the reader to learn from other's mistakes, rather than their own.

OBJECTIVES

At the end of this chapter, the reader will be able to:

1. Define the types and purposes of surveillance.

2. Explain terms commonly used in the industry.

3. Describe real life practical examples of common mistakes.

4. Debunk myths surrounding surveillance.

5. Identify the clients and situations that warrant the use of surveillance.

6. Explain how to blend in by choice of vehicle, apparel and actions.

7. Explain how to prepare for surveillance assignments.

8. Learn strategies of successful surveillance techniques.

INTRODUCTION TO SURVEILLANCE

Definition

Surveillance may be described as the clandestine or secret observation of persons or places in an endeavor to determine the activities of a person or place. More simply put, it is people watching with a purpose, a report, and a pay check, all without getting "burned" (detected).

Surveillance seems to be the part of the job that first comes to mind when people find out someone is a private investigator. "Wow, you must follow people around; wow, isn't it dangerous?" They stand wide-eyed until they hear about the fairly mundane tasks many investigators perform on a daily basis.

The next comment usually is, "Well, it must be very interesting work." A great opening for a conversation, yet most investigators are not as impressed with what they do in their jobs, as others seem to be. Actually, surveillance is one of the more interesting and stimulating activities in which private investigators engage.

From the Files of Diane Evans

"It was a dark and stormy night. You have absolutely no idea where you tailed your target to, yet you realize you are sitting alone in your car in a raunchy looking area and are freezing to death. Your windows are fogged up, you can hardly see outside and you really, really have to go… and not just to clean up the coffee you spilled in your lap. Welcome to the wide wonderful world of surveillance in the private sector."

While this account may be exaggerated just a bit, the picture isn't usually that dismal, nor is it near as comfy and glamorous as portrayed in the media. Those high tech surveillance vans are few and far between.

I promise you this story of my first surveillance assignment is absolutely true. It is a humorous account, yet please keep in mind the client was experiencing some mental health problems.

A female client, aged 45-50 comes into the office, and tells my employer that she has a problem with her former husband. She tells that her now ex-husband brings his lady friends over to her house, to have orgies while she is out bowling. (She bowls several nights a week.) The client knows this because there are orgy crumbs in the living room when she returns. (Some things you just don't ask 'cause you really don't want to know… like crumbs.)

The client wants someone to watch her house when she leaves for the bowling alley, in order to catch him in the act one evening. Being the new

From the Files of Diane Evans, cont

kid on the job, I got all the assignments no one else wanted. I had never actually conducted surveillance myself, nor had I been on a ride-a-long with another investigator, yet theoretically I knew what to do.

The evening before the surveillance was to take place, I drove by to canvass the area as I'd been instructed; I checked out the house and neighborhood. I was driving a full-size Ford F250 window van and hoping no one would notice me and "Big Blue" in their neighborhood.

The client's residence was a single story stucco home in a fairly well-maintained middle class suburban neighborhood. There was a three-foot chain link fence in the front of the house and across the driveway. It is still daylight; the curtains are closed and no interior lights are visible. There is nothing remarkable about the location.

My jaw dropped in amazement the next evening at dusk, when I arrived to conduct my assignment. I quickly established my pre-determined vantage point across the street, a few houses down, facing away from the residence. I planned to observe via my side and rearview mirrors.

Moments after arriving at the client's residence, I am struck with the rookie surveillance plague: PARANOIA. "All these people in these houses know I'm here, they see me and know what I'm doing." Anxiety sets in. Never mind it is getting dark, I am parked between two houses under a tree and have great cover.

I creep from my driver's hi-back seat; to behind the seat, where I hunker down and sneak a peak out curtained back windows. It is funny now, yet it was very real at the time. It's okay to laugh at my situation, as long as you remember to at least smile when you are out there the first time.

I am stoically looking around and taking in what I see, when the client opens her front door and looks up and down the street (for me, I presume). I am hoping she does not blow my cover by stopping by and saying "hi." She drives by my vehicle a few minutes later without making contact. Whew!

Now, back to the client's home. Today the gate across the driveway is tied open. That could have been her usual custom, I didn't know. Not a wise habit I thought, since it notified any burglar that the house was "open". As it becomes darker I realize all the lights in the interior are on, effectively deterring any rational burglar or errant ex-husband from entering the premises.

The most curious part of this scene was the lack of any visible window covering. There were bare-naked windows across the front of the house. Anyone passing by could see directly into her house which reminded me of a fishbowl. From my perspective, I could look directly into her bedroom closet. That was a sight! Mine is not near that messy.

I decide to take a closer look at the house in case there was something else I could see away from my vantage point. I had the foresight to remove my overhead light bulb, so the interior light didn't go on as I quietly emerged through the curbside cargo door. I closed the door leaving it unlocked, so I could get back in quickly, if necessary.

From the Files of Diane Evans, cont

> The rule is, **"Do not lose or give up your cover (your vehicle) unless it is the only way to continue visual contact and your assignment."** Well, I thought I might be able to learn something if I walked around for a while. It was okay.
>
> It was about 10 p.m., the street was quiet, and I thought what could go wrong (famous last words)? I walk down the street a block or so, and headed back to the van as this sleepy little suburban side street became a circus of activity.
>
> A vehicle was coming down the street in my direction, so I ducked out of view. I could see myself outlined on the front of the house by the car's headlights as it turns into the driveway where I sought refuge.
>
> My heart pounding in my chest; I headed back to safety when I became aware of another little obstacle. It seems the residents of the house about 20 feet from my vehicle had arrived home from a day of fun and surfing while I was out talking my stroll. There are about eight people standing around the garage and driveway laughing and talking while finishing whatever they had in their coolers. Great, now what will I do? It looks a bit suspicious if you see a person enter his vehicle and sit there.
>
> I had to take the chance of getting in or walk several miles home. It was now or never; I slipped in the driver's door then slid back to the safety of my little cubby breathing a sigh of relief. Well, it would have been suspicious if anyone sober had actually seen me; these guys didn't seem to notice. Nobody gave me a look, as the neighbors were more interested in talking about their day. The lesson was reinforced: **"Don't give-up your cover."** The rest of my assignment is unremarkable.

It is easy to appreciate the humor in my story, yet this situation raises another issue. Is this client rational? Should a firm take that kind of case and the client's money? This topic will get some more discussion the chapter "Laws & Ethics".

You will be hearing about a former co-worker, Gene (not his true name), who taught me numerous invaluable lessons. He is such an interesting field operative (surveillance guy), and such a rich source of things not-to-do.

Surveillance Beginnings

Surveillance was most of what there was to do back in the early 20th century when the profession of private investigations began to emerge in the United States. Like today's clients, their early counterparts wanted to locate bad guys, know what the school marm is up to, or if "William is paying undue attention to Maggie Sue, the preacher's wife."

Motor vehicles were non-existent and it would have been pretty tough to remain "invisible" on horseback or in a buggy. There were many foot surveillances and window peeping in those early days; earning our predecessors the nickname "gumshoe." Before Jim Rockford and Magnum PI, there was Thomas Marlow who always wore his trademark fedora. These references can conger up some great images, but the stories are primarily fictional. Several producers have tried to create a reality television show about private investigators, yet none have succeeded.

TYPES OF CLIENTS: INVESTIGATION IN THE 21ST CENTURY

Insurance Companies

False workers' compensation and disability claims cost insurance companies billions of dollars each year. Insurance adjusters would rather authorize $2,000 – 3,000 for surveillance, than continue to pay out thousands of dollars monthly to those who are healthy and only pretending to be injured.

Insurance companies and employers may contract with private investigators (neutral parties) that can help search out, then expose, and help prosecute the fakers and malingers. An employee who makes a false or inflated claim, pretends to be too injured to work, or works another job while collecting workers' compensation benefits, can find herself facing criminal charges.

Police departments with ever increasing on-the-job injury claims may hire investigators. In one instance, the Chief of Police in a fairly small department decided to investigate and prosecute employees who made false claims. Shortly after that he needed to hire new officers and claims fell from 58% down to around 12%. Those employees and officers paid a very high price for their dishonesty.

Traffic collision schemes are not accidents and a common method of bilking insurance companies out of moderate sums of money. There are rings of "victims" who stage accidents, then work with doctors, chiropractors, and physical therapists that create false reports, in order for attorneys to make claims and threaten law suits against the insured. These criminals know that when a claim is below a certain threshold, it is less expensive for the company to pay it, than investigate, and litigate it.

Homeowners may be tempted to exaggerate losses in order to satisfy deductibles and pick up a little extra cash. The bad news is that by being accountable to stockholders who invest to make a profit, insurance companies compensate for their losses by raising everyone's premiums. Watching the activities of these "suspects" is one of the best methods of determining whether the individuals are truly limited physically, or whether they customarily perform activities the alleged injuries should prevent.

Individuals

Although many of our states are "no fault" divorce states, jealousy, and infidelity still run deep. Husbands and wives want to check up on each other, as do boyfriends and girlfriends. Spouses may want to put themselves in better positions financially by verifying their spouse's infidelity.

Non-custodial parents want to know their children are properly cared for by the other parent and/or may seek to limit visits as a pay-back for the infidelity or divorce. Surveillance is an excellent method to determine what kinds of hours the family keeps, the types of activities at the location and visitors who are there when the children are present. Do the children attend school? Are they left alone for long periods of time? Investigators can tell them what they want to know. An inspection of the trash can indicate if there is excessive "partying" going on. There is usually no expectation of privacy when the containers are at the street for pick-up.

> Qwik-Tip:
> Some cities, counties and states are strengthening laws regarding "dumpster diving" due to the prevalence of identity theft. Although a subject's trash holds a plethora of information, it would be wise to familiarize yourself with state and local laws before digging in someone's trash. This will be covered in the Laws & Ethics chapter.

Partners want to know "for sure" before they break off a relationship. Others are suspicious and want to ease their minds; hoping an investigator doesn't catch the subject doing anything he shouldn't be doing.

It is difficult to earn a good living working exclusively on domestic fidelity cases. You get too little repeat business, and have to constantly market your services. It is time-consuming to educate new clients, yet for some investigators, domestic cases are all they want to do.

Businesses

An employer and/or business owner wants to find out who is stealing his inventory and how the thief is getting away with it. Large corporations may be suffering losses due to theft of product, or from unauthorized dissemination of trade secrets. A CEO needs to know if a pivotal employee makes unauthorized contact with one of her competitors. Is a field representative visiting his clients or his girlfriend during the day? Surveillance is a simple and effective answer to these dilemmas.

SKILLS, TECHNIQUES, AND METHODS

Required Skills

While it does not appears too difficult, surveillance can be demanding work. Not only do you have to locate and identify your subject, while you maneuver through mazes of traffic without drawing the subject's attention, then make notes, and be able to write a report at the end of your assignment. It takes some practice to follow far enough behind the subject so he does not realize someone is tailing him; then follow closely enough in traffic so that you are not caught at a traffic light or lose him at an intersection.

Meanwhile, you are considering what he might do or where he could go while placing your vehicle in the best position to be able to react to any of several actions he could make. Watch all his movements and traffic around you to avoid a traffic collision. You record details and provide an accurate report for your client. Multitasking skills come in very handy in this kind of work

Private Sector

Did I mention you will usually be in a vehicle by yourself? This is contrary to law enforcement surveillance in which several vehicles and officers are engaged in an assignment.

In the private sector, work is fee for service. We are not usually on retainer or have unlimited budgets. The client may be paying the agency $60-75 per hour per investigator with a mileage charge of 50 cents per mile traveled. At the lowest rate for an eight-hour day and 100 miles, the client will pay just over $500 per investigator and vehicle.

It is quite expensive to pay several investigators to conduct a multi-car surveillance. Multi-vehicle surveillances are usually reserved for "last chance" situations or when the target is "hinky" and/or difficult to follow.

Methods

Surveillance is conducted by having a person secretly watch for certain activities. If the agent is in a stationary position the assignment is referred to as a stakeout. If the client wants to know when and where the subject leaves and where he goes we conduct a mobile or rolling surveillance. A rolling surveillance can be conducted by foot, automobile, van, SUV, public bus, motorcycle, boat, airplane, horseback or snowmobile just to mention a few methods.

Unmanned video cameras can be installed inside and outside of workplaces to detect misconduct or illegal activity. Electronic devices allow persons and vehicles to be tracked by satellite and their position determined within a few feet. These Global Positioning Satellite systems are what General Motors places in many of their vehicles to give drivers a sense of security with the ability to summon aid or directions to where they are going.

Using any kind of tracking device on a subject vehicle could be a violation of state law. So we won't use those, yet we can obtain satellite photos that are close enough to see the junk in your subject's back yard.

QUALIFICATIONS & OPPORTUNITIES

Field Agents

There is a huge demand for field operatives and surveillance investigators, because there is such a large turnover in the workforce. It isn't that the work is too complex or difficult, but because employers have difficulty finding qualified people. In order to do this kind of work you need good observation and driving skills combined with an ability to produce a concise, accurate report in a timely fashion.

Another essential is the observer's ability to blend in with her surroundings. There should be nothing remarkable or memorable about her appearance, dress, physical characteristics, mannerisms, movements, or those of the vehicle she drives. If ones physical appearance is remarkable, such as bushy hair, a bright red beard, very large or tall or one has a prominent physical anomaly, he will have to be especially talented not be noticed by the person being observed.

The most important quality of a great field agent is his integrity. Surveillance is not difficult work, yet it is hard to find people who are dedicated and follow through with assignments, and who can write a literate report, conduct themselves properly, and arrive on time.

From the Files of Diane Evans

> This reminds me of Gene again, wouldn't you know? He was supposed to be on location at 7:30 am when our nurse subject was due to be arriving shortly after her hospital shift ended. He said he would be there at 8:00 am, which is the time he reports she returned home other days. I repeatedly told him 7:30 am. I knew he wouldn't be there, so I was.
>
> I watched as the subject, apparently on her day off, left the house at 7:40 am. I was also there when Gene pulled up almost in front of her residence and parked about 8:05 am. I hung out for another half an hour before returning to my office.
>
> He stopped by the office later that day to turn in his report. Gene noted he arrived at 7:30 am that day and that the subject arrived home at 8:00 am. It is customary to explore the area and conditions around a pickup location, and if the guy had done that he would have known not to falsify his report.
>
> He was a bit surprised that I was there and told him the subject departed before he arrived. I believe that was his last job for our firm. (My employer finally got the message that this guy was bad news.)

GAINING EXPERIENCE: LESSONS LEARNED

The field is the most common place to learn the rules, yet you can shorten your learning curve by taking advantage of other private investigator's experiences and save oneself the embarrassment.

From the Files of Diane Evans

> I had an instance where a husband wanted me to follow his wife, to see if she went where she said she was going late in the evening.
>
> "If she doesn't leave by 10:30 p.m. she isn't going," he tells me. That time came and went and I thought this client is paying for a minimum of four hours, so I can give another half hour, just in case.
>
> About 10:45 pm, I saw a vehicle matching the description and I verify the plate as she passes me. I am on it.

From the Files of Diane Evans

By all rights and our agreement, I could have left at 10:30 pm and legitimately kept the client's fee. This is one of those moral dilemmas that can be discussed later.

In another case the client said her "husband" would arrive about 11:00 pm, she described the vehicles he might be driving and said he would park in underground parking, stay there for a while, then leave and she wanted us to follow him after he left her house. This is one I had to cleanup after Gene had blown it.

The location was an apartment building situated 10-15 feet above the street level. The only way to enter the parking structure was from the alley and that is where Gene parked, in the alley. Not only could he be boxed in, but he had traffic tickets that had gone to warrant. Therefore, when one of the neighbors became suspicious of an occupied car parked in the alley and called police to investigate, you can believe it was an expensive evening for Gene.

The next night I arrived in the location and noted that from the curbside in front of the building, I could see through to the alley and had an unobstructed view of the parking entrance gate. This would allow me to cover the parking entrance from the relative security of the street.

The lesson I learned that night was "Clients don't always provide correct information." I was focused on the parking entrance, but happened to glance into the street to see a large man dressed in a suit crossing the street towards the front entrance. I looked behind him and there was a gold Mercedes as the client described, parked at the curb.

I almost missed him because I was not looking for him coming from that direction. The client assumed he would park in the garage; this time he did not. Fortunately, I was parked where I could see him enter the building. I would like to say that was planned, but it was really just dumb luck.

APPEARANCES

Vehicle

Your goal is to conduct your activities without the subject becoming aware. In other words, think invisible. Your chosen surveillance vehicle should likewise, be unremarkable and indistinguishable from hundreds of others on the road. Why do you think undercover police officers use plain sedans for fieldwork? There is nothing about the car to draw your attention. You want to avoid cars that are two-toned black and white since most of us can spot a police car a quarter mile away in our peripheral vision.

Avoid vehicles with primer spots, large antennas, metallic finish, bright or non-stock colors, fancy trim, loose parts, or memorable license plate frames. Grey, brown, silver, brown, tan, light green are good colors and tend to blend into the surroundings. Monster trucks or Hummers of any color are unsuitable. Custom license plates are memorable and especially ones like "SPY4U" or "PI4HIRE."

Some of the "old school" field agents have installed switches to alter the appearance of their vehicle at night. They can change the angle or intensity of headlights, put a headlight out, or even has a light that blinks or looks like it has a short. In a subject's rear view mirror, it does not appear that the same vehicle is continually behind them.

Most drivers do not pay much attention to who is behind them in another vehicle. Once someone has been threatened by an employer or spouse with "I'll find out what you are doing when you are not here" may be enough to arouse suspicion and to pay closer attention to other vehicles, at least for a while. This can make an ordinary surveillance into a real challenge.

The best surveillance vehicle for you is obviously the one you own or to which you have access. While the comfort of an air-conditioned motor home might be first choice, others insist on the maneuverability of a compact car. Some employers will hire only those with SUVs and vans, while others will not hire people with a SUV or van.

A mini-van may just be the greatest combination of all we are looking for in a surveillance vehicle. There are many on the road, the driver's view is higher than a passenger car, they are maneuverable, and there is room in the rear to set up a camera and any personal necessities you might need.

Take a walk around your intended surveillance vehicle to make a visual inspection. Check for any extra antennas, dents, dings, primer spots, front body damage, license plate frames, or stickers that someone might notice. It does not have to be spotless, but if it is very dirty, you might want to rinse it off with the hose and clean your windshield. If your vehicle is usually spotless, waxed and detailed to the max, you might have to drive down a dirt road to make it blend in better with other vehicles at the pick up.

You may, or may not have an opportunity to refuel during your assignment. Make sure your fluids are full. Do not pull a Gene and run out of gas. Fill up your tank before, if it is less than 7/8 full. Losing your target because of traffic is embarrassing enough; running out of gas is about the dumbest thing any surveillance guy or gal can do.

Do not be overly concerned about your own vehicle, because you can make due under less than ideal circumstances.

 From the Files of Diane Evans

I went with two associates for a surveillance assignment in Lake Havasu. It is a tourist area and the lake is actually in the desert surrounded by hills where everything is a shade of brown. The various elevations allowed us a choice of many observation points.

The client was a police agency and the target claimed knee injuries. Mike was lead and we drove together in his SUB and rented two more card at the airport when we arrived in town. We were on our way to our stakeout position the next morning when Ron gleefully radioed, "Did you know your lights are on?" 'What? I thought, oh no"; not that anyone would ever pay attention to a car following them all day with their lights on!

Mike took the close position near the house and concealed himself well in his vehicle. Ron and I established our respective positions and had the target's house surrounded. There was no way the target vehicle could leave without all of us seeing him. I'd found a nice little driveway near the main road where I tucked myself in. I could see the main exit road for several blocks. I assumed the homeowners at my location were either seasonal or at work, and I was fare enough from the the subject that I was not concerned that I would be noticed by the target.

The subject vehicle appeared in view then turned away from me on the main road. I started my engine and casually pulled out myself, in the sime direction. I would like to have kept my distance, yet that was not advisable because we were entering a commercial area.

Since I am the one with the headlights and without a camera, I pulled back some so Ron could overtake me and assume the close position. It did not happen quite that way, since Ron did not read my mind. He was an ex-police chief, but had never done this kind of surveillance. I wish I had had that information sooner.

We all lost visual contact temporarily, but drove around and picked up the subject going into K-Mart. the guys went into the store with cameras and got some good video. The target seemed to be walking and moving just fine. Proud of ourselves, we cut it off for the day and went back to the airport to exchange cars.

I was thinking we could not get any worse vehicles, but I was mistaken. The only vehicles Ron and I could rent were a red Neon and a purple Neon that stood out against the desert landscape like a giant cherry and a huge grape. I wouldn't have wanted either of those vehicles in an urban area with plenty of cover and other traffic. I had to look at the bright side: at least my lights were not on.

We were back on task the next morning and were watching as the target and his wife left their home in his Jeep. This time he limped and used a cane

From the Files of Diane Evans, cont

when they strolled into K-Mart. It was funny to watch, because he exited his vehicle and began to walk normally towards the store, then he remembered and started limping and returned to the Jeep to retrieve his cane, which he had apparently forgotten.

This alerted us that he was at least suspicious that he could be under surveillance. Mike was pretty close to their house with his SUV and they saw us the day before with cameras in the store. Regardless, we followed him home and resumed our positions. Before long, it got really interesting!

Ron had the foresight to look for another vantage point and was in place when the target drove his Jeep into his back yard behind his house where it was not visible from the street. I was a little bored and self-conscious in a residential driveway on the main road in by giant cherry. While I was canvassing the area, I spotted the grape and went to se what he had going. Ron had a pervect viewpoint from a house under construction. We were on a hill above the subject's house about 200 feet away. We watched and Ron taped, as the target put on white coveralls, then began shaking several spray cans of paint.

We could hardly contain our excitement as he bent to a squat and began to spray the undercarriage of his Jeep. He repeatedly squatted and returned to a standing position. At no time did he use the vehicle or the ground to assist himself in going up and down in excess of 25 times. After spraying, he went around the vehicle, again in a squat, apparently detailing it and wiping off any overspray. It would be a remarkable feat for a 25-year old man to do what he did, and this man was closer to 60 adn making a claim of a knee injury.

Our efforts were successful in spite of the vehicles we drove.

Subject Appearance

How the subject appears and is dressed can make a big difference. Style of dress can tell us what the subject may or may not do.

From the Files of Diane Evans

Gene learned this the hard way. I gave him a domestic assignment with a pickup 40 miles from his house. He called me midday to provide a verbal report that he had seen the subject, but that he did not leave his workplace for lunch... Under those circumstances, we called off the assignment for the day.

I phoned the client to tell her that her husband had not left the business by 1:00 p.m. and we called it off per our previous agreement. I was flabbergasted when she responded, "That's not true, he was standing in my

From the Files of Diane Evans, cont

kitchen at 11:00 a.m." She continued, "He had forgotten his glasses and had to come home to get them." I gulped and asked what he was wearing.

She reported he was wearing a green t-shirt, jeans and his boots. Gene took the description from the agent assignment sheet and reported it almost the same, "subject was wearing a white t-shirt, jeans, and white tennis shoes."

With a little more discussion I learned that what she calls a t-shirt has a collar and is what most of us refer to as a polo or golf shirt. The subject's trade was in metalwork, so I was confident he didn't wear white tennies or any other color athletic shoes. Steel toed boots seemed more likely.

Gene got to do the assignment again the next day, for free. He turned in a report, but claimed to run out of gas and lost visual contact shortly after the subject left work. If the decision was mine Gene would have been gone, the first time he reported that kind of nonsense. It was obvious to me that he just wasn't doing the assignments.

Personal Appearance

Your dress should be unremarkable as well, to blend in with the surroundings. Plain clothes, muted colors, conservative styles will usually suffice in urban areas. Avoid clothing with bright colors, stripes or logos, as well as black during the daytime and white at night. In resort areas dress like the tourists or if your target works in construction or a high-rise office building, dress accordingly.

Your pre-case briefing will give you an idea of where you might end up which will help you in choosing appropriate clothing. Moderate changes in appearance may be necessary when you have to risk a face-to-face in a restaurant, retail store, or other close quarters. In your car, put on or take off a jacket, shirt, cap, or sunglasses, if necessary. Do not wear sunglasses in bars or at night unless you want to look like a drug dealer.

If your target sees you in your Raiders' sweatshirt and cap once, he may not think much about it. He sees you again and may wonder if he has seen you before. The third time he knows and you will undoubtedly be approached by a suspicious and sometimes angry person. The same agent wearing a plain shirt and cap would likely go unnoticed.

Guys you will need to pull your pants up to your waist and fasten your shirt with only one or two buttons open. Body piercing and tattoos may go unnoticed in San Francisco, Hollywood, or Greenwich Village, but in other areas of the country, you may have to conceal or disguise facial decoration.

Jeans and a tee-shirt will fit in some bars and every Home Depot hardware store. As you make your preparations consider the weather and be prepared for changes. In springtime, you do not want to start out in Palm Springs wearing your tank top and shorts, ending up in the mountains at 7, 500 feet in the snow.

Restaurants, bars, retail stores, desert, mountains or tourist area, you cannot be sure where you will travel and end up at the end of your assignment. You may have an idea where the subject could go during the day and this will help you prepare to fit in there. If your target enters a restaurant or bar, you will want to be able to report with whom she is sharing her lunch.

The idea of a polo shirt and beige slacks with casual shoes, as an all around outfit for both men and women in an urban area, is generally a good rule. You can add a blazer or jewelry to dress it up, if necessary. A woman can easily slip a skirt over her shorts and be ready to follow the subject about anywhere. You should be able to easily slip into slacks or jeans over your shorts and add another shirt to cover up a tank top.

Remember to carry appropriate footwear. The fashion police will not arrest you, but you will definitely draw attention to yourself wearing business attire with white athletic shoes or flip-flops. Unremarkable, remember is your goal.

Try to layer clothing to compensate for moderate changes in temperature because it is important to be comfortable, but not at the expense of being inadequately prepared for all eventualities. You never can tell where you might end up on a weekend assignment: Las Vegas, Atlantic City, Boca Raton, New York City.

TOOLS OF THE TRADE

Compile a surveillance kit that you can easily assemble and update when needed. A backpack looks less business-like than a briefcase, and those passing by might think you are a student. No one who approaches your vehicle should be able to see any equipment lying in your seat. Be sure agent assignment sheets and notes are out of sight.

Compile a surveillance kit that is easy to conceal:

- Required equipment
  - Wristwatch/clock
  - Note pad
  - Pens or pencils
  - Maps
  - Binoculars
  - Caps, sunglasses, etc.
  - Alternate clothing
  - Beverages
  - $20 in small bills and change
  - Tissues or paper towels
  - Personal necessities
- Optional equipment
  - Still film or digital camera
  - Video camera
  - Tape recorder
  - Extra batteries, film, video
  - Small flashlight
  - Food and cooler
  - Compass
  - Credit card
  - Cell phone
  - Phone card

When an investigator doesn't have a way to tell the correct time, and a method of memorializing the subject's activity (or inactivity), he is going to have a difficult time preparing an accurate report of what transpired. It will be just as difficult to prepare a time and expense voucher, in order to be paid.

Maps come in real handy when an intended route is blocked by heavy traffic, and time is of the essence. In large cities, without maps it will be impossible to find a quick alternate route. When the attention of the driver is on another vehicle rather knowing where she is driving, it is easy to become disoriented and not even know which direction to head home. What a relief to find a Thomas Guide or other map under the seat. Field investigators now have the advantage of using global positioning systems in their vehicles.

Carry a cap, scarf, headband, and or a variety of sunglasses. A field agent can confidently leave his vehicle and not be overly concerned the subject will recognize him, even if she does happen to gaze in his direction. (Under no circumstances, does a field operative make intentional contact with the target.) He can also alter his hair by tying it back or combing it differently. (Ditch the wig changes.) Remember to reassume your car "look" when you are on the road again. Any alteration to appearance is quick and simple, so it doesn't detract from his purpose.

Parting Thoughts

Professionals carry a "quick change" outfit just in case a subject enters a retail establishment or office building. He can feign being a courier, but that "gag" likely won't allow him to stay around too long without arousing suspicion. Murphy's Law can and does prevail, when one is not prepared

Have a full tank of gas. Carry some small change and bills to take care of necessities as they arise. Having a credit card along, is not a bad idea either.

Bring something simple to eat and drink when an assignment is 4 hours or more. Tea, coffee and alcoholic beverages act as diuretics increasing urine production, and the possibility of dehydration. Soft drinks contain sodium that causes a body to retain fluids that will likely settle in the ankles. Keep food simple with cheese, crackers, vegetables, and fruit. Water is best for a primary beverage.

It is a mistake to think that withholding fluids will cut down on the rest room breaks. During hot spells, emergency rooms are filled with patients who dehydrate because they perspired more than they drank. Drink; just not the 44-ounce specials from the convenience store!

When working alone, as is the usual situation, an agent can't leave his vantage point to go to the bathroom. Short of using an adult diaper, you may wish to find alternate solutions to nature's call. Men carry a non-breakable container of adequate capacity with a screw on lid.

Women may be able to use a women's medicinal urinal. There is an expandable woman's urinal that contains a chemical that gels when it gets wet, and avoids spills. This device is available for purchase in camping or backpacking stores. Other devices and techniques to facilitate urination standing upright or the ability to aim at a specific location are available over the Internet.

Obviously if you are eating, drinking and taking care of other necessities there are likely to be spills. Paper towels and tissue come in very handy; as do "baby wipes."

Cameras, video recorders, and tape recorders all require power, film, tape, or disks. Have extras of all your consumables. Bring an extra shirt or something to conceal your equipment when not in use, just in case you get a visit from a concerned resident. Have a plan and a backup, in case something goes wrong.

Residents are usually wary of strangers and vehicles in their neighborhoods and are likely to call police to check up on the "suspicious" person. While stationery at your vantage point, you can quietly slip into your back seat or passenger seat to draw less attention. Just be sure you can resume your driving position in time to maintain contact with the subject when she leaves. Appear to be reading a map book, or studying papers or reports of some kind, to give neighbors a plausible reason to allow you to sit in by their house undisturbed.

Don't you pay attention when someone parks at the curb in front of your house? If possible avoid establishing a vantage point directly in front of an occupied residence. If you can, park on a side street, between two houses; away from windows; and under the shade of a tree, if you can find one.

No smoking, playing loud music, running air conditioning or heat while sitting in your vehicle. Sit low in your seat keeping your movements to a minimum. Since getting your battery jumped will draw some unwanted attention, don't listen to a TV, radio, tapes or CDs that run from your car battery. Use a portable or rechargeable battery source instead.

You have no idea who knows whom in the neighborhood you are in, and it is possible that your subject's best friend or brother-in-law lives a few houses down on the other side of the street where you are parked. Deny, deny, deny to curious neighbors without arousing suspicion. Have a plausible excuse ready when a neighbor taps on your window. Be pleasant and apologize for bothering them. Make up a story and hope they buy it. You can be a supervisor of a field crew of some type, a repairperson, or a cable company checking on employees. You can be taking a poll of how many birds land on the telephone lines. You can just being "cooling down" after a fight with your girlfriend, boyfriend, etc., and need some time alone.

In some states investigators cannot use a pretext or ruse to gain information in an investigation. Do not assume without checking, that you are also forbidden to use a pretext or misdirection to prevent yourself being identified as a private investigator. Those are two different situations.

If it bothers you to "lie," then you must know that information gathering in both the public and private sectors are facilitated by use of a pretext or ruse. Use of pretext is not immoral or illegal, except in limited situations.

Your can usually say just about anything, except that you are a police officer or private investigator. Save the truth, for when the neighbors get nervous and squad cars drop in on you with sirens screaming and lights a blazing.

If and when the police do roll, be polite and professional then ask her if you can get your identification to show them. Tell her you are a private investigator working on a case, yet don't be specific about identifying the subject or purpose, since you still have to protect the integrity of the investigation. If you tell them, you are trying to locate stolen property or some other criminal activity, they might be more sympathetic.

Location

In person or by using roadmaps, familiarize yourself with the area and location in which you are to begin the assignment. Note dead end streets, cul-de-sacs, and main routes to nearby Interstates or Freeways. Once you arrive near the pick-up location, drive around to canvass the area and become acquainted with the neighborhood.

Avoid situations where you follow a heated subject into a dead end only to be face-to-face with him as he is coming down, and you have no place to go, but turn around yourself. I advise that you to avoid getting trapped in a cul-de-sac, by someone who is checking to see if she is being followed. If this happens my best guess is that you have been burned, and better have a convincing story to tell him.

Before you leave for your assignment, use online directions and aerial map websites to expedite your drive. Plan your route to the pick-up location estimating your time to get there, allowing for traffic jams, toxic spills, detours and other obstacles. Plan to be 20-30 minutes early to give you some latitude in case Murphy's Law prevails.

Establish your vantage point. Your objective is to park where you can see the comings and goings of the occupants of the location and be able to identify your target as he enters or leaves the premises. You want to select a commanding perspective where you can see what you need to see, yet where the subject is unlikely to notice you.

You can conceal yourself in the shade, behind another vehicle, across an open lot, down a side road, position your vehicle facing away from the location and not in the likely direction, the subject will travel when he leaves. You want to be in a spot where you can start your engine, pull out then keep in visual contact without him noticing you.

CASE ASSIGNMENT

Now, to your first surveillance assignment. Your supervisor or case director will "brief" you on the case. You are called into your supervisor's office with, "Hey you, I have a surveillance assignment for you. Let me tell you about it in my office."

Ideally, you will receive a typed "agent assignment sheet" which provides the subject's name, address, identifying information, physical description, vehicles known to be driven by the target, where he parks, workplace, other hangouts, friends and places he'd likely go. You will learn his race, gender (male or female) approximate age, height & weight, build, complexion, eye color, hair color & style, facial hair or lack of, glasses, complexion, type of dress, any unusual characteristics, and any items usually carried.

You will always know when and where to begin your assignment; you will also know the purpose of the investigation, so you know how to prepare your report. If the target is purporting injuries, you will write your report including his difficulty or ease of movement.

With a domestic pursuit the husband wants to know where his wife, went and who she saw, complete with a description of person(s) she met along the way, plus any vehicle descriptions, license plate and direction of travel. Was there any smooching, intimate physical contact or adoring gazes? Those too, are part of your report. Depending on your instructions, you may continue to follow he, or possibly the person she met for lunch.

If Sandy goes home and begins putting a new roof on her house you will include it in your report, yet this is not significant information in a domestic case. Being on the roof and hauling up shingles and pounding away, would be of great interest to the client only if the subject was claiming physical injuries. Report the number and times she was up and down the ladder, how she swung the hammer, whether or not she appeared to be in pain or discomfort.

It is customary to arrive at the pick-up location 20-30 minutes in advance of your scheduled time. This is a "just in case" you run into traffic or have difficulty finding the location. In addition, it takes good common sense, the ability to anticipate what actions the target may take, and be ready to cover those alternatives. Quick reactions and good planning are essential to overcome any obstacles put in your way.

SUMMARY

This chapter not only provided some of the key techniques or methods needed for effective surveillance, it provided real life examples of these principles in action. Some of the highlights you should remember are; know the purpose of your assignment, study the agent assignment sheet, perform a reconnaissance mission, blend in, know your target, be prepared, have the proper tools, and develop street smarts.

DISCUSSION QUESTIONS

1. Describe your perfect surveillance vehicle, and how your own vehicle would fit in.
2. What are some types of cases where you will use surveillance as a tool?
3. What are some of the things you need to know about the subject before conducting surveillance?
4. Your assignment begins at 5:30 am at the subject's residence and ends when he is "down for the night," wherever that may be. His job is in construction 40-50 minutes from his home.

Chapter 8

Law and Ethics

OVERVIEW

We are presenting a brief overview of the history of U.S. laws along with an emphasis on the Bill of Rights and relevant federal laws that private investigators may frequently encounter. State laws will be discussed including the differences among some states in regulating the profession. Personal, business and professional ethics will be discussed and expanded upon.

OBJECTIVES

1. Explain the difference between the purposes of the federal Freedom of Information Act and the Privacy Act.

2. Describe relevant state and federal statutes regulating methods of investigation.

3. Discuss the ethics of this profession.

INTRODUCTION

American laws and concepts are patterned after old English law... or in spite of it. The first settlers came to America to escape religious persecution and the tyrannical government of England. Starting over and establishing a new government, the Pilgrims kept what they wanted from England then replaced the rest with personal freedoms for the people.

To escape the religious persecution of the time, Pilgrims began arriving here in 1620 on the ship Mayflower and began to make themselves at home. Many others crossed the "Pond" (Atlantic Ocean) to join them, as did, far too many rules and regulations from the King of England. England considered America to be merely an extension of "The Crown." The new settlers had different ideas. The king's continual "taxation without representation" was more than the colonists could bear.

It wasn't a quick or simple matter to break away, and it was some 150 years after their great-great-great grandparents arrived on our shores, before their sons began to prepare. The big step was taken in 1776 when the colonists declared their independence and set themselves up for the fight of their lives.

Written communications were hand-delivered by horseback from one point to another which was the fastest way to get information around at the time. Edison wasn't born yet; there was no Alexander Graham Bell standing in the wings.

"We the People of the United States, in Order to form a more perfect Union, establish Justice, insure domestic Tranquility, provide for the common defence, promote the general Welfare, and secure the Blessings of Liberty to ourselves and our Posterity, do ordain and establish this Constitution for the United States of America."

Written above is preamble to our US Constitution, adopted some 220 years ago in 1789. Our forefathers had the wisdom to create this nation of ours with a balance of power amongst its three branches of Executive, Legislative and Judicial. It remains today as a most remarkable document.

BILL OF RIGHTS

In all their wisdom and insight, there were some oversights on the US Constitution our forefathers added the *Bill of Rights* to insure personal freedoms, and to assure its citizens that the government could not violate its citizen's security, safety or property without legal cause.

That first *Bill of Rights* was extraordinary and still creates jobs for investigators in the 21st Century. The amendments that apply to the practice of private investigation are as follows:

Article I

> *Congress shall make no law respecting an establishment of religion, or prohibiting the free exercise thereof; or abridging the freedom of speech, or of the press; or the right of the people peaceably to assemble, and to petition the Government for a redress of grievances.*

The first amendment guarantees freedom of speech and the press, allowing the press to maintain confidential sources of information. Private investigators do not have the protection of secret sources of information. They are, however, free to confront and question witnesses.

Article IV

> *The right of the people to be secure in their persons, houses, papers, and effects, against unreasonable searches and seizures, shall not be violated, and no Warrants shall issue, but upon probable cause, supported by Oath or affirmation, and particularly describing the place to be searched, and the persons or things to be seized.*

Article IV forbids unreasonable searches and requires law enforcement to obtain a search warrant describing place to be searched and items to be seized. This only applies to the government and not to private citizens. Private persons and investigators could face theft or trespassing criminal charges.

Article V

> *No person shall be held to answer for a capital, or otherwise infamous crime, unless on a presentment or indictment of a Grand Jury, except in cases arising in the land or naval forces, or in the Militia, when in actual service in time of War or public danger; nor shall any person be subject for*

*the same offence to be twice put in jeopardy of life or limb;
nor shall be compelled in any criminal case to be a witness
against himself, nor be deprived of life, liberty, or property,
without due process of law; nor shall private property be
taken for public use, without just compensation.*

The article requires those being charged with a capital crime be
charged only after a preliminary hearing or Grand Jury indictment. Once
a defendant receives a "not guilty" verdict, the prosecution is forbidden
to prosecute again under the same circumstances. No defendant is
required to be a witness against himself. Personal property can not be
converted for public use without compensation.

Article VI

*The accused shall enjoy the right to a speedy and public
trial, by an impartial jury of the State and district wherein
the crime shall have been committed, which district shall
have been previously ascertained by law, and to be informed
of the nature and cause of the accusation; to be confronted
with the witnesses against him; to have compulsory process
for obtaining witnesses in his favor, and to have the
Assistance of Counsel for his defence.*

This amendment protects the most fundamental rights of an accused:
the right to a speedy trial, the right to know the charges against him, the
right to confront witnesses against him and the right to have an attorney
defend him whether he can afford it, or not.

Article VIII

*Excessive bail shall not be required, nor excessive fines
imposed, nor cruel or unusual punishments inflicted.*

Bail and fines must be in proportion to the alleged crime. Although a
defendant stands convicted of torture and mayhem, the government; is
forbidden to punish him in any cruel or unusual manner.

Article XIV

*All persons born or naturalized in the United States, and
subject to the jurisdiction thereof, are citizens of the United
States and the State wherein they reside. No State shall make
or enforce any law which shall abridge the privileges and
immunities of the citizens of the United States; nor shall any*

State deprive any person of life, liberty, or property, without due process of law; nor deny any person within its jurisdiction the equal protection of the laws.

While not part of the original Bill of Rights, The Fourteenth Amendment requires that all states provide equal protection and due process of law.

FEDERAL LAW

The US Constitution and federal laws are the "supreme law of the land." Local and state laws must be consistent with federal ones. If a state and federal law conflict, the federal law prevails, unless the state law is more restrictive. As the colonies and territories became states each established an independent state constitution with corresponding balances of power.

Laws of the nation and her states are made by Constitution, legislature, common law or case law, and in some states by voter initiatives placed on the state ballot. California used that process to impeach and replace its governor taking only a few months, in the early 2000s.

Many of the regulatory agencies such as the Food and Drug Administration, Federal Aviation Administration, National Transportation Safety Bureau are under Executive branch management. In addition, to Homeland Security, Federal Bureau of Investigation, Secret Service, Treasury Department and others, each federal agency has laws it regulates and investigators to identify and prosecute violators. Without all the laws and regulations of these government agencies, there wouldn't be much business for private investigators, nor there as many great sources of information.

RELEVANT FEDERAL ACTS

Most of the regulation of our profession is on a state or local level. There are, however a few relevant federal laws that may affect you as an investigative professional.

Freedom of Information Act

With all the federal regulation and documentation with three branches of government and personnel offices, service departments, property, procurement, clerks, files, etc. there are millions of documents generated, and information gathered on a daily basis.

The Freedom of Information Act (FOIA), enacted in 1966, generally provides that any person has the right to request access to federal agency records or information. Federal agencies are required to disclose records upon receiving a written request for them, except for those records that are protected from disclosure by any of the nine exemptions or three exclusions of the FOIA. This right of access is enforceable in court.

In 1996, Congress revised the Freedom of Information Act (FOIA) by passing the Electronic Freedom of Information Act Amendments (E-FOIA). The E-FOIA amendments provide for public access to information in an electronic format and for the establishment of electronic FOIA reading rooms through agency FOIA sites on the Internet. The primary source of FOIA-related information on the Internet is the Justice Department's FOIA website (www.usdoj.gov/foia), which contains links to the FOIA websites of other federal agencies.

Certain documents or portions of documents may be withheld when officials deem that releasing certain information might compromise national security, threaten the integrity of law enforcement investigations or violate the inherent privacy of personal and/or personnel records. Only recently were documents released from President Nixon's files. Many documents regarding President Kennedy and his family are still unavailable.

Privacy Act

In 1974 the federal Privacy Act permits the persons named in federal reports and records to view those documents that concern themselves. As you can imagine, these are not readily available and officials must hand search and review particular documents. This is generally a long process, often taking several months or a year.

The questions answered here are those frequently asked by persons who contact the Federal Citizen Information Center (FCIC) of the U.S. General Services Administration for information on the FOIA and the Privacy Act. The answers were compiled by the FCIC, along with the

Justice Department-the agency responsible for coordinating the administration of the FOIA and encouraging agency compliance with it. The Office of Management and Budget (OMB), which has a similar responsibility for the Privacy Act, reviewed the answers to questions on that law. (www.usdoj.gov/foia)

What is the Privacy Act?

The federal government compiles a wide range of information on individuals. For example, if you were ever in the military or employed by a federal agency, there should be records of your service. If you have ever applied for a federal benefit or received a student loan guaranteed by the government, you are probably the subject of a file. There are records on every individual who has ever paid income taxes or received a check from Social Security or Medicare.

The Privacy Act, passed by Congress in 1974, establishes certain controls over what personal information is collected by the federal government and how it is used. This law guarantees three primary rights:

1. The right to see records about oneself, subject to the Privacy Act's exemptions;
2. The right to amend a nonexempt record if it is inaccurate, irrelevant, untimely, or incomplete;
3. The right to sue the government for violations of the statute, such as permitting unauthorized individuals to read your records.

The Privacy Act also provides for certain limitations on agency information practices, such as requiring that information about an individual be collected from that individual to the greatest extent practicable; requiring agencies to ensure that their records are accurate, relevant, timely, and complete; and prohibiting agencies from maintaining information describing how an individual exercises his or her First Amendment rights unless the individual consents to it, a statute permits it, or it is within the scope of an authorized law enforcement investigation.

What information can I request under the Privacy Act?

The Privacy Act applies only to records about individuals maintained by agencies in the executive branch of the federal government. It applies to these records only if they are in a "system of records," which means they are retrieved by an individual's name,

Social Security number, or some other personal identifier. In other words, the Privacy Act does not apply to information about individuals in records that are filed under other subjects, such as organizations or events, unless the agency also indexes and retrieves them by individual names or other personal identifiers.

There are 10 exemptions to the Privacy Act under which an agency can withhold certain kinds of information from you. Examples of exempt records are those containing classified information on national security and those concerning criminal investigations. Another exemption often used by agencies is that which protects information that would identify a confidential source. For example, if an investigator questions a person about your qualifications for federal employment and that person agrees to answer only if his identity is protected, then his name or any information that would identify him can be withheld. The 10 exemptions are set out in the law.

If you are interested in more details, you should read the Privacy Act in its entirety. Though this law is too lengthy to publish as part of this book, it is readily available. The full text of the Privacy Act is available on the Justice Department's FOIA site on the Internet. Go to the Justice Department's website at www.usdoj.gov/foia (click on "Reference Materials," and scroll down to the "Text of the Privacy Act".

What is the relationship between the FOIA and the Privacy Act?

Although the two laws were enacted for different purposes, there is some similarity in their provisions. Both the FOIA and the Privacy Act give people the right to request access to records held by agencies of the federal government. The FOIA's access rights are generally given to "any person," but the Privacy Act's access rights are given only to the individual who is the subject of the records sought (if that individual is a U.S. citizen or a lawfully admitted permanent resident alien).

The FOIA applies to all federal agency records. The Privacy Act, however, applies to only those federal agency records that are in "systems of records" containing information about individuals that is retrieved by the use of a name or personal identifier. Each law has a somewhat different set of fees, time limits, and exemptions from its right of access.

If the information you want pertains to the activities of a federal agency, an organization, or some person other than yourself, you should make your request under the FOIA, which covers all agency records. If the information you want is about yourself, you should make the request also under the Privacy Act, which covers most records of agencies that pertain to individuals. Sometimes you can use the FOIA to get records about yourself that are not in a Privacy Act "system of records." If you are in doubt about which law applies or would better suit your needs, you may refer to both in your request letter. If you request records about yourself and the Privacy Act applies, the agency should process the request under both the FOIA and the Privacy Act and withhold requested information from you only if it is exempt under both laws.

Qwik-Tip
Any member of the public may make FOIA requests for government documents. Those seeking information on themselves will make requests citing the Privacy Act.

The required written requests follow a particular format and first requests are frequently denied, as policy. Repeated requests may be necessary and the wait for actual records may be from 6-18 months.

The government publishes pamphlets on FOIA, The Privacy Act and strategies for accomplishing FOIA requests. Check the US Government Printing Office website http://www.gpo.gov for ordering information. Various "freedom of information" or privacy organizations can offer further information.

Fair Credit Reporting Act (FCRA)

Three major bureaus, Experian, TransUnion and Equifax maintain consumer credit reports for business subscribers. The consumer is permitted one copy of his or her own report from each bureau per year.

In compliance with the FCRA an outside inquiry must concern a consumer debt, pre-employment check, professional licensing or other legitimate business purpose to legally obtain the credit report of another. Any pre-employment request must be accompanied by the consumer's signature, approving the request.

In addition to a person's credit account activity, the bureaus maintain header information (name, address, age, date of birth, spouse, and possible employer) that is public under FCRA as of this writing. As of

2001, there are limited permissible uses of Social Security numbers, by federal legislation.

The latest edition of regulations is on the Federal Trade Commission website. http://www.ftc.gov.

Gramm-Leach-Bliley Financial Privacy Act (GLB)

GLB requires that financial institutions issue privacy notices to customers and account holders customers to opt out of disclosures of non-public personal information to non-affiliated third parties. Banks, finance and mortgage companies make millions selling your information to marketers, as do the credit reporting bureaus.

Affecting us in the industry of private investigation, GLB forbids the use of pretext, false pretenses or ruse to gain financial information on a customer's bank accounts and balances. Private investigators cannot pretext account holders or financial institutions. The one exception to the pretext ban, is when an account locate is intended to satisfy delinquent child support.

FEDERAL WORKERS' COMPENSATION

Federal Employee Compensation Act

When a clerk is injured while working at the local FBI office in New Orleans, he or she is protected under workers' compensation for federal employees. Whether the employee is a cook in the cafeteria or head of a government agency the medical benefits are the same. It is common for these cases to be assigned to local investigation firms when fraud is suspected. With the exception of military personnel, FECA covers federal workers injured in the course of their official duties.

Non-government Federal Workers' Compensation

Federal laws cover workers in certain industries who are not federal workers, yet the nature of their jobs requires travel across state lines and/or international borders. These federal acts provide consistent treatment and benefits for those in the transportation and interstate commerce industries.

Federal Employers Liability Act

Passed in 1908, this law is intended to compensate railroad workers under certain circumstances. It is the investigator's job to determine if the railroad was involved with interstate commerce and crossed over state or international boundaries. The second requirement is to obtain evidence of negligence committed by any agent of the employer that could have resulted in the worker injury. If these two tests are not met, the worker is covered under the state's workers' compensation laws.

Jones Act of 1920

Jones protects some workers injured on a seaworthy ship on navigable waters when the worker is engaged in powering or navigating the ship. Those engaged in preparing meals, housekeeping and loading or unloading vessels are not covered under Jones.

Longshore and Harbor Workers Compensation Act

The Longshore and Harbor Workers Compensation Act covers those workers at sea who are not engaged in navigation of the ship and the workers who load and unload cargo from shore while engaged in their lawful duties.

MAIL TAMPERING

From the Files of Diane Evans

"You can look with your eyes, but not your hands!" comes to me since this is often what I was told as a child. The topic comes up at times, whether an investigator/private person can open another's mail box and see to whom the mail is addressed. Then someone will undoubtedly proclaim a law that forbids that, and then asks why anyone would want to do that.

The why may be your client's child was bitten by a neighbor's dog. The dog is known around the neighborhood and usually kept in the secured back yard with a sign posted on the gate "Beware of Dog." The client approached the house and the resident opened the door, and then slammed it in the client's face when she began to tell why she was there. There has been no sighting of the neighbor since and under the circumstances, the client may want to file suit against the dog's owner to cover the child's medical bills. Unfortunately she doesn't know to whom to serve legal papers.

As the investigator I can check property ownership and find the owner is listed as a bank. It may be a rental or recently changed hands and the bank will be of little use. After checking reverse directories and some proprietary sources, I still come up empty. Getting the resident's name from delivered mail may be a simple method of solving the client's dilemma.

Can I look at mail in a box if it is sticking out and I can see the addressee's name? I have no doubt that is not forbidden.

From the Files of Diane Evans, cont

> If I walk into an office and see mail on a receptionists desk and no one is around to stop me have I committed a federal crime? Nope, I don't think so, once mail is delivered it is no longer under postal service jurisdiction.
>
> If there is just the tiniest little lock that I can easily "pop" with my junior *Swiss Army* knife and won't damage the box, is that tampering? Well, I think we may have just found the breaking point.

Title 18, Part I, Chapter 83, section 1705 states:

"Destruction of Letter Boxes or Mail"

"Whoever willfully or maliciously injures, tears down or destroys any letter box or other receptacle intended or used for the receipt of delivery of mail on any mail route, or breaks open the same or willfully or maliciously injures, defaces or destroys and mail deposited therein, shall be fined under this title or imprisoned not more than three years, or both."

Common sense tells me not to be messing with anyone's mail, yet the postal regulations noted above concern tampering with or altering any mail receptacle or destroying mail.

Section 1725 forbids putting anything in a mail slot for the purpose of delivering it without paying postage. I knew there had to be a reason why service of process could not be legally completed by putting the legal papers in the mail slot, in the door.

If you are mindful that only the mail carrier can place items in the mail receptacle and the postal patron removes it, you will stay out of trouble. The argument can be made the mail is delivered and the postal services' job is complete. We are back to the question, "can we peek?"

The argument can be made that the postal patron has no expectation that their family mail will be secure when it is delivered in a small unlocked receptacles at their front door. Isn't that how a lot of identity theft begins, by stealing mail?.

Unless there is a locked gate or receptacle between the mail and the public I could not expect my mail to be secure from thieves or prying eyes and that is the argument I would use to defend my actions for peeking. That is why my mail comes through a slot in my front door and lands on the floor.

My interpretations of laws and regulations are meant to explain some of the basic principles of how to analyze. I am neither a postal official nor a lawyer and I never played either one on television, so nothing I write should be construed as legal advice or the right thing to do. As always, check with state or local laws that might also, apply to your actions.

STATE LAWS

Penal Codes

These will vary by state and no attempt will be made to provide penal codes from all states. For an interesting read you might locate the penal code from your state and read a few pages, beginning at the top. You will find out about the types of crimes, parties to a crime, plus the penalties for those acts.

Eavesdropping and Wire Tapping

Federal laws do apply, yet you may find the state laws are applicable to the professionals in your state. States are divided into two main categories regarding wire tapping and/or intrusion into others intended private conversations.

There are "one party" states, in which a person can covertly record conversations in which he is engaged. The following are "two party" states where all parties of an intended confidential conversation must be advised: Alaska, California, Connecticut, Florida, Illinois, Maryland, Massachusetts, Maine, Nevada, Hew Hampshire, Pennsylvania, Washington and Washington, Washington DC.

At a public meeting you don't have to get permission to record those speaking since their conversation is not intended to be private. An instructor may request that you do not tape record her lecture, yet no law is broken by making a recording. Of course, the lecturer has the right to remove anyone from that session, so to do so against her wishes would be in advisable.

Qwik-Tip
Here is a short cut to the various states wire tapping laws.
http://www.rcfp.org/taping/states.html

Arizona

Ariz. Rev. Stat. Ann. § 13-3005: Interception of a wire or electronic communication by an individual who is not a party, without the consent of someone who is a party to the communication, is a felony. The electronic communications referred to in the statute include wireless and cellular calls. The overhearing of a conversation by an individual who is not present, without the consent of a party to that conversation, is also a felony. Both violations are classified as "class 5" felonies, which are the second least serious felonies in Arizona.

Under the statute, consent is not required for the taping of a non-electronic communication uttered by a person who does not have a reasonable expectation of privacy in that communication. *See* definition of "oral communication," Ariz. Rev. Stat. Ann. § 13-3001.

A state appellate court has held that a criminal defendant's contention that police officers violated this law by recording their interviews with him without his consent was merit less because the defendant had no reasonable expectation of privacy in a police interview room. *Arizona v. Hauss*, 688 P.2d 1051 (Ariz. Ct. App. 1984).

In addition, a state appellate court has held that a mother who had a good-faith belief that it was necessary and in the best interests of her child may consent to taping the child's conversation with an alleged child molester. *State v. Morrison*, 56 P.3d 63 (App. Div. 1 2002).

It is unlawful for a person to photograph or film a person without consent while the person is in a restroom, locker room, bathroom or bedroom or is undressed or involved in sexual activity. Ariz. Rev. Stat. Ann. § 13-3019.

California

Cal. Penal Code § 631, 632: It is a crime in California to intercept or eavesdrop upon any confidential communication, including a telephone call or wire communication, without the consent of all parties.

It is also a crime to disclose information obtained from such an interception. A first offense is punishable by a fine of up to $2,500 and imprisonment for no more than one year. Subsequent offenses carry a maximum fine of $10,000 and jail sentence of up to one year.

Eavesdropping upon or recording a conversation, whether by telephone (including cordless or cellular telephone) or in person, that a person would reasonably expect to be confined to the parties present, carries the same penalty as intercepting telephone or wire communications.

Conversations occurring at any public gathering that one should expect to be overheard, including any legislative, judicial or executive proceeding open to the public, are not covered by the law.

An appellate court has ruled that using a hidden video camera violates the statute. *California v. Gibbons*, 215 Cal. App. 3d 1204 (1989). However, a television network that used a hidden camera to videotape a conversation that took place at a business lunch meeting on a crowded outdoor patio of a public restaurant that did not include "secret" information did not violate the Penal Code's prohibition against eavesdropping because it was not a "confidential communication." *Wilkins v. NBC*, Inc., 71 Cal. App. 4th 1066 (1999).

Anyone injured by a violation of the wiretapping laws can recover civil damages of $5,000 or three times actual damages, whichever is greater. Cal. Penal Code § 637.2(a). A civil action for invasion of privacy also may be brought against the person who committed the violation. Cal. Penal Code § 637.2.

Texas

Texas Penal Code § 16.02: So long as a wire, oral or electronic communication — including the radio portion of any cordless telephone call — is not recorded for a criminal or tortuous purpose, anyone who is a party to the communication, or who has the consent of a party, can lawfully record the communication and disclose its contents.

Under the statute, consent is not required for the taping of a non-electronic communication uttered by a person who does not have a reasonable expectation of privacy in that communication. *See* definition of "oral communication," Texas Code Crim. Pro. Art. 18.20.

Unlawful recording of a conversation, or disclosure of its contents with reason to know of the illegal interception, is a felony punishable by two to 20 years in prison and a fine not to exceed $10,000. Texas Penal Code § 12.33. A civil cause of action is expressly authorized for unlawful interception or disclosure. Texas Civ. Prac. & Rem. Code § 123.002. The plaintiff may be entitled to $10,000 for each occurrence, actual damages in excess of $10,000, punitive damages and attorney fees and costs. Texas Civ. Prac. & Rem. Code § 123.004.

The U.S. Court of Appeals in New Orleans (5th Cir.) held in 2000 that a television station and reporter who had been given illegally obtained tapes of telephone conversations, but who had not participated in the illegal recording, could nonetheless be held civilly liable under the federal and Texas wiretapping statutes. *Peavy v. WFAA-TV, Inc.*, 221 F.3d 158 (5th Cir. 2000). The case was appealed to the U.S. Supreme Court along with two other cases raising similar issues. The Supreme Court refused to hear the Texas case but decided in one of the other cases, *Bartnicki v. Vopper*, that media defendants could not be held liable for publishing information of public concern that was obtained unlawfully by a source where the media were blameless in the illegal interception. Following the *Bartnicki* decision, the parties in the *Peavy* case settled out of court.

Florida

Fla. Stat. ch. 934.03: All parties must consent to the recording or the disclosure of the contents of any wire, oral or electronic communication in Florida. Recording or disclosing without the consent of all parties is a felony, unless the interception is a first offense committed without any illegal purpose, and not for commercial gain, or the communication is the radio portion of a cellular conversation. Such first offenses and the interception of cellular communications are misdemeanors. *State v. News-Press Pub. Co.*, 338 So. 2d 1313 (1976), *State v. Tsavaris*, 394 So. 2d 418 (1981).

Under the statute, consent is not required for the taping of a non-electronic communication uttered by a person who does not have a reasonable expectation of privacy in that communication. *See* definition of "oral communication," Fla. Stat. ch. 934.02.

Anyone whose communications have been illegally intercepted may recover actual damages or $100 for each day of violation or $1,000, whichever is greater, along with punitive damages, attorney fees and litigation costs. Fla. Stat. ch. 934.10.

A federal appellate court has held that because only interceptions made through an "electronic, mechanical or other device" are illegal under Florida law, telephones used in the ordinary course of business to record conversations do not violate the law. The court found that business telephones are not the type of devices addressed in the law and, thus, that a life insurance company did not violate the law when it routinely recorded business-related calls on its business extensions. *Royal Health Care Servs., Inc. v. Jefferson-Pilot Life Ins. Co.*, 924 F.2d 215 (11th Cir. 1991).

Ordinarily a civilian cannot secretly eavesdrop on, nor record an intended confidential conversation to which one is *not* a party, in any state. Some states permit recording of intended confidential conversation when one is a party to the conversation; others require permission of all parties before taping.

There may be exemptions and exceptions; however, depending on the circumstances. In California you may secretly record a phone conversation in which you are engaged when another party is revealing plans for a crime or making threats of serious bodily harm.

The issues we are concerned with are whether an act is illegal which would negate any evidentiary value and whether we have invaded a person's privacy as a basis for a civil suit. Any evidence obtained illegally is inadmissible, and as the individual who obtained and prepared it for trial may be charged criminally.

ETHICS

The states are empowered to regulate professional and licensing activities within that state. You can refer back to Chapter Two for a refresher on which states require licensing and those that do not.

A state sets standards for its professionals and determines whether or not, a particular vocation shall be licensed. Licensing exists in an endeavor to protect the consumers from unlawful, untrained and/or unethical individuals in a profession.

In our various states the duties of licensed professionals quite similar. Each licensed investigator is required by virtue of her license, to act in a certain way not required by other citizens.

Merriam-Webster

Main Entry: eth·ic

Pronunciation: ʻe-thik

Function: *noun*

Etymology: Middle English *ethik,* from Middle French *ethique,* from Latin *ethice,* from Greek *EthikE,* from *Ethikos*

> 1 *plural but singular or plural in construction* : the discipline dealing with what is good and bad and with moral duty and obligation
>
> 2 a : a set of moral principles or values; b : a theory or system of moral values present-day materialistic *ethic;* c: *plural but singular or plural in construction: the principles of conduct governing an individual or a group; d : a guiding philosophy*

Delving into the concept, we can relate ethics to good sportsmanship. "It's not whether you win or lose; it is how you play the game." Many adults and children do not agree, believing instead that getting to the top, regardless of the cost is what is important in life. If someone else falls off on their way up to the top that is just the way it goes sometimes.

There are a steady stream of stories in the news of parents fighting over their children's sports and activities. Reports of a father beating another father to death over child's athletic team are reported in the news. One mother was so deranged she planned to have her daughter's competitor killed in order to guarantee her little darling a place on the cheer squad. The need for ethics in children's sports is overwhelming and many groups are de-emphasizing winning in favor of having fun playing the game.

"It's not whether you win or lose, but how you play the game," may be a forgotten concept. Hockey is one of those sports where physical violence is encouraged. Pro players missing most of their front teeth, may trip an opposing player or give him a not so-friendly"high stick" just for fun. Professional pitchers are known to throw for a batter's head and football players hit a quarterback "hard" after he released the ball. It seems winning that game, the championship or a Super Bowl ring is everything and disabling a few players on the way is no big deal.

Tennis, golf and bowling are more gentle sports combing ethical standards with that desire to win. With few exceptions, pro tennis players play their hearts out to beat an opponent. If an opponent knows the other player has a lousy backhand he will play to that player's weakness and force him to return with backhand shots. Is that unsportsmanlike conduct? Should we teach players to play to the opponents weaknesses? Of course, that is one of ways we win by being stronger than our opponent. We aren't out to win by crippling him, just by outplaying and outlasting him.

In bowling there is etiquette that one player does not approach the lane while an opposing team member is preparing his shot.

Golf is a game of integrity and honesty. The rule book is huge and any player who even unknowingly violates the rule will pay the price. There was a pro golfer who won the tournament, but walked away without signing his score card and the "win" was taken away along with a sizeable check. Can you imagine a hockey team giving up a win over something like that?

Throwing a golf club down in anger is looked upon as poor sportsmanship. Unlike hockey, if a player on a golf course struck anyone with a club, they would likely face criminal charges.

Ethical people play the game of life fairly. They hone their skills and make the best of a situation, yet not at the expense of crippling another. They are honest in their dealings and don't resort to manipulation or undue pressure. Respect for the competition never falters, nor does their self-respect that prevents them from resorting to unfair tactics to achieve their goals.

Business Ethics

The news also provides a steady stream of shady business deals, political corruption and insider trading. As a country our business ethics fail miserably Homemaker expert Martha Stewart served a federal prison sentence for lying in court about insider trading amounting to only a few thousand dollars.

ENRON will be remembered for a long time since it separated elderly retirees from their live savings. Just as illegal insider trading prospers, so"the rich get richer". There is sometimes an attitude exhibited by the very wealthy that they play life by their own set of rules.

Shortly before hotel empress Leona Helmsley was sentenced for tax evasion she remarked. "Taxes are for the little people."

Doesn't anyone play by the rules anymore, or is it just the little people who live ethically. Come to think of it, we've all read news stories of welfare fraud in which a poor family becomes rich by collecting welfare for more than one family. Is it really alright to take more money from the government than you are due?

It's not really a big deal if you claim a couple extra items stolen on your insurance claim, is it? Should you keep too much change from a clerk? Would you let a bank error go unreported, if it is in your favor? Will you return an item to a store when it ends up in your cart, although you didn't pay for it? The boss has plenty stamps and envelopes, so it is no big deal if I borrow a handful occasionally to pay my bills. Yes, or no? These are concerns of ethics.

If you are the clerk, will you want someone to tell you you gave them change for a $20 rather than the $10 they gave you? As a store owner do you want your products going out the door without money in your cash register?

Since no one wants the expense of preparing payroll, maybe we should be smart and just pay workers "off the books." There's no sense having that extra expense. We can pay them on a 1099 and let them worry about their own taxes. Workers' compensation insurance is so expensive; we can hardly afford it, so let's just subcontract workers.

Before you make the decisions above you may will to consider some possible financial consequences. The law requires an employer to deduct taxes and pay workers' compensation insurance premiums on legitimate employees. Should a legal issue arise, the government decides who is an employee and who is a legitimate subcontractor. It makes no difference how the employer classifies a worker.

When an employer misclassifies a worker as a sub-contractor and fails to make required deductions the employer will have to pay withholding, Social Security, unemployment and workers' compensation for past periods of employment. Should that employee be injured on the job it is the employer who is responsible for the employee's medical care and benefits… for the rest of his life if permanently disabled. For some it is not a matter of ethics, but of economics. In at least one state, failure to carry workers' compensation or otherwise be prepared to take financial responsibility for your employees is considered fraud and a basis for license revocation.

There is an element of private investigators that tend to lack in legal and ethical concerns, as well. It could be the thrill of the chase or the buzz from the risk that prevents some from performing ethically.

There were two unlicensed investigators in Southern California working for a wealthy client who wanted a divorce and was looking for "dirt" on his ex-wife. The investigators went so far as to send the victim a "clock radio" that she "Won" in a drawing. Inside the working radio was a tiny video camera that recorder all activity in her bedroom. These fellows also followed her around and generally stalked her making her extremely stressed. The two were prosecuted, yet received sentences of less than one year of house arrest.

A well-known "investigator to the stars," Anthony Pellicano earned a federal prison sentence for possession of illegal hand grenades. What could he have been thinking? He will likely earn additional prison time for wire tapping charges.

Before the computer age, in the mid 1980s there was a ring of investigators and Social Security employees who were in the business of selling SS information for a fairly large fee. As it happened, some 20-25 investigators and workers were arrested from New York to Florida, Arizona, California and places between all within minutes of each other. There were many convictions, investigators lost their licenses and SS workers lost their jobs and pensions.

Each knew that what they were doing was illegal, yet somehow each was above the law. The sense of right and wrong was skewed for each of them. We can only wonder if after all was said and done, if it was worth it to them.

The term "mala in se" refer to acts that are bad by the very nature of the act; stealing for example. Failing to register you vehicle with the state would be mala in prohibita; there is nothing evil in not doing it, yet it is bad because the law requires it. Is it unethical? What if the reason for not registering a vehicle, is because the owner does not have insurance?

A toddler doesn't understand that it is wrong to keep something that does not belong to him. Many pre-school aged kids hit other children and may cause injuries, yet at such young ages the responsibility lies with the adults in charge; the children must be taught. "Do unto others as you would have them do unto you" is a premise of ethics, yet it is become widely ignored as we leave childhood.

Values are taught, by parents and teachers, yet rejected by the child later in life. There are news accounts every day involving someone in a position of trust who violates that trust. A person who hasn't learned his lessons may see others who are profiting and adopt another's unethical strategy as his own. Post ENRON investigation, business schools began to think about offering classes on business ethics.

As a professional working on behalf of a client, the licensee has a different responsibility than an employee. He is now responsible to the client, not to an employer. The professional has superior knowledge with an obligation to act in the client's best interest. A business professional is morally obligated to lawfully take the high road and place the client's interest above his own personal values. If a firm is not able to do that then, ethically they must refuse the case.

For an example, when considering working a criminal defense case for an accused child molester while hoping the guy gets his due, it is appropriate to withdraw.

 From the Files of Diane Evans

A supervisor assigned me a case that I had no idea how to work and didn't have the resources to find out. (No World Wide Web or internet to turn to) A $1,000 retainer was paid upfront and when the client didn't get what he wanted, he refused to pay the $1,000 balance. In turn, my employer threatened to sue the client for the balance owed.

In my view this was not an appropriate case for an investigative firm. The client had a raw source of a substance and wanted to know how to refine and process it for sale. Had it been within my control, I could legally charge a consultation fee and sent him to a chemist. I probably would have just sent him to the library after talking with him over the phone.

Some other serious ethics breech occurred with some colleagues, one of whom I was acquainted. I received a call from a client on a Sunday who had a court date in a few days. Mrs. Webster (not her true name) was involved in a custody matter involving her daughter and grandchildren.

From the Files of Diane Evans, cont

> She spoke with another licensed investigator over the phone providing the investigator the detail of the case. The investigator, Gwen, had her husband call and cancels the meeting. Mrs. Webster was in rather a panic. I agreed to do the work for her and had it ready for the hearing. The day of her court date, I received an angry call from an upset Mrs. W, accusing me of violating client confidentiality. Whoa, that did not happen and I knew it, so rather than react, I let her get it all out.
>
> Some derogatory information from the opposition that came out in court included information she gave me. When we began to talk, and as I understood what transpired I was able to put the rest together myself.
>
> It seems that when Mrs. W. was divorced she hired, Frank, a local licensee to investigate her then husband. Now, Frank was working for her daughter. (Law #1: We cannot take a case that is adverse to a client or former client) She now confides to me that she gave Frank almost $10,000 on the divorce case and that she never received a receipt or report. (Law #2: Once the fee is paid we must provide the client a report. Is she lying or is he very slick?) The plot thickens when she confesses that they also slept together
>
> Mrs. W. got Beth's name from the phone book and had a long conversation with her over the phone. What I threw into the mix was my knowledge that Beth and Frank are buddies. One of two things likely happened; either Beth was innocently discussing interesting case facts with a colleague, or she knowingly and willingly spilled all she knew when she discovered her buddy was on the case.
>
> A third possibility is that Frank kept quiet about his role and let her talk, then used the information for his client. All those scenarios would be unethical, at least. (Law #3: Confidentiality begins when the conversation is about a potential client retaining professional services.) Ethically, Frank should have stopped Beth and told her he was working for the daughter. It isn't totally unethical to discuss a case as long as names and pertinent details are omitted, but you do have to be extra careful in a small town.

Since ethics are not inherent in each of us, professional organizations create *Codes of Ethics* for its members to follow.

The National Association of Legal Investigators has strict application requirements including examinations and a requirement to write a "paper" on an investigative topic. Their code of ethics likewise sets high standards for members.

NALI CODE OF ETHICS

Preamble

A legal investigator is dedicated to a search for truth and the furtherance of his employer or his client's interest consistent therewith. This search for truth makes possible the establishment of the American ideals of fairness and justice for the benefit of the client in every case that the investigator works on. It should be the intention of every investigator to deal honestly, justly and courteously with all with whom he comes in contact and to practice his profession according to this Code of Ethics.

Professional Relations

Section 1. The Legal Investigator will extend the effectiveness of his profession by cooperating with other investigators and related professions and by the exchange of information and experience so long as the interests of his clients or employers are not violated.

Section 2. He will not advertise his work, skill or merit in an unprofessional manner or in a dramatic, misleading or exaggerated fashion, and he will avoid all conduct or practice likely to discredit or do injury to the dignity and honor of his profession.

Relations with the Public

Section 3. The Legal investigator will, when the appropriate opportunity presents itself, explain to the public the role of his profession in the furtherance of the administration of justice.

Section 4. He will not knowingly violate any right or privilege of any individual citizen which may be guaranteed or provided by the United States Constitution, and State Constitution, or the laws of the State and Federal Governments or any subdivision thereof.

Section 5. He will make all his reporting based upon truth and fact and will only express honest opinions based thereon.

Section 6. He will not disclose or relate or betray in any fashion that trust of confidence placed in him by client, employer or associate, without his consent.

Section 7. He will not suggest, condone or participate in any fashion or degree, for any purpose whatsoever, in entrapment.

Section 8. He shall refrain from accepting an assignment or employment if a personal conflict of interest lies therein.

Section 9. He will deal fairly and equitably with his client or employer, and will clearly explain his duties and the basis for his charges in each undertaking.

Section 10. He will guard against employing those techniques, or utilizing such equipment or devices, that may threaten the life, limb or safety of another.

Section 11. He will not accept commissions or allowances, directly or indirectly, from independent contractors or other parties dealing with his client, employer or associate in connection with work for which he is responsible.

Section 12. He will not allow personal feelings or prejudices to interfere with factual and truthful disclosures on the assignments in which he has been employed or consulted.

Section 13. The Legal Investigator will endeavor to provide the opportunity, education and skill for the professional development and advancement of investigators in the profession.

Section 14. He will not directly or indirectly injure the professional reputation, prospects, or practice of another investigator. However, if he considers that an investigator is guilty of unethical, or unfair practice or designs, he will present the information to the proper authority for action.

Section 15. He will uphold, and never abuse, the principle of appropriate and adequate compensation for those engaged in investigative work.

Section 16. He will not criticize another investigator's work except in the proper forum for technical discussion and criticism.

Section 17. He will not compete illegally with other investigators in the solicitation of work.

Section 18. He shall not engage in the unauthorized practice of law.

Section 19. He shall not solicit clientele for any attorney.

The North Carolina Association of Private Investigators and many other state associations borrowed NALI's code as shown above. One of the longest ones is from the Private Investigator's Forum.

1. TO perform all assignments and case examinations in a moral, ethical, and legal manner;

2. TO work entirely within the framework of the law;

3. TO NOT knowingly support, affiliate with, or agree with any group or firm or individual whose teachings or practices are contrary to or opposed to those accepted by IPIU;

4. TO NOT knowingly make a false statement of material fact;

5. TO NOT engage in conduct involving dishonesty, fraud, deceit or misrepresentation;

6. TO NOT unlawfully obstruct another party's access to evidence or unlawfully alter, destroy, or conceal a document or other material having potential evidentiary value and to not counsel or assist another person to do any such act;

7. TO NOT offer evidence that I know to be false, and if I have offered material evidence and come to know of its falsity, I shall take reasonable remedial measures;

8. TO NOT falsify evidence or assist a witness to testify falsely, or offer an inducement to a witness that is prohibited by law;

9. TO immediately inform the appropriate authority when knowledge exists of another private investigator that has committed a violation of the standards of professional conduct, as set forth herewith, that raises a substantial question as to that person's honesty, trustworthiness, or fitness as a private investigator or case examiner in other respects;

10. TO NOT commit an act that reflects adversely on my honesty, trustworthiness or fitness as an investigator in other respects;

11. TO NOT state or imply an ability to influence improperly a government agency or official;

12. TO verify all paperwork, documents, statements, evidence, and facts that may lead to a wrongful arrest, detention, civil action, or criminal action whether it involves an individual or organization;

13. IN REGARDS TO MY FEES, I PLEDGE that my fees shall be reasonable. The factors to be considered in determining the reasonableness of my fee include the following:

(1) time and labor required, the novelty and difficulty of the questions involved, and the skills requisite to perform the service properly;

(2) likelihood, if apparent to the client, that the acceptance of the particular assignment will preclude other assignments by myself;

(3) The fee customarily charged in the locality for similar services;

(4) The amount involved and the result obtained;

(5) The time limitations imposed by the client or by the circumstances;

(6) The nature and length of the professional relationship with the client;

(7) The experience, reputation, and ability of myself or others performing the services; and

(8) Whether the fee is fixed or contingent.

(9) When I have not regularly represented the client, the basis or rate of the fee shall be communicated to the client, in writing, before commencing the assignment.

1. IN REPRESENTING A CLIENT, I SHALL report all facts developed in a case promptly and timely;

2. I SHALL NOT use means that have no substantial purpose other than to embarrass, delay, or burden a third person;

3. I SHALL NOT use methods of obtaining evidence that violate the legal rights of such a person;

4. I SHALL NOT present or participate in presenting criminal charges solely to obtain advantage in a civil matter; or

5. I SHALL NOT threaten to present criminal charges in order to obtain advantage in a civil matter;

6. I SHALL NOT fail to disclose a material fact when disclosure is necessary to avoid assisting a criminal act by my client;

7. I SHALL NOT enter into a business transaction with a client or knowingly acquire an ownership, security or other pecuniary interest adverse to a client unless:

(1) the terms on which I acquire the interest is fair and reasonable to the client and is disclosed in writing to the client in a manner which can be reasonably understood by the client;

(2) the client is given a reasonable opportunity to seek independent counsel in the transaction; and

(3) the client consents in writing thereto;

1. I SHALL NOT use facts relating to representation of a client to the disadvantage of the client unless the client consents;

2. I SHALL NOT prepare an instrument, or take part in an instrument, giving myself or a person related to me any substantial gift from a client, including a testamentary gift, except where the client is related to the donee;

3. I SHALL NOT provide financial assistance to a client in connection with pending or contemplated litigation, except that:

(1) I may advance court costs and expenses of litigation, the repayment of which may be contingent on the outcome of the matter; and

(2) in representing an indigent client may pay court costs and expenses of litigation on behalf of the client.

1. I SHALL NOT accept compensation for representing a client from one other than the client unless the client consents;

2. I SHALL NOT represent a client if the representation of that client will be directly adverse to another client, unless:

(1) I reasonably believe it will not adversely affect the relationship with the other client;

(2) each client consents;

RESPONSIBILITIES

Professional ethics go well beyond any applicable law. In states that don't require licensing, then a professional is morally obligated to hold oneself out as a professional with high standards. It does make a difference how you play the game, and the public deserves a level playing field.

Although as private citizens private investigators are not required to protect anyone's civil rights, morality does not permit one to trample on another's right to privacy or the right to be free from harassment. Professional investigators would not do anything to cause harm to an adversary or subject of an investigation. It is wise to become a member of a professional organization to remain abreast of new laws, networking and a source for continuing information.

A licensee has a fiduciary responsibility to his client to act in the client's best interest. He must be truthful in his dealings with a client, and refrain from making exaggerated claims about his investigative abilities. Investigative endeavors must always be within the law.

Activities on behalf of a client are confidential, unless the client releases the licensee from that requirement. Of course, the investigator will have to provide the subject name to others in order to search public records, conduct interviews, and otherwise make inquiries.

Client information and the goal or purpose of the assignment should never be revealed when making inquiries. When assigning cases to subordinates or subcontractors there is no need to provide a client name. Professionals must take sufficient care that identities of clients or case facts, do not become visible to a casual observer, who happens by. Some firms keep case files in a locked cabinet when the office is closed to protect the privacy of clients and subjects alike.

In discussing case requirements with the client, the professional is obligated to provide the client a reasonable estimation of the costs involved, hourly fees, expenses, etc., yet no one is not obligated to reveal how the end result will ultimately be obtained. We are under no obligation to reveal *sources* or *trade secrets*.

The firm's owner must stay informed of the requirements of the profession in his state. He is obligated to inform employees of requirements and insist that applicable laws be followed. It is the employer's responsibility to be diligent in supervising employees.

Licensees must include license number, agency name and contact information in advertisements, or other printed material representing the business and cannot use an unapproved business name. Any license must be posted at the place of business.

Each must be diligent and complete a thorough investigation within the case budget. No one is obligated to go to the ends of the earth for a few hundred dollars.

There are principles that vary widely among the states, such as use of badges, firearms, pretext or ruse, and insurance requirements. Florida permits use of badges by licensed investigators, yet the badge cannot include the state seal. Florida has an insurance requirement, while

California does not unless the firm engages in armed personal protection. Arizona requires a $2,500 surety bond issued in the owner/ firm name.

Qwik-Tip
Another method of learning the resident's last name and when they moved in is by looking at the top of the gas meter. Often the installer will write that info on top of the meter in grease pencil. If the meter readers can use mirrors, so can you.

In order to get the specifics of a particular state it is necessary to conduct research of that states laws and regulations as those apply to private investigations.

SUMMARY

You have been enlightened with a refresher of the foundation of our laws and specific examples of federal laws affecting the investigation profession. State laws were discussed as well as, specifics of techniques utilized in the course of investigations. The topic of ethics is explained further and summarized as it may apply to private investigators in the respective states.

DISCUSSION QUESTIONS

1. Explain the differences in the FOIA and the Privacy Act.
2. A worker is injured while lawfully engaged in his duties on an oil drilling platform 3 miles off the Texas coast. What is the jurisdiction for this case? Does it meet the test of Jones or LHWCA?
3. A worker is injured on the ferry he uses to transport workers to and from the same platform.
4. How does GLB affect gathering financial information?
5. How are laws and ethics related?

Chapter 9

Organization of a Private Investigation Firm

CHAPTER OVERVIEW

In this chapter, we will be looking at how to set up and organize a private investigation business. Due to the wide variety of disciplines within the private investigations industry, the organization and approach can vary dramatically.

However, there are disciplines within private investigations that are more common or where there is a greater chance of employment. We will endeavor to provide a brief overview of these areas. In the last part of the chapter, we will cover what could be called the "business infrastructure" and other aspects of the business that are common to most investigations firms.

SELECTING THE PATH

Private investigation is the investigation of life. Where there is a profession, a business, or virtually any other activity, there will be in need for private investigators. Think about it for a minute. Is there any place where you can think that investigation would not be needed? health care, financial, corporate, industrial, sports, production, restaurants, and hotels, insurance, transportation, medical, and virtually every other aspect of life contains the possibility for controversy, disagreement or other need for independent research. As such, it is not really possible to provide a template or boilerplate solution to setting up the private investigator's business.

Choosing the Right Path

The first question to be asked is: what do you enjoy? This is often one of the most overlooked questions as a person considers the private investigation industry. The common motivators are the glamour, excitement, and money. However, quite often the work can be rather unglamorous and routine.

This will not be the case if you have carefully thought out a specific area that you know you would enjoy. Do you enjoy working with people? Are you a technical whiz? Do you prefer doing research or similar activities where human interaction is limited? Does the idea of doing surveillances excite you? Are you a number cruncher? Do you enjoy a particular subject matter? These may or may not be questions you can answer right away. As mentioned above, there are many different areas where private investigators are needed. Thinking about what you enjoy is a good place to start.

As we cover some of the more common areas in this chapter, you can also be thinking about these areas as possible options.

Keeping the Lights On; Paying the Bills

One other very important factor initially is running a business that pays the bills. If you have properly thought out the first question (what you enjoy), you will most likely be successful and competitive. However, that may not always be the case. Certain areas are known to be more lucrative than others. In fact, many private investigators simply enjoy investigations for the sake of investigation. As such, they next ask – where can I make the most money? Or - where can I be assured of making a decent living? That is a question that can only be answered by specific research into the area you're considering. Nevertheless, most of the areas we will be covering specifically in this chapter are known to have a strong and continuous need for good investigators.

Before getting into common areas of practice, you need to determine if a license is required. In the previous chapter we identified the states that do and do not require licensing. Don't forget that even if you live somewhere that doesn't require state licensing, your city or county may. In addition, there are still business license and insurance issues. Licensing is usually a consumer protection issue to ensure that the investigators in the marketplace are of the highest quality. This is important because in many states to practice without a license is a crime.

COMMON AREAS OF PRACTICE

Workers' Compensation Insurance

Workers' compensation is one area where there is usually plenty of work for private investigators. Workers' compensation is usually mandated by the state in order to provide employees with a more streamlined approach to obtain compensation for work related injuries. On the employer side, workers' compensation provides dollar limits and other safeguards to protect against frivolous or fraudulent claims. Because it is state mandated, is often one of the largest sectors of the insurance industry. And, it is wrought with fraud.

Work in this area can be looked at from either the plaintiffs or the defense side. On the plaintiff's side, the injured worker will approach an attorney who sues the employer. The employer then contacts their workers' compensation insurance carrier. The plaintiff's attorney will hire a private investigator or will have an in-house legal investigator interview the injured worker and prepare the case for trial. The plaintiff's private investigator better be certain however that the claim is not frivolous or fraudulent. This is where those superior interview and interrogation techniques we discussed earlier become necessary.

On the defense side (the employer) the workers' compensation insurance carrier has in-house investigators, often called a special investigations unit, or they will hire an outside private investigator who will interview the injured employee. As with the investigator for the plaintiff, the defense investigator will also review the case for frivolity and fraud. In addition the investigator will determine that the case falls within the scope of the insurance contract. This scope of investigation typically involves checking to see that the injury occurred while at work and during the course of employment. If the investigator and claims adjuster are satisfied that the claim is legitimate and proper they will pay out the claim.

If the defense is not satisfied the claim is valid, the workers' compensation insurance carrier may decide to initiate additional interviews. If the insurance carrier believes that the injury is false or inaccurate, the carrier may initiate a surveillance of the injured employee. Here is where surveillance skills from the earlier chapter come in. Often these surveillances turn up proof that the injury did not occur, was exaggerated, or that the employee is no longer injured yet continues to collect benefits.

As you can see, workers' comp is a very investigation intensive area. And, due to the volume of cases, many beginning private investigators find more work than they know what to do with. The only catch is that the pay is often on the lower end of the scale.

Personal Injury/Wrongful Death

We've all seen the advertisements on television; the ones with the attorney asking people "Have you been injured in an accident? Call us; we can get you money for your pain and suffering". Ethical issues aside, personal injury cases provide those who have been hurt, compensation for medical expenses, lost wages, pain and suffering among other possible damages. These cases typically revolve around some sort of tort legal theory such as battery or the negligence of someone else. These include slip and fall cases, dog bites, or barroom brawls, etc. However, the large majority of personal injury cases are based on automobile accidents.

In the majority of cases the plaintiff will be represented by a personal injury attorney and the defendant will be represented by their insurance carrier. The approach is really rather straightforward. The private investigator, whether plaintiff for defense, typically interviews the injured party, any witnesses, and anyone else who may have information about the incident. Very often the investigator will revisit the scene of the incident to help provide a context for what happened. Private Investigators specializing in this area are typically well equipped with cameras and are very skilled at using them. In fact, some private investigators make their living doing this alone. It is not uncommon for these investigators to have several cameras worth thousands of dollars. Of course, interview skills, especially in the area of eyewitness evidence, are paramount.

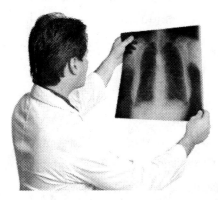

There are many people from the medical profession who crossover into the private investigations profession. Nurses, paramedics, and even medical doctors have been known to become private investigators since they are especially skilled at determining the nature and extent of injuries. They are most able to spot fraudulent or exaggerated claims of injury. What other profession would make for natural in auto accident investigations? Quite often retired law enforcement officers find their way into this field. They unfortunately have been to many auto accidents injuries and fatalities.

In the more extreme cases, the injured party will die as a result of their injuries. This will give rise to what is called a wrongful death claim. Depending on state law, certain members of the decedent's family may sue for damages on behalf of the injured party. The obvious difference in kind of case is that the injured are no longer available to be interviewed. Typically the county coroner will be contacted for relevant information.

This area of law can mean big bucks. Often the plaintiff's attorney will take the case on a contingency basis, that is, they will be paid a percentage of the money that is recovered for the injured party. It is not unusual for this percentage to be anywhere from 30% to 50%. If the case brings in $1 million, using the same percentage amounts, the attorney would make from $300,000 to $500,000.00. The attorney may only have put in little more than a few hundred hours. Because these cases are so factually intensive, the private investigator is a key part of its success. As such, the stakes are high, the skill sets must be keen, and the competition can be fierce.

Criminal Defense

This is another area where there's usually plenty of work to go around. Although the pay in some situations can be exceptionally high, it generally runs in the middle of the average hourly rates.

Criminal cases will be handled by different governmental bodies —at the local, state and federal level. The large majority of cases though will be generated by city or county government.

Here, the plaintiff becomes the prosecution and is the district attorney (DA). In criminal cases the state takes on the case as the victim or on behalf of the victim. The prosecutions investigator will either be the lead police detective or an investigator who works directly for the district attorney. Due to high caseloads and low budgets, it is difficult for these entities to give every case as much attention as they would like. Because their budgets are paid by tax dollars, they are not at the whim of market forces. Therefore, there is a regular stream of criminal prosecutions to provide the private sector with plenty of work.

On the defense side of criminal cases, it is rather common to find a retired law enforcement officer working as the defense investigator. This is because they are in the best position to understand the legal issues and to have familiarity with the approaches, tactics, and strategies of their former profession. They are now on the opposite side of the fence. Nevertheless, many investigators in this area have no prior law enforcement experience at all and are equally as valuable and successful.

Common criminal cases include theft, drugs, burglary, rape, battery and arson. More serious crimes typically involve kidnapping, drug trafficking, manslaughter and murder. In each of these different areas of criminal law we find people that specialize in one area only. It is common in the more serious cases to involve specialists and expert testimony. Drug cases may require involvement of medical doctors or pharmacist. An arson case might need someone with a firefighting background.

Private investigators working in criminal defense rely heavily on their interviewing skills and their ability to detect deception in a client. It is imperative that the investigator obtain the truth and to do so they must be sure they are getting this from the client. While most clients are honest, many are not. Because of this, the client interview is typically initiated by the defense attorney. This is because their discussions are absolutely privileged, that is, the attorney cannot be called as a witness against his client in this area. While the private investigator's interviews may provide similar protection, for example under attorney work product, it is not the same. The client defendant is more likely to feel safer talking with the attorney.

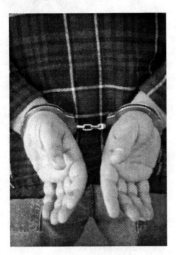

The stakes are high in criminal defense cases. The downside for the client can be imprisonment, fines, a criminal record and lost privileges, such as the right to vote or to hold a license (such as private investigator!). Being that these cases are factually intensive, the private investigator plays a major role in its success. The investigators capabilities and skills must be top notch.

Domestic Cases

Conducting surveillance to determine spousal infidelity keeps many private investigators busy. There are some people who do this kind of work as their sole source of income. Private investigators specializing in this area benefit from having two or more vehicles for the purposes of conducting surveillance. Typically, surveillance will span several days. Having multiple vehicles gives the private investigator an advantage as it makes it less likely that the subject will notice they are being followed.

These specialized private investigators often have sophisticated video recording equipment and are skilled at obtaining photographic evidence. Investigators who do surveillance must be very good at thinking on their feet and must have good hand-to-eye coordination.

Following someone in a vehicle can be very difficult. Getting the right shot or video images takes skill and patience.

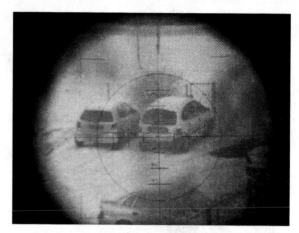

However, not all surveillance in domestic cases will involve following a subject. Some spouses are watched from a stationary position. These situations require the private investigator to conduct stakeout surveillance. The ideal setup for a stationary surveillance is to have a van equipped with cameras and video equipment with long range capabilities. These vans and equipment can cost many tens of thousands of dollars. And, this work can involve many hours of sitting in one place, necessitating a mobile toilet of sorts and plenty of food and water. Investigators who do surveillances are often doing their work at odd hours.

While a majority of work is in surveillance, there is plenty of work in other aspects of divorce and child custody. Some cases involve a spouse who has taken a child without permission and the private investigator is tasked with finding them. Other cases involve spouses who had hidden assets or money from the other spouse. Someone skilled in financial investigations is often used in these kinds of cases.

Financial Investigations

The need for private investigators in conducting financial investigations is rapidly growing. With the increases of major corporate fraud such as Enron, WorldCom, and Tyco, new laws such as Sarbanes-Oxley have created an entire industry around financial investigations. There is a dual side to this area. One is on the proactive and preventive side; auditing. This is usually done by certified public accountants or others skilled in analysis of financial statements. On the other side, it is reactive. This occurs after malfeasance has been detected by a whistleblower or an auditor. It is the private investigator that will be called in to assist or to take charge. It is not uncommon for private investigator working in this area to be a certified public accountant. In fact, there is a designation that is available to any professional who qualifies and passes the test; it is called the Certified Fraud Examiner or CFE. Highly regarded, people with this designation are often hired to audit for fraud or to investigate fraud. For more information, contact the Association of Certified Fraud Examiners (ACFE; www.cfenet.com).

Financial investigations can come in many forms; they are not limited to the high profile or large corporate fraud scandals. If it has to do with monetary issues and needs to be investigated, then it is a financial investigation.

One area that does not involve malfeasance or wrongdoing is due diligence. Due diligence involves an investigation of the assets and liabilities of the company. This is usually done for the purpose of deciding whether not one company will purchase the other. What kinds of assets are owned? Are they owned outright, leased, mortgaged? Does the company own intellectual property and does it the company employ competent professionals? Is the company being sued, has it filed for bankruptcy, or does it have any current contractual obligations? Does it have subsidiaries or is it a subsidiary? These are all questions that must be asked prior to a purchase and to help establish a price.

Other topical areas within financial investigations include securities fraud, real property scams, money laundering, counterfeiting, check, and credit card fraud and any other topic that might be defined as "financial."

Medical Malpractice

The area of medical malpractice has a fair amount of crossover with personal injury. These cases differ in that they typically involve the competence and the reasonableness of the actions of someone in the medical profession. The legal causes of action closely resemble negligence and turn on whether or not actions by medical professional were above or below certain standards. If the actions were below standards, the medical professional is liable for damages. If not, there is no liability. The determination of whether or not the actions are above or below the standard is aided by expert investigators. Typically these are medical doctors, nurses or others who have extensive knowledge in the area. Damage amounts are typically very high. To be involved in this area, the private investigator must be skilled at interpreting medical data.

Information Services

There are companies whose sole reason for existence is maintaining current and accurate information about assets and people. The typical customer is a private investigator, collection agency, or attorney, but there are numerous other professions that seek these services. Often during the course of their work, private investigators and attorneys will need to locate people or assets. With the arrival of the Internet, a large majority of these resources have become available through online databases. Certain records are still stored in paper form or on CD-ROM or similar media. This may sound familiar from the Sources and Resources chapter. Typically, these information service providers purchase their information, e.g. records, from government agencies in bulk. They then convert it to a form usable in an online format or comparable set up. The information that may be obtained from these companies can include but may not be limited to:

- Weapons searches – certain databases contain records indicating who holds a license to own or carry a gun. It is important to know whether someone owns a weapon or not when suspicion of violence is an issue.
- Birth index – these records simply show birth certificates containing dates of birth and locations. These are often accessed to verify a subject's identity.

- State tax records – these records characteristically show any outstanding debts or liens that a person may owe to a state taxing authority. This information can show whether somebody is in bad financial condition or whether a piece of property, real or personal, is encumbered by a lien.

- Marriage records – marriage and divorce records can be obtained from these databases. This can be done to establish ownership of property, for example whether not it is separate or community property, to track name changes and to be certain someone is divorced before remarrying.

- Civil index – these records can reveal whether or not someone has sued or been sued, i.e. plaintiff or defendant. Does this person have a history of suing other people? Has this person been sued many times? Are there many pending lawsuits against this person or company? These records might be used to decide whether to hire someone, to involve them in a business transaction or whether to purchase a company owned or controlled by the person.

- Corporate and business entity records –in most states certain business entities are required to apply and register with the secretary of state or similar governmental body. Typically corporations, limited liability companies, and limited liability partnerships will be required to do this. This information indicates who owns the company, what its purpose is and other important information.

- Criminal index – federal, state and local criminal records can sometimes be accessed through the services. Most often they are accessed to determine someone's eligibility for a license or employment.

- Death index – a person's death can be verified to death records and sometimes used to end a search for a person thought to be alive.

- Fictitious business name – where a person does not use their own name for business, they will use a fictitious business name. Who owns the business? When was it set up? Was it set up at all? Information about a business can be verified here.

- Professional licenses – professional licenses such as private investigator, attorney, medical doctor, and many others can be verified through state and local records. These records are often used in hiring decisions and to look for possible disciplinary actions by the licensing body.

- Real and personal property indexes – state and local records are kept regarding the ownership of real and personal property. These records should provide the chain of prior sales and purchases of a piece of property as well as records indicating those who have a security interest in the same property. These records are used to establish a person's worth, whether not to buy a piece of property, and to demonstrate legal or financial responsibility of the person; this may be shown by the existence or nonexistence of tax liens and other encumbrances.

- Eviction records – these records expose whether someone has been evicted from a place of residence or commercial property. These records are most often used to establish a person's financial responsibility.

There are many other records to numerous to list. Suffice it to say, there are countless things that can be done and learned through the use of these services.

As discussed in our previous chapter, usually, the services will require a private investigator license, attorney license, or proof of a similar business purpose before the service will allow you access to the records. The propensity for fraud and abuse is tempting. The legitimate purposes a private investigator uses these information services for are as a means of locating assets and people. Many of these investigators do this as their sole means of income. There is truly an art and skill requiring practice.

Information Security and Computer Forensics

This area is highly specialized and usually performed by people with a strong technical background. Some states will usually require that these people have a private investigator's license. Often, these investigators work for local, state or federal law enforcement. They seek out and assist in prosecuting those who create and spread computer viruses and other malicious software. They also go after those who snoop around on networks and computers for confidential data and similar illegal activities. They are usually broken down into two categories, network forensic examiners and computer forensic examiners.

Network forensic examiners will watch for traffic moving across networks and on and off of servers. They are looking for illegal activity, collection of evidence, and locating and prosecuting perpetrators.

Computer forensic examiners usually limit themselves to individual computers such as the computer's hard drive. They will search for evidence of various crimes and other activity.

Technical Counter Surveillance Measures (T.C.S.M.)

This is a highly specialized field where the technician is looking for those who eavesdrop, place electronic bugs, and otherwise invade the privacy of people or businesses

Perpetrators here are looking to obtain confidential information that will either provide them with profit or provide them opportunity to do harm. For example, inside traders might use confidential information to buy or sell securities at the right time and amount. A perpetrator might learn of an important business decision or learn of proprietary data that can be sold. Or, the perpetrator might learn of embarrassing or private information and will extort money by threatening to publicly disclose information. As such, offices, automobiles, and other areas must be examined and searched for bugging and similar devices.

We've covered several of the major and most common areas within private investigations. There are numerous other specializations that typically fall along professional lines. If you are or have been involved in a specialized profession or line of work, you may well find a field of private investigations that will suit you well. For example, someone with experience as an auto mechanic or auto body shop repair might find a lot of work in insurance investigations; for example, where it is necessary to determine how damage occurred to a vehicle in an accident and the cost of that damage. Someone with a nursing background might find a lot of investigations work in personal injury. The possibilities are nearly limitless.

BUSINESS INFRASTRUCTURE

No matter what you do, you want to be certain that you are compliant with local and state requirements. The first thing you should consider is whether not your state requires licensure for the practice of private investigations. It is very common for a state to require a certain minimum number of hours of experience, a thorough background check, and perhaps a test. For example, in Ohio the Department of Public Safety and Homeland Security govern the licensure of private investigators and security officers. Their laws and rules state that in order for an individual to obtain license they must have a good reputation for integrity, have not been convicted of a felony within the last twenty years or any offense involving moral turpitude, and have not been adjudicated incompetent for the purpose of holding the license. The applicant must have been engaged for at least two consecutive years in investigatory or security services work for a private investigator, or for a law enforcement or other public agency engaged in investigatory activities, or engaged in the practice of law, or has acquired equivalent experience as determined by rule of the director of public safety. The applicant must demonstrate competency as a private investigator by passing an examination. The full text of Ohio laws and rules can be found at www.homelandsecurity. ohio.gov

It is also common for a state to make it a crime to practice without a license. There may be an exception such as practicing without pay or if you are working for certain kinds of employers. However, the specifics of the requirements for licensure and any exceptions should be checked with the proper authority.

The next issue has to do with a business license. Some city, municipal and county governments require that anyone engaged in business obtain a business license. The requirements can vary dramatically. It may be simply filing an application and a fee or it could require an interview process and more in-depth statement of your business purpose.

Some jurisdictions may require that you obtain a fictitious business license as well. When in doubt of any of the above issues, it is best to check with local jurisdictions and/or an attorney specializing in business law.

The Office

Probably the biggest question to ask the outset is whether not you want work from your home or rent space in a commercial setting. If you choose to rent on office by yourself, you are adding an enormous amount of overhead. This may be worth it if you need the space and, for credibility reasons, you want to meet clients in a more professional setting. It might not be possible to work your home if your business activity is of a nature that will conflict with residential zoning regulations. Fortunately there are many companies that are set up for the purpose of providing cost-effective solutions here. These companies provide an answering service, mail forwarding, and meeting rooms for business and client meetings. You would not have a permanent office. You would simply use meeting rooms as needed. This kind of arrangement can run a fraction of the cost of having your own office.

Many investigators though do not have a need to meet with clients at their own office. In fact, this is true of most investigators. Typically, the investigator will travel to the client's place of business or will simply communicate by phone, e-mail, fax or will meet in a restaurant or coffee shop. Obviously working at home is the least expensive alternative; it is also a very short commute.

Support Staff

Next you will need to determine whether or not you will require support staff. Many private investigation firms have administrative assistants, surveillance personnel, in-house information research professionals, or other depending on the type of business. You'll need to determine their hourly rate, health care insurance, workers compensation insurance, tax withholdings, and safety and working condition issues which are mandated by law. It may be possible to farm these tasks out to independent contractors rather than employ someone so that you do not have such a large overhead. Typically though independent contractors charge higher hourly rates but they will be responsible for taking care of tax, insurance, and other expenses.

Equipment

The next step is to think about equipment for your office. You'll definitely need a dedicated phone line. A fax line and an Internet connection; preferably a high speed, are most likely need as well. Very few businesses these days can get by with less. You should also have a decent computer system, a locking file cabinet for evidence and sensitive or confidential material. A paper shredder is a must and perhaps a fireproof safe. A laptop computer will be beneficial if your information needs are mobile, and then there are the more obvious equipment needs such as desks, chairs and lighting equipment.

Other equipment will depend on your specific line of investigation profession. The majority of private investigators will need a camera and possibly video and audio recording equipment. The cost and sophistication of this equipment can vary dramatically. You may also need audio recording equipment.

One other very important tool for the investigator is their automobile. It is a rare case that an investigator is not spending a lot of time on the road. An inexpensive and reliable automobile is the best way to go. It can be a good idea to equip this car with items appropriate to a mobile office. Things such as a notebook, plenty of pens, a flashlight, measuring tape, binoculars, cameras, audio or video recording equipment and anything else you think you may need a moment's notice. If you are in the business of doing surveillances, you want an automobile that is especially reliable and inconspicuous. You also equip it with items appropriate to long periods of surveillance such as a portable toilet, coolers to hold food and drinks, and a cell phone, etc.

The type of equipment that an investigator might need can vary dramatically depending on the area of specialization. If you have questions, seek out and local private investigations association for a contact in your area of specialty. That person will likely be able to give you better information about equipment needs and costs.

Examples of specialization are those companies that are set up primarily to seek out eavesdropping, electronic bugging or similar activity. This is typically called technical counter-surveillance countermeasures or T. C. S. M. This equipment typically costs tens of thousands of dollars. However, it can be very lucrative and potentially interesting.

Insurance

Many private investigators obtain what is called "errors and omissions" insurance. These policies will protect a private investigator in the event of a lawsuit. If the investigator has done something in an investigation that another person alleges is negligent, there is a potential for a malpractice suit against the investigator. When this occurs, the insurance company will either hire an attorney for you or they will have an in-house staff attorney represent you in the lawsuit (either without charge or at a reduced cost). The policy often covers payment of damages awarded in a lawsuit. Premiums, policy coverage and limitations vary dramatically, so it is best to contact an insurance company for specifics. It is also highly recommended that you get a referral by someone you trust as not all insurance companies or agents in this area will be right for you.

Getting Business

There is one effort that should be done before any serious investment in the business — that would be a business plan. You can obtain books on creating a business plan from your local library. It is common sense that one must have an idea of one's market, the competition, expenses and potential income level. If you cannot make a profit, what is the point?

We will endeavor to give you some common methods of finding and gaining business. This will depend largely on who your anticipated client is. However, certain things work for virtually any client base.

Yellow Pages – the Phone Book

If you are anticipating selling your services to the general public you should consider this resource. The costs will vary depending on the size of your ad. An ad can be anywhere from a few lines to a full page. Costs can range from a few tens of dollars to many thousands. Experimentation will help, but it is a good idea to talk with other private investigators in your area about the successes they have had. Many P.I.'s find the Yellow Pages to be a diminishing return while others swear by it. Most people who advertise here are advertising to the general public. Domestic cases, finding missing persons and background checks are services commonly advertised here.

Industry or Professional Journals and Periodicals

If your clientele exists in a specific industry or profession, it makes more sense to advertise directly to them rather than a general newspaper or phone book. Attorneys, insurance company professionals, and many other vertical markets have newsletters, newspapers, magazines, and similar periodicals which offer advertising. Again, rates and size of the ad can vary dramatically. A good place to find these rags and periodicals is with the reference librarian at your local library.

Radio and Television

Although these are available for most businesses, it is very rare that a private investigator would use either of these media for advertising. The costs are high and the audience too broad.

Direct Mail Marketing

This is another area where you will probably find that others have had very mixed results. If it is not done correctly, it is doomed to fail. Trial and error is usually the key, along with a lot of patience

Direct mail marketing involves sending leaflets, letters, or brochures to a targeted audience. These documents will contain information about your services, costs and other reasons why the recipient should choose you. The cost of this type of advertising can be among the highest per person. This means; if you advertise in a newspaper for $20.00 that reaches 10,000 people, the cost is pennies per reader. But direct mail marketing may cost you a thousand dollars to mail to only a few hundred people. However, direct mail marketing also has some of the highest return rates. Using the newspaper example above; you may only get a few phone calls that might turn into a paying client. Typical return rates on direct mail marketing can be much higher.

It is highly recommended that you select someone who does direct mail marketing for a living. Direct mail marketing requires expertise in choosing who to send material to, and how to layout and prepare content. They can decide how best to send the material, for example bulk mail, postcard or brochure. Be sure to shop around for the right direct mail marketer to be sure he or she has your best interests at heart.

Cold Calling

This involves picking up the phone and calling people either out of the phone book or a list of names with phone numbers purchased from a broker. Direct mail marketers can often obtain information like this from various brokers, e.g. a list of attorneys, insurance company contacts. Again the cost per name will be higher but the potential clientele will be more targeted resulting in better return rates.

Generally this kind of advertising effort is frowned upon. A large majority of people do not like receiving these phone calls for any reason. Unless you know what you are doing, this may not be your best first choice. Most that do cold calling do so as a follow-up to printed materials sent previously.

Joining Professional Associations

One of the most effective ways of meeting potential clients and customers is by joining professional associations. Many state and local bar associations allow non-attorney members to join and participate. As a private investigator, this is a great way to pass out your business card, brochure or similar and explain what you offer in-person. Often called "networking", this is probably one of the most cost effective ways of growing business. By joining the professional association not only do you get to know others, you show a commitment to their industry or profession and you stay abreast of recent news and activity.

Networking with attorneys over general advertising has its advantages. For example, if you specialize in relationship infidelity and only advertise in the yellow pages, you may get a distraught husband wanting you to prove or disprove an affair. You do surveillance on the wife. You discover she has been secretly getting voice lessons so that she can surprise her husband at their anniversary party. The husband is satisfied client. You get paid and now what? While it's good to have client a that will recommend or use you again, what are the chances he will feel the need to check up on his wife again, or tell his friends about what he's done? You need repeat business; you need someone who is interested in infidelity all the time, a divorce or custody lawyer.

Let the attorney do the advertising and bring in the jilted spouses or parents fighting over custody issues. When expert surveillance is needed to uncover whether a parent is fit or not to have custody of a child, the lawyer will bring you in. Network with a couple of attorneys who specialize in domestic issues and you could very well be working three or four cases at a time.

There a several good ways to initiate working relationships with attorneys. Check with the local colleges in your area for classes taught by attorneys. Contact them and offer to be a guest speaker. Offer to be on-call as a stand in speaker for those occasions when they have to go to court. Not only will this get you in with the attorney, but you may make good contacts with students who are working their way through school clerking at law firms.

Contact the local bar association and ask for a list of the attorney organizations in your area. These professional organizations frequently have quest speakers at their meetings. Put together an entertaining and informative presentation of your services. Highlight one of your best cases as an example of what you can do for them. Follow up by passing out business cards and possibly a small brochure with your services.

Attorney organizations, like other professional associations often have conferences that provide training for attorneys. Follow the attorney trade journals and find a conference that covers a topic you are interested in. Attend the conference, and again, pass out cards and brochures. The attorneys will recognize your efforts to learn about the topic or have received specific training the area. This might make you very appealing to them over hiring another PI that isn't up to speed on the latest trends in this area.

Professional associations can also include associations that cater to other investigators. There are; local, state, national and international organizations where you can stay top of the latest P.I. trends, that is, what areas are lucrative and hot, and learn from other private investigators what advertising works and doesn't. It is not uncommon for the more established private investigators to have more work than they can handle, often called "overflow" work. Many investigators make a living or supplement their income with overflow work referred to them. This is often called "subcontract" work.

Here a just a few of some of the organizations available to join and some of the benefits of membership:

- AMIA – American Medical Investigators Association
  This is a national and international organization, all investigators and medical professionals are invited to become members. The AMIA is striving to improve the field of Medical Investigations. They can be located at AmerMedAs@aol.com.

- ACI – Association of Christian Investigators
  One of the benefits offered by membership in the ACI is a non-competitive environment fostered on trust in which business challenges can be openly discussed and problems solved by sharing other's experiences. More information can be found at www.a-c-i.org

- NAFI – National Association of Fire Investigators
  The National Association of Fire Investigators includes members from every U.S. state, Canadian province and over 15 foreign countries. Its key purposes are to advance the skills and enhance the knowledge of members engaged in the investigation of fires, subrogation, explosions, fire prevention, arson, and related fields, and in the litigation which results from such investigations. The NAFI offers the following certifications: Certified Fire and Explosion Investigator (CFEI), Certified Fire Investigation Instructor (CFII), and Certified Vehicle Fire Investigator (CVFI). For more info log on to www.nafi.org

- NCISS – National Council of Investigation & Security Services
  This national organization works with businesses and associations that provide investigation and private security services to the legal profession, business community, government and the public. They work to raise the standards and image of the security and investigation profession by addressing excessively restrictive legislation regarding training and standards, creation of legislation necessitating local licensing, public misconceptions and misinformation about the role and involvement of private investigators and security services. Their website can be located at www.nciss.com

- NCIA – National Construction Investigators Association
  The NCIA is a national organization that encourages communication and fosters interaction between investigators and prosecutors. They work to protect the public from transient criminals, who travel the country engaging in fraudulent schemes while posing as contractors. More information can be found at www.nciassociation.org

Pre-Approved Lists

There are certain lists maintained by various entities that contain the names of approved private investigators that will be called upon as needed for work. The most common of these are insurance companies and government defense agencies, such as the public defender.

Insurance companies that deal particularly in fraud, personal injury and workers' compensation areas, have a tremendous workload where it concerns investigations. Often they will have an internal special investigations unit (SIU) and sometimes the workload exceeds what their internal investigators can handle. Many insurance companies do not even have staff investigators at all. In either case, an insurance adjuster will maintain a list of local investigators, one of which might be you. Typically you can call the insurance company to find out about their list and how to on it. The criterion for being placed on the list is usually nothing more than having a license; however, this is not always the case. The claims adjuster, when choosing investigator for a case, will either pick someone they like, someone who is especially skilled in a particular area, or will simply to loop through the list one after the other without deference. Many investigators make their living entirely in this way. The hourly rate is not usually very high, but it is competitive and the regular work makes up for any loss in rate.

Many government criminal defense entities such as the public defender also maintain these lists. Here, the reason is not usually because of a lack of internal investigators but because of a conflict of interest. These lists are often termed "conflicts" lists or panels. If the public defender or similar entity has a legal conflict with a criminal defendant they are representing, such as an adverse prior representation, they will not legally be able to represent them directly. As such, the case is referred out to the "conflicts" attorney who in turn will hire an investigator. Getting onto these lists a similar to that of the insurance companies. You would put a call into the government agency and find out the procedure for getting on that list. Investigators are typically chosen for their skill or they are chosen one after the other on the list.

Internet and Online Advertising

This is fast becoming one of the most effective and cheapest ways to advertise. Setting up a web page, e-mail marketing, and search engine submissions can be inexpensive and highly effective. However, as in any advertising effort, it must be done properly. It is highly recommended that the investigator hire a professional to help them with an effort such as this.

Unique to online advertising and marketing, it is possible to track in real time who is visiting your site and how they found out about you. With this information, it is possible to narrow when, where, how and to whom to market to. Many investigators find this method of advertising brings in up to 50% of their business.

A word of encouragement is in order here. There are still many P.I.s who either do not own a computer or who have not joined the online community. While many of these investigators enjoy satisfying and lucrative careers, this approach is fast becoming outmoded. If you have not already done so, you should purchase a computer, learn to use it, and get involved online. You will then be able to search the Internet for professionals who can help you advertise your business.

Word of Mouth

The cheapest, most common, and by far the best method of getting business is by word of mouth. If you do good work, and stick around long enough, people will begin to know you as a "go to" a person. This is a matter of treating each client with the utmost care and responsibility. That client then becomes your best form of advertising. Initially, the business will be sporadic and inconsistent. However, if you have enough satisfied clients floating around they will be a referral source for more clients. At some point, you will find you have more work than you can handle and will begin to provide overflow work to other private investigators. The coin has two sides however. If you do substandard work for clients then that bad news will travel quickly. You'll find that you never get off the ground. And, unfortunately, many investigators either do not have the proper work ethic or are not cut out for the investigations business at all. As such, it is the investigator with a good reputation that will become a funnel for all of the good business.

Your First Client

Bringing together everything that we've covered so far this chapter, you may feel well equipped to take on your first client. However, there are some important points that one should know before starting off.

The most important thing you can do for client is to listen and listen carefully. This is probably the most overlooked need that a client has. Most clients will be very pleased with your work if you listen to what they expect, provide them with a detailed list of goals that are realistically consistent with their expectations, and then execute on those goals.

The client might have a legal position to assert or other conclusion that they hope to find; it is your job to provide them with the truth whatever it may be. Clients will respect you for providing objective, independent and factual results.

You must be certain to have other issues clearly defined. How much is as client willing to pay you? Are they agreeable to your hourly rate and the number of hours that you estimate it will take to complete the task? Are they willing to involve other professionals if need be? Will this client reimburse you for expenses and if so how much? Will this potential client provide you with a retainer up front? All of these questions have to be answered clearly and adequately. A written fee agreement with the scope of representation is always a good idea.

From the Files of Jeff Bachtle

After being in the PI business in AZ for over 10 years, I would recommend the following:

Always remember, this is a customer service business, therefore you must respond almost immediately or the potential customer will find someone else. With today's wireless technology; you can get email, phone calls, etc. most anywhere. Communication is extremely important.

Research the area and make sure your rates are comparable to other PI Agencies.

Specialize in a certain area and make sure you are not spread too thin, i.e. superior court or federal court criminal defense work. If you are in & out of the court house, records department, etc, you can work 2 or 3 cases at a time without making a special trip. You should be able to bill accordingly.

Retainers are important. If you don't have the retainer, don't complete the job. You may start working a case, and a day or two later, the matter was resolved! Now you have time & money in a project but NO compensation.

Referral - Remember, this is a customer service business, so answer ALL CALLS & listen to all potential clients. I have had potential clients that tell me they don't have enough money to retain me, but sometimes ten minutes on the phone goes a long way. If they don't retain you, they will keep you in mind or refer you to someone that may retain you. In the ten years or so in the business, I don't need to advertise. Most all my business is referral or repeat clients.

Good luck

Jeff Bachtle

Jeff Bachtle and Associates

Arizona DPS Private Investigator ID # 9706004

LLC, Investigations & Legal Support Services

http://www.bachtlerandassociates.com/

You'll want to discuss timelines and report formats in detail. Stick to these and you'll be in good shape. In other words, use common sense, good business ethics, and do what you are trained to do and you will do well.

A word of caution - some clients can be more trouble than they are worth. You may be eager to get started and take the first client that comes through the door. However, you will quickly learn that there are people you should probably pass on. If the client seems uncomfortable with your fee, your approach, or seems to have an ulterior or bad motive in seeking your services, then you should be more careful in deciding to take the case. It is also good idea to ask who the client has talked to about their case before. If you find that he or she has been to many investigators about the same case, this should be a red flag that the client may be a problem. This is one of those common sense areas that will become honed over time.

From the Files of Greg Bailey

Although I have many years of experience in law enforcement, my career in private investigations only spans a few years. Being in law enforcement most of my adult life, I never had to worry about budgets or time allocation. If I needed more report forms or a new flashlight, I just went to the sergeant and got a new one. Being in business is much different. I have to pay for the supplies, the batteries, and all the software, etc.

Most of the investigation that PIs do could be learned by almost anyone. It doesn't take years of law enforcement duty or street smarts to get what you need. It does take business knowledge, marketing technique, and a sense of being an entrepreneur. PI work is feast or famine. When you have a feast, you better put some away, because there is a good chance you won't get any more work for weeks.

I do not believe that former police officers necessarily make the best PIs. Yes, it is true that they have a work history and training in dealing with people, investigations, interviewing, forensics, and the like. A lot of former police don't make it in the private sector. Most have never had to balance a business budget or do all the things that have to be completed to start a business. This causes a slow start up and you spend precious hours learning the business ropes, when you should have been out getting business. Those hours turn into a financial loss.

Police officers are trained to deal with people and their issues. Because they have a power of removing people that are not conforming, some tend to be overbearing in the private sector and that does not get you return business. It's the "my way or the highway" issue. The people you deal with in the PI biz are your clients, not just "citizens." If you give your clients a [poor quality] video of their husband fooling around, or you loose someone in traffic, they let relatives and friends know about their experiences and soon they rap your business. That hurts the bottom line.

PI work is somewhat like police work, but not a flamboyant job. If you were like Tom Selleck in Magnum PI with a red, Ferrari, how would you ever be successful doing surveillance? People would "make" you the moment you drove out of the garage. PIs have to be "unnoticeable." T-shirt and blue jeans most of the time, except when meeting with clients, court or associates. Instead of a new car, you should have an older car that looks OK, earthen colors, but has a good running engine that can keep up with fast drivers and is highly maneuverable. You have to "smooze" people most of the time. If you want information, you have to be able to show up at the right time, at the right place and have the gift of winning people over. Sometimes police can threaten people with being an accessory and incarceration if they don't tell you what you need to know. If you are not good at subterfuge, you better learn. Here is an example.

I followed a person to an apartment house, and saw the person go in a particular apartment. I had to go back at night to get the apartment number. All of the names were missing off the mailboxes, so you can surmise what sort of neighborhood I was in. I had to learn who was in the apartment. I could call the manager, but the likelihood of the manager telling me who was in the apartment was not good and they would probably tell the occupants that someone was asking about them. I had to try several reverse address searches until I came up with a name and a cell phone number. I also needed to know who the live in boyfriend was. I called her cell phone number at about 4:30PM and told her I was Bill Smith with a made up pizza restaurant. Never use a real business name because of possible legal issues. I told her that if she would answer a couple of questions about pizza, I would send her a free certificate for pizza. She said, "Sure." I then asked her some questions and then I got to ask her name and address. She supplied both. I then told her that if she had other adults living in her home, I could send them a certificate. She gave me the name of her boyfriend, telling me that he lived there, however she was moving out in a couple of weeks and gave me her new address! Those names led to local criminal history checks which gave me dates of birth, physicals, cars driven, signatures and a bunch of other stuff I could not have learned from reading the crime reports.

Greg Bailey

BAILEY ENQUIRIES, LLC

A Private Investigation Firm

Greeley, Colorado

http://home.comcast.net/~baileyenquiries/index.htm

Member of: PPIAC, CCDB, AIASS

SUMMARY

In this chapter, we took a brief overview of how to select an area within investigations, covered some of the more common areas and what they involve. We also looked at how to set up and organize a P.I. business with some pointers on how to advertise and get your first client. It cannot be emphasized enough how important is to talk to other private investigators about the area that you anticipate entering, and how best to run the business and how to obtain clients. And, as with anything, practice makes perfect.

DISCUSSION QUESTIONS

1. Using the Internet, investigate a local private investigator organization and then a national or international one. List some of the benefits of each. What are the benefits of a local organization over a national and visa versa?

2. What are some of the first steps a person should take if they are planning to get into the private investigations business?

3. If you were going to hire a private investigator what would qualifications or traits would you look for?